THE GEOGRAPHY OF THE EUROPEAN COMMUNITY

The EC does not exist just at a point or in a vacuum, rather it is made up of a mosaic of regions of various sizes, shapes and functions. The attributes of each region and its location in relation to other regions are as vital for each area's existence and development as is the way in which each is managed. Geography draws attention to the features and locations of regions and to their implications. People, natural resources and means of production are distributed in complex ways and people and products move from place to place. Increasingly, the influence of the Community is being felt in the 12 member states and a new geography is emerging, with pressure to achieve convergence if not homogeneity.

The purpose of the book is to identify and assess the problems and prospects of the various regions of the EC and also to view the Community as a system of interdependent regions. Increasingly, in a changing Europe, the Community has become important both economically and, more recently, politically; with the break-up of the former Soviet Union and applications for Community membership by various 'neutral states', its enlargement also seems imminent. Therefore, attention is given throughout the book to the activities and influence of the EC in the broader context of Europe and neighbouring parts of Africa and Asia. Its influence globally seems likely to grow and this must also be taken into consideration.

John Cole is Professor of Human and Regional Geography at the University of Nottingham, and has taught for short periods in the USA, Mexico, Brazil, Chile, China and Spain. His research interests have included regional aspects of Italy and of Europe in general, the USSR, and Latin America. He has written widely and is the author of over 20 books, including *Geography of World Affairs* (Penguin), *Italy* (Chatto & Windus) and *A Geography of the USSR* (Butterworths). **Francis Cole** is a freelance interpreter based in Brussels. He graduated from the University of Cambridge in 1981 and has since worked for the European Commission and the European Parliament. He has lectured and written on the EC, and has also visited China, the USSR and Taiwan in a professional capacity.

THE GEOGRAPHY OF THE EUROPEAN COMMUNITY

John Cole and Francis Cole

London and New York

First published 1993
by Routledge
11 New Fetter Lane, London EC4P 4EE

Simultaneously published in the USA and Canada
by Routledge
29 West 35th Street, New York, NY 10001

© 1993 John Cole and Francis Cole

Typeset in 10pt September by Leaper & Gard Ltd, Bristol
Printed and bound in Great Britain by
Biddles Ltd, Guildford and King's Lynn

British Library Cataloguing in Publication Data
A catalogue reference for this book is available from the British Library.

0-415-07992-6
0-415-07993-4 (pbk)

Library of Congress Cataloging in Publication Data
has been applied for.

0-415-07992-6
0-415-07993-4 (pbk)

CONTENTS

PLATES

FIGURES

TABLES

PREFACE

Great changes have taken place in Europe during the time this book was being written. As far as possible, changes such as the momentous unification of Germany and the decisions at the Maastricht Summit have been incorporated in the text. There will undoubtedly be further major changes in the next few years. EC publications are numerous, and for UK readers, these can be traced through HMSO.

The authors wish to thank three reviewers appointed by the publisher for their helpful comments and suggestions for improvements. They are also greatly indebted to Kieran Bradley of the Legal Service of the European Parliament for his close scrutiny of several chapters, especially with regard to organisational and legal aspects of the EC. Mrs E. O. Wigginton's great help in typing most of the chapters at least once and Mrs R. Hoole's efforts in getting them into a word processor are greatly appreciated. The maps and diagrams have been drawn by Chris Lewis and Elaine Watts, whose patience was frequently tried as changes in the EC meant adjustments almost across the board. Four years of undergraduates in the Department of Geography, Nottingham University, who took the courses on the EC, unknowingly also made a major contribution.

CONVENTIONS

Countries The English version has been used throughout the book for names of countries, however the reader should note that in EC publications initials for the 12 EC Member States are often used and these start as in the national spelling (e.g. E for España, Spain). These initials are given in Table 1.1 of the text.

Regions The names of EC regions are given throughout the book in their own languages (e.g. Sicilia rather than Sicily, Corse rather than Corsica, Bretagne rather than Brittany). Readers who intend to use EC regional data sets need to recognise these names.

Italy is subdivided into four main regions: Italia Settentrionale, Centrale, Meridionale and Isole. These have been written with initial capital letters as North, Central, South and Islands. Northern and southern Italy are used in a more loose sense. Western Europe refers to EC and EFTA countries, Central Europe (formerly Eastern Europe) to countries between Western Europe and the USSR.

Cities For names of cities, the English version has been used, but the reader will obviously meet the names in their own languages in the literature and when travelling. Among EC cities with English equivalents are the following: Germany – Köln (Cologne), München (Munich), Hannover (Hanover); France – Marseille (Marseilles), Lyon (Lyons); Italy – Firenze (Florence), Genova (Genoa), Milano (Milan), Napoli (Naples), Roma (Rome), Torino (Turin), Venezia (Venice); the Netherlands – Den Haag (The Hague); Belgium –Brussel (Flemish), Bruxelles (Walloon). Brussels has been used to avoid choosing one of the two spellings. In Belgium, note also Antwerpen/Anvers and Gent/Gand; Denmark – København (Copenhagen); Greece – Athinai (Athens), Thessaloniki (Salonika); Spain – Sevilla (Seville); Portugal – Lisboa (Lisbon), Porto (Oporto). Note too that Luxembourg refers both to the Grand Duchy (GD) and to a province in Belgium.

TERMS AND ABBREVIATIONS

TERMS AND ABBREVIATIONS

billion	(shortened to bln, bn) is one thousand million
ha	hectare(s)
kg	kilogram
km	kilometre
km/h	kilometres per hour
kW	kilowatt
kWh	kilowatt-hour
Motorway	This refers not only to British motorways but also to Autobahnen, Autoroutes, Autostrade, etc.
sq km	square kilometre
t.c.e.	tonnes of coal equivalent
t.o.e.	tonnes of oil equivalent
tonne	a metric ton

ACRONYMS/INITIALS

ACP	African, Caribbean and Pacific countries (the Lomé Convention)
ASEAN	Association of South East Asian Nations
CAP	Common Agricultural Policy
CCT	Common Customs Tariff
CFC	Chlorofluorocarbon
CFP	Common Fisheries Policy
CIS	Commonwealth of Independent States (most of former USSR)
CMEA	Council for Mutual Economic Assistance
COMECON	see CMEA
DOM	Départements d'outremer (French overseas departments Guadeloupe, Guyane, Martinique, Réunion)
EAEC	European Atomic Energy Community

EAGGF	European Agricultural Guidance and Guarantee Fund
EC	European Communities (often Community)
ECSC	European Coal and Steel Community
ECU	European Currency Unit (also Ecu, ecu)
EDF	European Development Fund
EEA	European Economic Area
EEC	European Economic Community
EFTA	European Free Trade Association
EIB	European Investment Bank
EMS	European Monetary System
EMU	Economic and Monetary Union
EP	European Parliament
EPC	European Political Co-operation
EPU	European Political Union
ERDF	European Regional Development Fund
ERM	Exchange Rate Mechanism
ESC	Economic and Social Committee
ESF	European Social Fund
EUR 9, 10, 12	European Community 9 without Greece (10), Spain and Portugal (12)
Euratom	see EAEC
Eurostat	Statistical Office of the European Communities
FRG	Federal Republic of Germany (West Germany)
FAO	Food and Agriculture Organisation (of the United Nations)
GATT	General Agreement on Tariffs and Trade
GDP	Gross Domestic Product (see also GNP)
GDR	German Democratic Republic (East Germany)
GNP	Gross National Product (GNP measures the resources available after the transfer of factor incomes such as interest payments and dividends but unlike GDP is not used at regional level)
IT	Information Technology
JET	Joint European Torus
LUFPIG	Land Use and Food Policy Inter-Group
Maghreb	Usually refers to Algeria, Morocco and Tunisia
NATO	North Atlantic Treaty Organisation
NCI	New Community Instrument
NUTS	Nomenclature of units of territory for statistics (levels 1, 2, 3 frequently used in EC publications)
OECD	Organisation for Economic Co-operation and Development
PPS	Purchasing Power Standard
PRB	Population Reference Bureau (Washington)

R and (T)D	Research and (Technological) Development
RSFSR	Russian Soviet Federal Socialist Republic (Russia)
SEA	Single European Act
TACIS	Technical Assistance to the CIS
TEU	Treaty on European Union
TFR	Total fertility rate
TGV	train à grande vitesse
TOR	Treaty of Rome
UN	United Nations
UNDP	United Nations Development Programme
UK	United Kingdom of Great Britain and Northern Ireland
USA	United States of America
USSR	Union of Soviet Socialist Republics
VAT	Value Added Tax
WEU	West European Union
WPDS	World Population Data Sheet (see PRB)

1

INTRODUCTION

THE HISTORICAL BACKGROUND OF THE EUROPEAN COMMUNITY

This book is intended to serve as a basis for the study of the European Communities (hereafter referred to as the EC or the Community) within a broader European and global context. Since its foundation in the 1950s, the EC has developed and grown into an international entity whose scale and scope of activity outweigh those of any other comparable unit in the world. Nevertheless, it is an entity with a future very much under debate, in a fast-changing continent, and with increasing pressures upon it from other regions of the developed and developing worlds. The geographical approach is used in this book to analyse and evaluate the EC and the greater Europe in their major economic, social and political areas. In order to establish the framework for the book it is appropriate first to put the EC in its European and global contexts.

The EC has appropriated the word Europe(an) for its title, so it is necessary to define the limits of the so-called 'continent' of Europe (see Figure 1.1), of which the EC occupies only about one-third. Europe reaches eastwards to the Ural Mountains of Russia, the Ural River and the Caspian Sea. In the south it is separated from Africa by the Mediterranean, and from Asia by the Bosporus, the Black Sea and the mountains and rivers south of Transcaucasia. The limits to Europe are conventionally associated with physical features, but these precise limits are not barriers of great note politically, militarily or culturally. The former USSR and Turkey each has territory in both Europe and Asia. Cultural contacts across the Mediterranean between Europe and North Africa have been considerable in the last 100 years, while trade is at present very large, and migration northwards is increasing. While the conventional limits of the 'continent' of Europe are culturally without significance in the east and south, the concept of Europe as a region of the world has existed for a long time, and the influence of Europe on the rest of the world has been enormous during the last 500 years.

In 1494 the Pope divided the world beyond Europe between Spain and Portugal in the Treaty of Tordesillas. Christian Europe thus effectively gave itself a mandate to conquer anywhere in the world. The empires of the Western

1

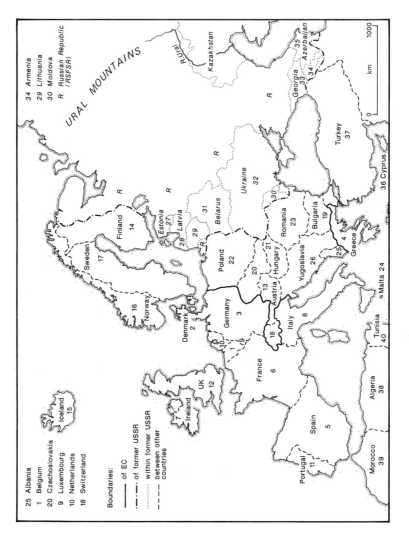

Figure 1.1 The countries of Europe, including the European Republics of the former USSR, Cyprus and the Maghreb. The numbering of the countries corresponds to that in Table 1.3. No distinction is made between the various Soviet Socialist Republics of the former USSR

European countries continued to grow in some parts of the world into the twentieth century, but more than 200 years ago they started to disintegrate with the War of American Independence. EC countries such as France, Belgium and the UK have lost most of their colonies over the last few decades. Ties have been maintained, however, through the Lomé Convention, linking the African, Caribbean and Pacific (ACP) countries into the EC through trade and development co-operation agreements. The British Commonwealth and the French Community (which links France with many of its former colonies in Africa) also help to retain ties between the EC and former colonies.

While Spain, Portugal and, subsequently, other Western European countries were acquiring colonies in various parts of the world from the sixteenth century onwards, Russia was expanding in several directions in the eastern half of Europe, and in the seventeenth century it conquered much of what is now Siberia. In the early 1990s the Soviet Union, inheritor of the Russian Empire, in its turn disintegrated, as various non-Russian peoples sought and achieved independence. Such a development seems at the time of writing to have particular significance for the EC, since several former Soviet Republics, aspiring to independence, look towards the Community for support, and even aspire to eventual membership.

For the last five centuries European powers have frequently been in conflict both in Europe itself and elsewhere in the world. Since the Second World War, and during the last stages of the disintegration of their empires, Western European countries have come together in the North Atlantic Treaty Organisation (NATO) and through economic co-operation. The creation of the supranational bodies of the EC has brought together former rivals and enemies in a completely new situation. In the European Parliament, which at the time of writing is a body with limited powers, politicians of similar political views from the 12 Member States of the EC form transnational groups or alliances. The same politicians are regrouped and allocated to delegations, each vested with the care of the Parliament's relations with the parliament and/or responsible national authorities of a particular country or group of countries elsewhere in the world. Such strange bedfellows would have been unthinkable 60 years ago.

In the present book, the EC is considered both as an entity moving, sometimes against historical traditions, towards greater unity, and as a region of the world coming to terms rapidly with a new situation in Europe and likely also to be influenced increasingly by regions outside Europe. Early in the twentieth century, the British geographer Halford Mackinder (1904) suggested that future historians might call the period 1500–1900 'the Columbian epoch':

Broadly speaking, we may contrast the Columbian epoch with the age which preceded it, by describing its essential characteristic as the expansion of Europe against almost negligible resistances, whereas mediaeval Christendom was pent into a narrow region and threatened by external barbarism. From the present time forth [1904] we shall again have to deal with a closed political system, and none the less that it will be one of world-wide scope. Every explosion of social forces, instead of being dissipated in a surrounding circuit of unknown space and barbaric chaos, will be sharply re-echoed from the far side of the globe, and weak elements in the political and economic organism of the world will be shattered in consequence.

We are now well into the post-Columbian epoch. If Mackinder's view of the world has turned out to be correct, then in the future Western Europe's global position may soon be more like its position in the pre-Columbian epoch than it was the Columbian epoch. From now on there will be pressures from outside: from the USA and Japan to maintain innovative and competitive industry; from Central Europe and the former USSR to help in their economic restructuring; and from the developing countries to be more forthcoming with assistance. There is also growing economic and social pressure from immigration both out of former Council for Mutual Economic Assistance (CMEA) countries and from the developing world. Since the Second World War, a feature of world affairs has been the emergence of supranational blocs in various parts of the world. Apart from the recent demise of CMEA, the process continues, with much of the economic power of the world concentrated in a few countries or groups of countries, including for example USA/Canada (280 million inhabitants) and the Association of South East Asian Nations (ASEAN, 320 million inhabitants). Whether or not such a process will lead to greater pressure on the EC remains to be seen, but it is worth bearing in mind that between 1990 and 2010 the combined population of the developing countries of the world is forecast to grow by about 1.7 billion, adding the population of five ECs in that time – the equivalent of a new EC every four years.

Before 1989 the EC concentrated on internal integration, building towards the completion of the Single Market by 1993; since 1987, it has refused to consider new applications for membership until after 1993. The collapse of Soviet influence in Central Europe and the emergence of new democracies in the former Communist states of Central and Eastern Europe have, however, led to a reappraisal of the future composition and scope of the EC. The debate over whether the EC should widen or deepen, or both, has become a central issue in the Community.

In spite of the great impact of Western Europe on the rest of the world for several centuries, its area is very small in relation to the total land area of the world. The area of the EC of 2,360,000 sq km (including GDR, the former German Democratic Republic) is only 1.74 per cent of the total land area of the world of 135,840,000 sq km. Its share of total world population has been declining for several decades, and seems destined to decline still further for several more. In 1990 its population of 345 million (including that of the GDR) was 6.5 per cent of the total population of the world. Fifty years ago the present Member States of the EC had over 10 per cent of the total population of the world. By the year 2030 the same 12 countries are expected to have only 3 per

4

cent of that population. On the other hand, the EC accounts for about 18 per cent of total world Gross Domestic Product (GDP), which is one of the keys to its global influence.

With regard to natural resources, the EC is comparatively poorly endowed. Details will be given in later chapters, but it may be noted here that it has less than 1 per cent of the world's proved oil reserves, about 2 per cent of the proved natural gas reserves, and about 6 per cent of the commercial coal reserves. It has a small or negligible share of almost all major non-fuel minerals. The extent and quality of agricultural land in the EC is more favourable, but agricultural production has risen in recent decades almost entirely through an increase in yields rather than through the growth of the area cultivated.

In order to compare its size and shape with those of its main rival, the EC is shown in Figure 1.2 on the same scale as the eastern part of the USA. It is less than a quarter of the area of the USA. If squeezed into a more compact shape, the EC would fit more than nine times into the former USSR. It is smaller in area than the single state of Western Australia, which only has about 1.5 million inhabitants.

The global technological and military superiority of Europe since the end of the fifteenth century was based initially on inventiveness, organisation and indigenous natural resources. Subsequently some other regions of the world have caught up with Europe, while some have natural resources in far greater abundance in relation to their population size. In the post-Columbian epoch, Western Europeans will have to work hard to retain their position, and the integration and expansion of the EC is expected to give them greater strength to do so.

THE ORIGINS OF THE EC

The 12 Member States of the EC are listed in Table 1.1 in their 'European' alphabetical order, together with the remaining countries of Europe. Elsewhere in this book the 12 Member States are listed in the order used in the EC publication COM 87-230 (1987), the order in which they joined, which is considered by the authors to be more appropriate historically than the arbitrary alphabetical order used here and in some EC publications. The location of all the countries is shown in Figure 1.1. Although the principal subject of the book is the EC, reference will be made, where appropriate, to non-EC countries, in particular to the members of the European Free Trade Association (EFTA) and to those countries of Central and Eastern Europe most likely to become associated with the EC in the 1990s.

The origins of the European Communities, now more commonly referred to as the European Community (EC), date back to the Europe that emerged in 1945 from the turmoil and devastation of the Second World War. Deeply influenced by wars dominated by Franco-German conflicts, which had ravaged continental Europe, the founders of the EC saw closer economic and political ties between these two historical protagonists as being the best way of reducing the risks of a

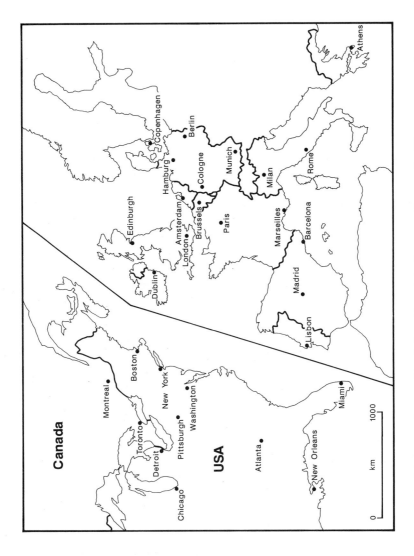

Figure 1.2 A comparison of the areas of eastern North America and the European Community. The maps are on the same scale. Only EC countries are distinguished

Table 1.1 The countries of Europe, 1992

European Community[1] (date of joining)				EFTA[2]	Former CMEA[3]
English name	Own name				
Belgium	België/Belgique	B	1952	Austria	Bulgaria
Denmark	Danmark	DK	1973	Finland	CSFR[4]
Germany	Deutschland[5]	D	1952	Iceland	Hungary
Greece	Ellas	GR	1981	Norway	Poland
Spain	España	E	1986	Sweden	Romania
France		F	1952	Switzerland	Former USSR[6]
Ireland	Eire	IRL	1973		
Italy	Italia	I	1952		
Luxembourg		L	1952	Other	Other 'socialist'
Netherlands	Nederland	NL	1952	Malta	Albania
Portugal		P	1986	Turkey[6]	Yugoslavia
United Kingdom		UK	1973	Cyprus[7]	

Notes: 1 1952 – ECSC; 1958 – EEC/Euratom
2 European Free Trade Association
3 Council for Mutual Economic Assistance, also referred to as COMECON, disbanded 1991
4 Czech and Slovak Federal Republic (formerly Czechoslovakia)
5 + former GDR 1990
6 in both Europe and Asia. Estonia, Latvia and Lithuania became independent in 1991
7 strictly part of Asia

repetition of such a conflict. This vision led the 'Father' of the EC, Robert Schuman, French minister for foreign affairs, to propose on the 9 May 1950 that Franco-German coal and steel production should be placed under a joint High Authority in an organisation to which other European nations could belong. At that time, the coking coal of Germany and the iron ore of France complemented each other in the context of geographical proximity and environmental similarities.

The first of the European Communities, the European Coal and Steel Community (ECSC), was founded in 1952, following the signing of the Treaty of Paris on 18 April 1951. The first six Member States were West Germany, France, Italy, the Netherlands, Belgium and Luxembourg, with the four official languages being Dutch, French, German and Italian. The Treaty established the institutions for the management of resources, production and trade in ECSC coal and steel, the High Authority (later the Commission), the Common Assembly (later the Parliament), the Council, and the Court of Justice.

Since one of the fundamental objectives of the founders of the EC was to ensure peace and stability in postwar Europe, there was also an attempt to develop a parallel European Defence Community, but proposals foundered when, in 1954, they were rejected by the French Assemblée Nationale, which

Table 1.2 A summary history of the EC

Year	Event
1945	End of the Second World War
1950	The Schuman Declaration
1952	The ECSC founded
1958	The EEC and Euratom founded
1960	EFTA founded
1973	The UK, Ireland and Denmark join EC
1979	First direct elections to the European Parliament
1981	Greece joins EC
1986	Spain and Portugal join EC
1987	Single European Act enters into force
1990	Unification of Germany
1991	Treaty of Maastricht on European Union
1992	Completion of the Single Market

saw it as a threat to national sovereignty. Proposals for further co-operation in the area of defence and security were then shelved until the negotiations at the start of the 1990s over future political union of the EC with agreement in Maastricht (1991) on a fledgling common defence policy.

The success of the ECSC led the six founding Member States to commit themselves in June 1955 to further integration in other sectors. Following two years of negotiations, the Treaties of Rome were signed on 25 March 1957, setting up the European Economic Community (EEC) and the European Atomic Energy Community (Euratom). The EEC Treaty laid down a series of objectives in various economic and social areas, governed by the principle, presented in the preamble, of reducing economic divergences between regions of the Community, and improving the living standards of its citizens. The Euratom Treaty dealt specifically with research, production and safety in the nuclear energy sector. Both Treaties contained more detailed provisions governing institutional and administrative procedures for the attainment of their objectives and, together with the ECSC Treaty, they form the corpus of EC primary law which has governed the activities of the EC over the subsequent three decades.

During the period of the establishment of the EEC, the United Kingdom made attempts to join, but negotiations failed to produce conditions acceptable to it, partly owing to obstacles created by France, led by General de Gaulle. In 1959–60 a frustrated UK was instrumental in the creation of the European Free Trade Association (EFTA), signed with Austria, Denmark, Norway, Portugal, Sweden and Switzerland (Liechtenstein, which has a customs union with Switzerland, is also an associate member). Finland took associate membership in 1961 and Iceland joined in 1970. Although more limited in scope of activity than the EC, concentrating primarily on the removal of trade barriers between members, there is no doubt that EFTA was a significant counterweight organisation. In spite of the fact that the UK, Denmark and Portugal have now joined the EC, it has played a major role in areas of economic and commercial co-operation into the 1990s. In 1991 the remaining EFTA Member States moved closer to membership of the EC, through the European Economic Area (EEA) and individual applications for EC membership.

The EC continued to attract other European countries, and in 1970 the UK, the Republic of Ireland, Denmark and Norway applied for membership. In a closely fought referendum the population of Norway decided to remain outside, but the other three countries joined in 1973, bringing the EC up to nine Member States, with six official languages. Greece applied in 1975, and joined in 1981, followed by Spain and Portugal which applied in 1977 and joined in 1986, making up the current total of 12 Member States, with nine official languages.

The activities of the EC over its first 30 years were substantial in a wide range of areas such as agriculture, international trade, harmonisation of customs procedures and, latterly, co-operation in energy policy and in research and development. Nevertheless, it was felt in the course of the 1980s that insufficient progress was being made towards more fundamental objectives of the Treaties, such as the reduction of regional and social inequalities and the harmonisation of legislation to establish a single internal market. Following negotiations, which coincided with the accession of Spain and Portugal, the Single European Act (SEA) was signed in 1986, entering into force on 1 July 1987. It was the first significant reform of the substantive law of the EC since its foundation.

The SEA set the agenda for the following years of EC activities, establishing a timetable for the completion of the Single Market by the end of 1992 (Art. 8a EEC), and the development of EC policies in such areas as transport and environmental protection. The need for 'economic and social cohesion' (Art. 130a EEC) has been regarded as a central priority for the further development of the EC. Moreover, experience of lengthy negotiations and slow decision-making over previous decades had shown the need for legislative procedures to be speeded up, so the SEA also contained provisions for rendering EC decision-making and institutional relations more efficient and democratic. In particular, it extended qualified majority voting in the Council, strengthened the executive powers of the Commission, and gave a more substantial role to the Parliament (SEA Articles 6–9).

Since the signing of the SEA, there have been substantial impetus and a greater sense of urgency in the policy-making and integration of the EC. The Commission's White Paper on the Internal Market, which predated the SEA by eight months, set the objectives for the completion of the Single Market, with 282 directives being stipulated as essential for its legislative and technical framework. During this period there has also been an ongoing process of continual negotiation for Treaty reform, with initiatives such as the Delors Committee proposals for Economic and Monetary Union, and initiatives to create the Social Charter. This process culminated at the end of 1991 in the completion of the intergovernmental conferences on political union, and economic and monetary union, and the agreement on the Treaty on European Union signed in Maastricht.

Developments in 1989 in Central and Eastern Europe, resulting in the unification of Germany in 1990, with the rapid and almost automatic accession of the territory and population of the former GDR to the EC over a period of months, led to a substantial reappraisal of the future direction and scope of the EC. Membership of the Community is now becoming increasingly attractive to other European countries in EFTA and in Central Europe, leading to the debate on crucial issues of the enlargement and continued integration of the EC. Some governments talk of further integration into a deeper federal union, whereas others prefer the concept of a broader and shallower confederation of European states in an EC based more on co-operation and decentralised decision-making, with limited central decisions based on consensus, rather than a full political and economic union.

Increased trade between the countries of Western Europe can perhaps be regarded as both a cause and an effect of greater economic integration. Since the Second World War it has expanded relative to the total foreign trade of all the present Member States and, indeed, in general also between these and the Member States of EFTA. In order to justify entry into and integration within the EC, a number of advantages of membership in a large supranational entity have been identified. The economies of scale resulting from the existence of a large single market, in which standards and legislation are harmonised, and the possibility of achieving a high level of regional specialisation in various economic activities and of allowing comparative advantage to occur, have been presented as benefits of membership of the EC. Accordingly, all barriers to the movement of people, goods, services and capital are to be removed in the 1992 programme.

In his series of influential reports on *Research on the Cost of non-Europe* (summarised in *The European Challenge 1992*), Paolo Cecchini (1988) argued that the completion of the Single Market was crucial to the future development of the EC, since it would 'propel Europe onto the blustery world stage of the 1990s in a position of competitive strength and on an upward trajectory of economic growth lasting into the next century'. Many, however, argue that the benefits to be gained from centralisation and large-scale integration are limited. The concept of subsidiarity, which entails responsibilities and powers being exercised at the lowest appropriate level, has gathered support during the recent debate on the future integration of the EC.

It is clear from the foregoing account of the development of the EC since the 1950s that the leaders of various Western European countries have perceived entry into the Community to be desirable. It is difficult, however, to quantify objectively the advantages of joining, and it is a matter of speculation as to what path a Member State would have followed had it not joined. The process of economic integration observed in various parts of the world in the past has not followed a clearly defined series of steps. Earlier cases, such as the unification of Italy or Germany in the nineteenth century, show some features similar to the more recent development of the EC. In Latin America, a Free Trade Association established in the early 1960s has virtually ceased to exist. On the other hand, in the late 1980s, the USA and Canada formed a 'Customs Union' with atypical haste. Even the argument that the great size of the EC, particularly in economic terms, has led to greater prosperity, can be questioned. On average, the six Member States of EFTA, with a combined population of only about one-tenth that of the EC, are considerably more wealthy than the 12 Member States of the EC. On the other hand, the much poorer former GDR was a member of a larger bloc than the EC, at least in population size, CMEA, in which many of the advantages of international collaboration were supposed to work for the benefit of its members.

THE OBJECTIVES AND ACTIVITIES OF THE EC

A more detailed analysis of the principles and objectives of the EC, past and present, will now be presented. The account begins with the Treaties of Paris and Rome. In their statement of principles and tasks for the EC, the three founding Treaties, of which the EEC is the most comprehensive, share the same basic aims of the EC:

> The Community shall have as its task, by establishing a common market and progressively approximating the economic policies of Member States, to promote throughout the Community a harmonious development of economic activities, a continuous and balanced expansion, an increase in stability, an accelerated raising of the standard of living and closer relations between the States belonging to it.
>
> (Art. 2 EEC)

In order to meet these basic objectives, the EEC Treaty goes on, in its next article, to list the following priority activities:

(a) the elimination, as between Member States, of customs duties and of quantitative restrictions on the import and export of goods, and of all other measures having equivalent effect;

(b) the establishment of a common external customs tariff and of a common commercial policy towards third countries;

(c) the abolition, as between Member States, of obstacles of freedom of movement for persons, services and capital;

(d) the adoption of a common policy in the sphere of agriculture;

(e) the adoption of a common policy in the sphere of transport;

(f) the institution of a system ensuring that competition in the common market is not distorted;

(g) the application of procedures by which the economic policies of the Member States can be co-ordinated and disequilibria in their balances of payments remedied;

(h) the approximation of the laws of Member States to the extent required for the proper functioning of the common market;

(i)   the creation of a European Social Fund in order to improve employ-
      ment opportunities for workers and to contribute to the raising of their
      standard of living;
(j)   the establishment of a European Investment Bank to facilitate the
      economic expansion of the Community by opening up fresh resources;
(k)   the association of the overseas countries and territories in order to
      increase trade and to promote jointly economic and social develop-
      ment.

(Art. 3 EEC)

Similarly, the ECSC Treaty established priorities governing production, trade
and working conditions in the coal and steel sectors for the EC, concentrating in
particular on measures to abolish state aid and restrictive market or price-fixing
activities (Arts 3 and 4 ECSC). The Euratom Treaty also contains a series of
objectives and activities related to research, safety, supply, production and trade
in the civilian use of nuclear energy (Art. 2 Euratom).

The Common Market

In spite of the fact that the EC has been referred to since its establishment as 'the
Common Market' in various languages, it is a misnomer. As far as the establishment of a common market is concerned, the SEA and the 1992 deadline was an
admission that during the first 30 years of the EEC the original aim of a market in
which goods, persons, services and capital could circulate freely had not been
fulfilled. The original deadline had been 12 years (Art. 8 EEC), an unrealistic goal
due to continued protection of national interests and cumbersome decision-
making procedures. The accession of six new Member States in the last two
decades contributed to the delays in creating a single market. The SEA, with its
new deadlines and procedures, was essential if such a market were ever to exist.

The Common Customs Tariff and commercial policy

In this area the EC has been more successful, with the establishment of a
common tariff for all Member States and a commercial policy co-ordinated
centrally by the EC Commission. Thus, in the General Agreement on Tariffs and
Trade (GATT), the EC is represented by the Commission, which negotiates with
other trading partners on behalf of the 12 Member States. The Common
Customs Tariff (CCT) and harmonised customs nomenclature systems mean that
imports from third countries are subject to the same duties regardless of where
they enter the Community, and their identification and description is facilitated
through a single nomenclature. In this area, the framework for a single market is
now in place.

Common sectoral policies

The policies set out in the Treaties have had mixed success. The ECSC has been successful in co-ordinating the coal and steel sectors of the Member States, in particular in concluding negotiations on the running down of the steel industry through its particular crisis in the 1980s (see Chapter 6; 'Iron and steel, and shipbuilding'). Without it, there is no doubt that national subsidies would have been used to prolong and aggravate the crisis. Similarly, Euratom has been successful in co-ordinating strategies and policies in the nuclear energy sphere.

The Common Agricultural Policy

The provisions in the EEC Treaty establishing the Common Agricultural Policy (CAP) were aimed at increasing productivity, stabilising markets, ensuring availability of supplies and guaranteeing farmers' incomes and reasonable prices for consumers. Food rationing after the Second World War and the fear of shortages of food supplies in the future led to the establishment of an extremely comprehensive and productive policy. Productivity increases through techno-logical advances indeed turned out to be far higher than expected, and the EC was left with huge surpluses of some products, for which it still had to pay producers. The accession of new Member States, and a strong farming lobby, aggravated the problem. The CAP has ended up taking well over half of the limited EC budget (see Chapter 2; 'The EC budget') and is now the subject of a major debate over its reform, in particular due to its impact on world agricultural markets (see Chapter 4; 'The Common Agricultural Policy and its reform').

Other policies

Transport policy has hardly developed at all since 1957 owing to the fact that many sectors of transport are state owned and, therefore, subject to strong protectionist tendencies in most Member States. As far as industrial sectors are concerned, there has been very little policy development, except in the field of research and development (R and D) in new industries, where the EC funds and manages programmes co-ordinating efforts of Member States. In terms of actual funding, however, the sums involved are small when compared to those provided in the USA or Japan.

In the social and regional policy areas, the EC has had insufficient financial resources to make a major impact on social and regional imbalances and here, also, the accession of the most recent Member States to join, especially Greece and Portugal, has tended to aggravate the problem (see Chapter 10). The SEA also drew attention to past failings by setting new objectives in such imbalances, as well as in environmental protection and health, which were largely disregarded in the 1950s as international issues, when the Treaties were signed. Development policy, established in EEC 3(k) has also had limited success, owing to lack of funds, although some useful progress has been made in relations with developing countries through the Yaoundé and Lomé Conventions.

Other activities

The ambitious objective of closer co-ordination of economic policies of Member States is still far from being a reality, although the creation of the European Currency Unit (ECU) and the European Monetary System (EMS) have prepared the way for closer monetary co-operation. There are still major divergences in overall economic and fiscal policy between Member States, although the move towards Economic and Monetary Union (EMU) agreed in Maastricht (1991) is a clear indication of the intention in the EC to move towards a single currency. In the course of 1992 further doubts were expressed about the economic convergence conditions being fulfilled by enough Member States for EMU to become a reality. The Maastricht Treaty on European Union also lays down the framework for a common foreign and security policy for the EC, regarded as being increasingly urgent as a result of developments in the former Soviet Union and of crises in the Middle East and Yugoslavia.

With regard to the legislative and judicial framework of the EC, the principles of the Treaties are actively policed by the Commission and the Court of Justice (see Chapter 2; 'The EC institutions: structure, powers and activities'), which are particularly strong in areas such as competition and state aids. Nevertheless, the risk that Member States will revert to national interest and protectionism, and attempt to distort competition, is never far from the surface. There have also been difficulties in getting EC legislation properly implemented in Member States, with the UK and Denmark particularly assiduous in transposing EC directives into national law when compared to Italy and Greece.

There has, however, been progress in areas of culture and education, with efforts to develop an EC identity among the citizens of Europe. There is now much more awareness of, and contact with people from, other Member States, especially among the young, although fears have also been expressed that national identities and cultures are being eroded as a result.

The debate over the future of the EC will have to cover all the various aspects referred to above as its objectives and activities are revised and assessed over the coming decade. In later chapters of this book, sectors and issues will be addressed in more detail.

DEMOGRAPHIC AND ECONOMIC FEATURES OF EUROPE

An analysis of the EC must take place within a more general European setting, and comparisons must be drawn with the countries that aspire to eventual membership. The purpose of Table 1.3 is to introduce some of the main demographic and economic features of the countries of Europe and to allow a broad comparison of the countries within the EC and of these countries with the rest.

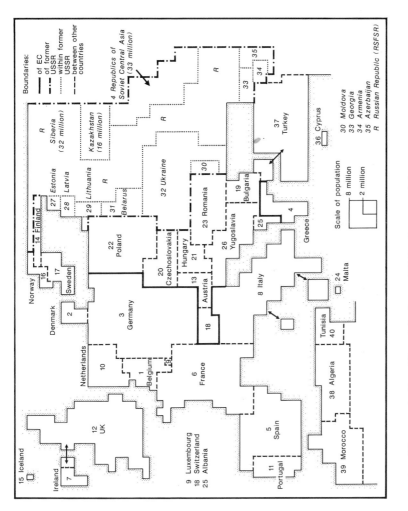

Figure 1.3 The countries of Europe, the Republics of the former USSR, Cyprus and the Maghreb, represented according to population size. The numbering of the countries corresponds to that in Table 1.3

Table 1.3 Data set for the countries of Europe and other selected countries

(1) Political units	(2) Official or main language(s)	(3) Area in 000s sq km	(4) Estimated population in millions			(5) Total fertility rate 1990	(6) Total GDP 1987	(7) Real GDP per head 1987	(8) Infant mortality rate 1990	(9) % in agriculture 1989	(10) Energy consumption per head 1988
			1990	2000	2020						
European Community (EC)											
1 Belgium	D, F, G	31	9.9	9.9	9.4	1.6	130	13,140	9.2	1.9	5,590
2 Denmark	Danish	43	5.1	5.2	4.9	1.6	77	15,120	7.8	4.9	5,010
3a Germany (FRG)	German (G)	248	63.2	65.7	62.3	1.4	899	14,730	7.5	3.8	5,590
b Germany (GDR)	German	108	16.3	15.5	15.0	1.7	134	8,000	8.1	8.3	7,760
4 Greece	Greek (GR)	132	10.1	10.2	9.9	1.5	55	5,500	11.0	24.8	2,820
5 Spain	Spanish	505	39.4	40.7	40.7	1.5	351	8,990	9.0	11.3	2,310
6 France	French (F)	574	56.4	57.9	58.7	1.8	776	13,960	7.5	5.5	3,670
7 Ireland	English[1]	70	3.5	3.5	3.4	2.2	30	8,570	9.7	13.9	3,560
8 Italy	Italian (I)	301	57.7	58.6	56.1	1.3	613	10,680	9.5	7.5	3,620
9 Luxembourg	French[2]	3	0.4	0.4	0.4	1.4	7	18,550	8.7	see Belgium	11,760
10 Netherlands	Dutch (D)	34	14.9	15.3	15.0	1.5	185	12,660	7.6	3.8	6,810
11 Portugal	Portuguese	92	10.4	10.7	10.7	1.6	58	5,600	14.9	16.9	1,550
12 UK	English	244	57.4	59.1	60.8	1.8	697	12,270	9.5	2.0	4,950
European Free Trade Association (EFTA)											
13 Austria	German	84	7.6	7.7	7.6	1.4	94	12,390	8.1	6.0	4,020
14 Finland	Finnish	337	5.0	5.0	4.9	1.7	63	12,800	5.9	8.4	5,791
15 Iceland	Icelandic	103	0.3	0.3	0.3	2.3	5	16,330	6.2	7.1	5,860
16 Norway	Norwegian	324	4.2	4.3	4.3	1.8	67	15,940	8.4	5.5	6,660
17 Sweden	Swedish	450	8.5	8.8	9.0	2.0	116	13,780	5.8	4.0	4,910
18 Switzerland	G, F, I	41	6.7	6.8	6.9	1.6	102	15,400	6.8	4.2	3,780

Former CMEA countries excluding USSR

19	Bulgaria	Bulgarian	111	8.9	9.0	9.1	2.0	43	4,750	13.5	12.7	5,730
20	Czechoslovakia	Czech/Slovak	128	15.7	16.3	17.0	2.1	121	7,750	11.9	9.7	6,170
21	Hungary	Hungarian	93	10.6	10.6	10.4	1.8	48	4,500	15.8	12.1	3,810
22	Poland	Polish	312	37.8	38.9	41.7	2.1	151	4,000	16.2	21.5	4,740
23	Romania	Romanian	238	23.3	24.5	26.0	2.3	69	3,000	25.6	21.1	4,710

Other Europe

24	Malta	Maltese	0.3	0.4	0.4	0.4	2.0	2	4,190	8.0	3.9	1,920
25	Albania	Albanian	29	3.3	3.8	4.7	3.2	6	2,000	28.0	49.1	1,310
26	Yugoslavia	Various	256	23.8	25.1	26.3	2.0	117	5,000	24.5	22.6	2,500

Baltic Republics

27	Estonia	Estonian	45	2	2	2	2.2	18	9,230	12.4	10.0	4,000
28	Latvia	Latvian	64	3	3	3	2.2	26	8,680	11.0	10.0	3,000
29	Lithuania	Lithuanian	65	4	4	4	2.2	30	7,570	11.5	15.0	3,000

Other former Soviet
Socialist Republics of Europe

30	Moldova	Moldavian	34	4	5	5	2.8	21	5,340	23.0	25.0	2,500
31	Belarus	Belarussian	208	10	11	11	2.1	67	6,650	13.1	15.0	5,000
32	Ukraine	Ukrainian	604	52	54	55	2.1	297	5,720	14.2	20.0	6,500
33	Georgia	Various	70	5	6	6	2.3	27	5,450	21.9	25.0	2,000
34	Armenia	Armenian	30	3	4	4	2.6	15	4,890	25.3	15.0	2,000
35	Azerbaijan	Various	87	7	8	10	2.9	25	3,600	27.0	30.0	3,000

Table 1.3 continued

(1) Political units	(2) Official or main language(s)	(3) Area in 000s sq km	(4) Estimated population in millions 1990	2000	2020	(5) Total fertility rate 1990	(6) Total GDP 1987	(7) Real GDP per head 1987	(8) Infant mortality rate 1990	(9) % in agriculture 1989	(10) Energy consumption per head 1988
Extra-European countries											
36 Cyprus	GR, T	9	0.7	0.8	0.9	2.4	4	5,210	11.0	21.1	2,610
37 Turkey	Turkish (T)	781	57	69	94	3.6	215	3,780	74.0	49.1	940
38 Algeria	Arabic	2,382	26	33	46	6.1	68	2,630	74.0	25.0	1,230
39 Morocco	Arabic	444	26	31	43	4.8	46	1,760	82.0	37.5	350
40 Tunisia	Arabic	164	8	10	14	4.1	22	2,740	59.0	25.2	700
Former Union of Soviet Socialist Republics (USSR)											
All USSR	Russian, many others	22,402	289	312	355	2.5	1,734	6,000	24.7	13.6	6,890
Other countries for comparison											
USA	English	9,373	251	268	294	2.0	4,421	17,615	9.7	2.4	10,060
Japan	Japanese	373	124	128	124	1.6	1,629	13,135	4.8	6.8	3,920

Notes: 1 official language Gaelic or Irish
2 official language Luxemburgish

Definitions of the variables in Table 1.3

(1) All the sovereign states of Europe are included apart from some very small units (e.g. Andorra, San Marino).
(2) In many countries in the table, minority languages are in use in addition to the main or official languages listed. In the former USSR there are about 100 languages altogether (many in the Asian part), some of which form the basis for the former Soviet Socialist Republics.
(3) Area in thousands of square kilometres.
(4) Estimated population in millions in 1990, 2000 and 2020. The Population Reference Bureau estimates for 2000 and 2020 are based on past trends.
(5) Total fertility rate (TFR) is 'the average number of children a woman will bear in her lifetime assuming that current age-specific birth rates will remain constant throughout her child-bearing years' (PRB definition), 1990.
(6) Estimates of GDP in billions of US dollars for the countries of the world. These vary considerably according to the way in which they are expressed and there is always delay in producing data for some countries. The Central European countries and the former USSR did not calculate the value of their total product in the same way as Western countries. In this table, 1987 data published in the UNDP (United Nations Development Programme) Human Development Report (1990) have been used because they are 'real' values rather than values produced by conversion of US dollars at official exchange rates of the time. Values for the Soviet Republics have been based on the UN estimate for the USSR as a whole of 8,000 dollars per capita and scaled according to Soviet data for retail sales per head of population in each Republic.
(7) Real GDP in US dollars per inhabitant, 1987.
(8) Infant mortality rate is the annual number of deaths of infants under the age of 1 year per 1,000 live births, 1990.
(9) Economically active population in the agricultural sector as a percentage of total economically active population in 1989.
(10) Consumption of commercial sources of energy in kilograms of coal equivalent per inhabitant in 1988.

Sources of the data in columns (4) to (10) in Table 1.3

(4), (5), (8) Population Reference Bureau Inc. (PRB), *1990 World Population Data Sheet*, Washington, DC, 1990.
(6), (7) United Nations Development Programme (UNDP) *Human Development Report 1990*, pp. 128–9, New York, 1990.
(9) United Nations, *Food and Agriculture Organisation Production Yearbook Vol. 43, 1989*, Table 3, Food and Agriculture Organisation, Rome, 1990.
(10) United Nations, *1988 Energy Statistics Yearbook*, New York, 1991, Table 1.

Given the close association of Turkey and the Maghreb countries with the EC, these have also been included, together with those former Soviet Socialist Republics of the USSR located in the European part of the country. Their inclusion does not, however, imply that the authors consider their entry into the EC imminent. The USA and Japan have been included for comparative purposes. Table 1.3 is accompanied by technical notes on the source and the precise definition of each variable. There follows, column by column, a brief commentary on salient features that emerge from the data.

Language

The main language(s) of each country has/have been noted in col. (2) of Table 1.3 in order to show the linguistic and cultural complexity of Europe compared with that of its main rivals among the developed countries, the USA and Japan, each with one main language only. Most of the non-EC countries that have already applied for membership of the EC or are likely to do so in the near future would bring at least one new language each, increasing the burden of translating and publishing texts in all official languages and of interpreting at meetings.

Area and population

The countries of Europe vary greatly in area and population size. These differences are shown clearly in Figures 1.1 and 1.3. Luxembourg, Iceland, Malta and Cyprus each have under 1 million inhabitants, while Germany, France, Italy and the UK all have over 50 million inhabitants, as do the Ukraine and Turkey. This difference has clear institutional and political implications for the status of individual sovereign states within the supranational union. The population projections show that little change is expected in the total population of most countries of Europe, but that the populations of Turkey and the Maghreb countries are growing fast and could double in a matter of three or four decades. The total fertility rate (column (5)) shows that if present trends continue, the population of several European countries will start to decline in a matter of years.

Gross Domestic Product (GDP)

GDP is widely used to measure the total value of goods and services produced in a country or a region. Total GDP, column (6), varies according to both the absolute size of country and the amount per inhabitant, column (7). The total GDP of Germany, for example, is several hundred times that of Malta. Figure 1.4 shows graphically the enormous differences in the 'economic' size of countries, and the dominance of Western Europe in the continent as a whole. The large development 'gap' in Europe is clearly shown by the values per inhabitant. In Western Europe the extremes are Luxembourg with 18,550 dollars per inhabitant and Greece with 5,500. Most Central European countries, and the

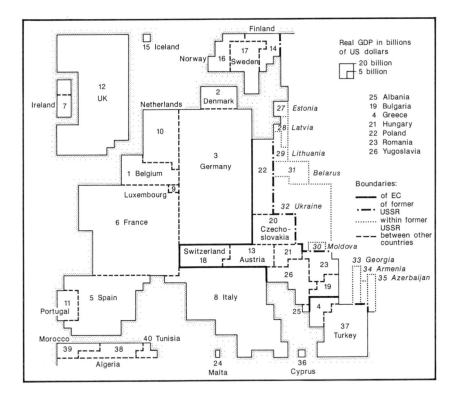

Figure 1.4 The countries of Europe, the Republics of the European part of the former USSR, Cyprus and the Maghreb represented according to size of total Gross Domestic Product (GDP) in 1987

Republics of the former USSR, are close to or some way below Greece, while Morocco, with 1,760, the poorest of all the countries considered, has about one-tenth of the Luxembourg level (but is still far above Zaïre's 200).

Infant mortality

Infant mortality is a rough guide to the quality of healthcare facilities in each country. By world standards, all the EC and EFTA countries except Portugal have very low levels of infant mortality. Among the countries of Central Europe and among the former Soviet Republics of Europe, variations are considerable. Turkey and the Maghreb countries have far higher rates, Morocco being near the average for all less developed countries in the world.

Employment

Employment in the agricultural sector is a guide to the extent to which a country has developed and modernised. In all the countries of Europe, the share of total economically active population in the agricultural sector has declined sharply in the last few decades whereas the area cultivated has not changed much. The number of people working in agriculture cannot be expected to diminish much more in the UK and Belgium, where it is now only about 2 per cent of all employment, but it is likely that in Greece, Portugal, Spain and Ireland the number of jobs lost in agriculture will be considerable in the next two decades. Most Central European countries and most former Soviet Republics can also be expected to continue losing jobs in the agricultural sector.

Energy consumption

Until the widespread alarm felt about the possible negative effects of pollution and 'greenhouse' gases on the environment in the 1980s, growth in the consumption of inanimate sources of energy, mainly fossil fuels, together with nuclear and hydro-electric power, was regarded as a measure of progress. The data for energy consumption per inhabitant of all commercial sources illustrate several aspects of the economic life of the country: the use of machines in various sectors of the economy; the need for domestic heating, especially in the colder areas; the unavoidable production of pollutants. A comparison of GDP per inhabitant and energy consumption per inhabitant for each country (see Figure 9.1) shows that the Central European countries use their energy much less efficiently than do the Western European ones.

THE GEOGRAPHICAL VIEWPOINT AND THE STRUCTURE OF THE BOOK

Due reference is made in this book to political, economic and social aspects of the EC, but the authors concentrate primarily on a geographical approach. Spatial aspects of regions and the relationship of humans to the environment are two of the most prominent traditions in geography. Two distinct features of a region, whatever its size, determine its performance and prospects: first its attributes and second its location in relation to other regions in a given context.

The *attributes* of a region include features of climate, relief and soil, and the availability of commercial minerals, as well as features of the population and its activities. The EC contains some relatively backward agricultural regions, other regions that depend heavily on industry, whether long established or newly developed, as well as some of the largest and most sophisticated service-based urban complexes in the world. One of the general aims of the EC is to work towards convergence. That does not mean that conditions in all regions should be exactly homogeneous, but it does mean that the standard of living, employment

22

opportunities and the quality of life should be broadly similar throughout the Community. In the present book it will be shown that there was still great diversity in the EC in the early 1990s.

The *locational advantages and disadvantages* of a place may be influenced by its position in relation to the centre and periphery of the EC. In Figure 3.3 (Chapter 3), circles with a radius of 500 km are centred on four cities in the Community. Over 40 per cent of the total population of the EC is contained within a circle of that radius if it is centred, for example, on Strasbourg, but only a few per cent if it is centred, for example, on Lisbon or Athens.

In addition to the attributes and location of the various parts of the EC, trends over time in a wide range of human activities will also be noted, since they affect the current situation and future prospects. These activities are represented within the following principal themes covered in the subsequent chapters of the book.

Chapter 2 The organisation of the EEC   A gradual transfer of powers to supranational bodies from national governments and a growth in membership since 1958 with additions in 1973 (UK, Ireland, Denmark), 1981 (Greece), 1986 (Spain and Portugal) and 1990 (the former GDR).

Chapter 3 Population   Little change in total population, a gradual increase in average age, moderate internal migration, a possible sharp increase in the rate of migration from extra-EC areas. Unemployment has tended to change since the 1960s in a cyclical manner.

Chapter 4 Agriculture   Little change in the arable area in use, increases in yields of crops and livestock, increasing mechanisation, but a decrease in the number of people employed.

Chapter 5 Energy   Increasing consumption of energy but a decline in the use of coal and an increase in the use of nuclear power.

Chapter 6 Industry   A gradual decline in the number employed in this sector since the 1970s, a sharp decline in some sectors, a rise in others.

Chapter 7 Services   A growth sector to the present.

Chapter 8 Transport   The relative decline of rail transport, a sharp increase in road transport, and increasing air travel.

Chapter 9 Environment   Great increase in the 1980s in concern over pollution of various kinds.

Chapter 10 Regional issues   The relative positions of rich and poor regions has not changed much since the 1960s. The entry of new Member States has stretched regional disparities.

Chapters 11, 12 Enlargement and the global setting   Can the EC both expand and become more integrated without encountering insurmountable difficulties? What will the future role and identity of the EC be in a changing global setting?

The reader will find that the amount of material on relations between the EC and other parts of Europe and the world varies between chapters. Thus, for example, energy is dealt with in a broader context than services because about half of the EC's energy is imported whereas the Community is largely self-contained with regard to services.

FURTHER READING

Clout, H., Blacksell, M., King, R. and Pinder, D. (1989) *Western Europe: Geographical Perspectives*, Harlow: Longman.

European Communities (1992) *Europe in Figures*, (3rd edn), London: HMSO.

Eurostat (1989) *Europe in Figures*, deadline 1992 (1989/90 edition), Brussels-Luxembourg/London: HMSO.

Heseltine, M. (1989) *The Challenge of Europe: Can Britain Win?*, London: Weidenfeld & Nicolson.

McDonald, J. R. (1991) *The European Scene: A Geographical Perspective*, Englewood Cliffs, NJ: Prentice-Hall.

Masser, I., Sviden, O. and Wegener, M. (1992) *The Geography of Europe's Futures*, London and New York: Belhaven Press.

Minshull, G. N. (1990) *The New Europe*, London: Hodder & Stoughton.

Pinder, D. (ed.) (1990) *Western Europe – Challenge and Change*, London: Belhaven Press.

2

THE EC: A COMMUNITY AND ITS REGIONS

THE EC INSTITUTIONS: STRUCTURE, POWERS AND ACTIVITIES

As explained in Chapter 1, the founding treaties of the EC, subsequently amended by the Merger Treaty and the Single European Act, laid down objectives and activities for the EC and established an institutional framework to perform the tasks required. The EEC Treaty set up the institutions, namely: a European Parliament (EP), a Council, a Commission, a Court of Justice, assisted by an Economic and Social Committee with an auditing role carried out by a Court of Auditors (Art. 4 EEC).

The Merger Treaty of 1965 merged the Council and Commission into single institutions for all three Communities, as the 1957 Convention on Common Institutions had done for the Parliament and the Court, and laid down provisions for their appointment and/or composition. The powers and roles of the institutions remained largely unchanged through the successive enlargements of the EC until the Single European Act in 1986, which gave some enhanced powers to the European Parliament, the Council and the Commission at the expense of the governments of the individual Member States sitting in the Council of Ministers, and later the Treaty of Maastricht, which extended further the powers of the EP and the Council in some areas.

The roles of the institutions in the decision-making and legislative process of the EC can be summarised as follows:

- *The European Council* (heads of state and government) the supreme political body;
- *The Council of Ministers* the legislative body;
- *The Commission* the executive and administrative civil service, with sole power to initiate legislation;
- *The Parliament* the democratically elected assembly, with a largely consultative role in the adoption of legislation and more extensive budgetary powers;
- *The Court of Justice* the judiciary which supervises the proper application of EC law by institutions and Member States;

- *The Economic and Social Committee (ESC)* an appointed consultative body;
- *The Court of Auditors* the external auditor of EC expenditure;
- *The European Investment Bank* provider of loans and guarantees for certain categories of EC projects.

The European Council

The European Council is composed of the heads of state and government of the 12 Member States of the EC, meeting at least twice a year; the presidency is held by each Member State in turn for a six-month period in the order determined by the Treaties. A special arrangement for the Republic of France means that the president and prime minister are present, hence the reference to the head of state. Other Member States are represented by their prime ministers.

As the supreme political body, the European Council takes decisions on key political and institutional issues not resolved in the Council of Ministers. Its existence was first formally recognised in the SEA (see Art. 2) although it had been meeting periodically since the early 1970s. It usually meets for one day every six months in the country of the current holder of the presidency, and for one additional session in Brussels. The European Council should not be confused with the Council of Europe, which is a separate non-EC organisation in Strasbourg with 26 member countries, covering co-operation in areas such as social and cultural affairs.

The Council of Ministers

The key legislative and decision-making body of the EC, comprising one minister from each of the 12 Member States of the EC. It meets in various forms on a more or less permanent basis, grouping together the respective ministers from the policy areas concerned, as for example agriculture ministers for the CAP, and social affairs ministers for social policy. Ministers alone would not have the time or expertise to deal with all the technical aspects of EC legislation, so preparatory work is done in working groups, committees and COREPER, the body of EC ambassadors from the 12 Member States who meet in almost permanent session to clear the ground for ministerial meetings.

The presidency of the Council of Ministers is held for six months by each of the Member States in an alphabetical order which during 1987–92 was based on the spelling of the country's own name in its own language: Belgium, Denmark, Germany, Spain, France, Greece, Ireland, Italy, Luxembourg, the Netherlands, Portugal, UK. This order has been modified from 1993 onwards to ensure that each Member State holds the presidency for the first half of the year (which is considered productive due to fewer holiday periods) once in a 12-year cycle. In the event of the accession of new Member States, further modifications will be needed. The outgoing, current and incoming presidencies form the Troika, an unofficial but influential trio of foreign ministers active in the early 1990s in foreign policy activities outside the EC territory in such places as Kurdistan and Yugoslavia.

Subject to the blocking powers enjoyed by the EP under the co-operation and assent procedures, and those matters passed up to the European Council as too politically sensitive to resolve, the Council has the power to adopt all primary legislation, taking decisions and passing laws or resolutions on EC policy or activities. The power of the Council to enact legislation is generally conditional on the submission of a proposal by the Commission, and there is a large number of policy areas in which it is obliged to conduct prior consultation of the EP and the ESC, although the influence of such consultation is limited.

Decisions are taken in accordance with Art. 148 of the EEC Treaty either by simple majority, a qualified majority or unanimously, depending on the area of activity to which the legislative act applies. For simple majority decisions, each Member State has one vote. Where the Council acts by a qualified majority, the weighting of the votes is as follows:

Germany, France, Italy and UK	10 votes each
Spain	8 votes
Belgium, Greece, the Netherlands and Portugal	5 votes each
Denmark and Ireland	3 votes each
Luxembourg	2 votes

Fifty-four of the 76 votes cast must be in favour for the decision to be adopted. Most decisions taken are by qualified majority, although unanimity is still required in some areas. The Council is also one branch of the Community's budgetary authority, the other being the EP; as such, it can determine budgetary expenditure in many areas of Community activity, accounting for more than 60 per cent of total expenditure, although its decisions are subject to Parliament's power to reject the draft annual budget as a whole.

The Commission

The EC Commission has over 16,000 permanent members of staff and uses several thousand additional people on a freelance or expert basis. It is based in Brussels but also has several departments in Luxembourg and research establishments elsewhere in the EC. Its structure is a classic civil service type, with 23 directorates-general covering main policy areas and several services. The Commission comprises 17 commissioners, two from each of the five larger Member States (Germany, Spain, France, Italy and the UK) and one from each of the remainder. The commissioners are appointed by common agreement of the governments of the Member States and, by tradition, the larger countries appoint one from the political party in government and one from the main opposition party. Under the terms of Art. 157 of the EEC Treaty, commissioners must be independent in the conduct of their duties, although this does not preclude their maintaining allegiance to their own political party.

The powers of the Commission can be divided into the categories of initiative, supervision and implementation. The EEC Treaty vests the following powers in the Commission:

> – to ensure that the provisions of this Treaty and the measures taken by the institutions pursuant thereto are applied;
> – to formulate recommendations or deliver opinions on matters dealt with in this Treaty, if it expressly so provides or if the Commission considers it necessary;
> – to have its own power of decision and participate in the shaping of measures taken by the Council and by the European Parliament in the manner provided for in this Treaty;
> – to exercise the powers conferred on it by the Council for the implementation of the rules laid down by the latter.

(EEC Art. 155)

The Commission is the only institution with the right to initiate legislation, an important power both in terms of the speed and the direction at which EC legislation moves. Its supervisory powers lead to the Commission being called 'The Guardian of the Treaties', supervising the implementation of EC law in the Member States, and bringing action against states or other entities in case of infringement. The Commission is also responsible for supervising the implementation by the national administrations of the common policies of the EC, such as the Common Agricultural Policy (CAP) and the structural funds, and managing more directly joint programmes and actions in a wide range of areas such as research and technological development (R and TD), development aid and vocational training. In addition, the Commission is responsible for the negotiation of certain agreements with third countries and for maintaining relations with other international organisations (Art. 229 EEC), such as the GATT, in which Member States do not participate individually, but speak 'with one voice' through the Commission.

The EC Commission is an institution based on collective responsibility, and decisions taken in the pursuance of its tasks are adopted in the weekly meetings of the commissioners on a collegiate basis. The portfolios are shared out at the first meeting of the new Commission, at present appointed every four years but to be extended to five under proposals contained in the Treaty of Maastricht. The president of the Commission is also agreed upon beforehand by the Member State governments.

Commissioners are responsible for areas of Community activity, and administer them using a small advisory cabinet and the overall structure of the directorate-general for the area concerned. In the initiation process for legislation there is a substantial amount of consultation of committees of national government officials, the social partners and other interested parties, and the Commission holds in excess of 50 multinational and multilingual meetings on most days. The Commission is answerable to the European Parliament and commissioners

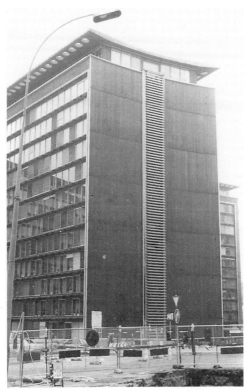

Plates 1, 2 The Berlaymont of the European Commission, Brussels, in 1992, undergoing surgery for the removal of asbestos. The Berlaymont is arguably the best-known twentieth-century building in Western Europe

regularly attend its standing committees meeting in Brussels and plenary sittings in Strasbourg, to answer questions from MEPs. In the last resort, the EP has the power to sack the entire Commission with a two-thirds majority in favour (Art. 144 EEC), although such action has not been taken to date.

The Parliament

Originally a consultative assembly with appointed members, in 1979 the European Parliament became the world's first international parliament to be elected by direct universal suffrage, following the implementation of the Act of 1976. Following the accession of Greece, Spain and Portugal, the number of members of the EP reached its present level of 518, distributed as follows between the Member States:

Belgium	24	Spain	60	Luxembourg	6
Denmark	16	France	81	Netherlands	25
Germany	81	Ireland	15	Portugal	24
Greece	24	Italy	81	UK	81

Elections to the EP take place every five years. There is no single electoral system for the election of MEPs, but a variety of proportional representation and constituency-based systems is found among the Member States, and often the political balance in national delegations is very different from the domestic political situation. Most members, from over 80 national parties, join multi-national political groups in Parliament, composed as follows in 1991, including the nationalities represented (in brackets):

- *Socialist*   180 members (all)
- *EPP (Christian Democrat)**   125 members (all)
- *Liberal, Democratic and Reformist*   46 (all except UK and Greece)
- *European Democratic (Conservative)**   34 (UK and Denmark)
- *Greens*   28 (Belgium, Germany, Spain, France, Italy, the Netherlands, Portugal)
- *European Unitarian Left (soft 'Communist')*   28 (Denmark, Spain, Greece, Italy)
- *European Democratic Alliance (Gaullist)*   22 (Spain, France, Greece, Ireland)
- *European Right*   12 (Belgium, Germany, France)
- *Left Unity (hard 'Communist')*   14 (France, Greece, Ireland, Portugal)
- *Rainbow (Regionalists)*   14 (Belgium, Denmark, Germany, Spain, Ireland, Italy, UK)
- *Non-attached*   15 (Germany, Spain, France, the Netherlands, UK)

Note: *in Alliance as of May 1992

The European Parliament has its own administration, with over 3,000 officials working in Brussels and Luxembourg, divided into seven directorates-general and a legal service. The treaties establishing the EC originally granted the Parliament supervisory and consultative powers in the legislative process which were extended in 1987 with the entry into force of the Single European Act. Although limited in scope, barring the power to dismiss the Commission (see above), the supervisory powers of the EPs are such that Commission and Council are bound to come before the House in order to present proposals and account for action or lack of it. As far as the legislative process is concerned, Parliament's opinions take the form of amendments to the legislative proposal, which the Commission accepts as often as not and undertakes to defend in Council.

The EP is actively involved in the procedure for the adoption of the budget and in supervising its implementation (see p. 34, 'The EC budget'). Since 1975, a conciliation procedure between Council and the EP has been possible, although there have been difficulties in its application. In addition, the co-operation procedure now applies to a considerable part of the legislative process; under this procedure the EC has two readings of the legislative proposal, and its amendments carry greater political weight. The assent procedure (Arts 237 and 238 EEC) also provides the EP with powers in the admission of a new Member State or the signing of association agreements, where the assent of Parliament by a majority of its members is required. The Treaty of Maastricht gave the Parliament the right to veto on limited categories of laws in areas such as consumer protection, education, the single market, environment, and R and TD. Overall, however, especially considering the fact that the EP is the only democratically elected EC institution, its powers are still extremely limited in the legislative and administrative process, with the balance still tipped very heavily towards Council and Commission.

The European Parliament conducts its business very much like a national parliament, in spite of two major handicaps, first the fact that everything is conducted in nine languages and, second, the fact that it still has no fixed 'seat', and is forced to operate in three places of work: Brussels, Luxembourg and Strasbourg. Parliamentary committees and political groups meet in Brussels, the plenary sittings, or 'part-sessions' are held in Strasbourg, and the Secretariat is largely located in Luxembourg. This renders the functioning of the EP costly and inconvenient, and there are frequent efforts to centralise activities in Brussels, where the other main political institutions of the EC are located, but these are consistently thwarted by the powerful French lobby, which insists on continuing to use Strasbourg (see p. 41, 'Current and future issues in the EC').

A normal month in the life of the EP consists of one week of group meetings, two weeks of meetings of standing committees and delegations, and one week of plenary. Most members are full or substitute members of several committees and delegations and tend to be actively involved in a variety of different policy issues and geographical areas. There are 19 standing committees, including Agriculture, External Economic Relations and Social Affairs, and 26 delegations for relations with parliaments from individual or groups of non-EC countries such as the USA or the Maghreb. Although not official organs of Parliament, there are

Plate 3 The new European Parliament under construction in
Brussels, 1992. It will have a circular auditorium capable of
holding 750 Euro MPs

also a large number of 'intergroups' which deal with more specific areas of interest such as animal welfare or land use.

The EP produces reports on proposals for EC legislation, when consulted by the other institutions, and also produces reports at its own initiative. A draft report is prepared by the Committee rapporteur and discussed and voted on in Committee; it may be amended in plenary before being adopted. The EP also discusses and passes resolutions on topical or urgent matters and tables a large number of oral and written questions to Council and Commission.

Although the EP has been more involved in the legislative process since 1986 and is likely to become even more so following Maastricht, a fact borne out by the increasing number of lobbyists and journalists following the institution through its peripatetic existence, doubts are expressed as to whether the EP could actually cope, in terms of efficiency and working methodology, with being vested with any more significant powers.

The Court of Justice

The Court of Justice, located in Luxembourg, is the EC institution responsible for the interpretation and correct application of EC law, both in disputes between different parties, such as institutions, Member States or individuals, and in preliminary rulings on questions of EC law referred to it by national courts. The

Court consists of 13 judges (one from each Member State and an extra judge appointed by one of the large Member States in rotation to keep the total number uneven) and six advocates-general. Both are appointed by a common agreement of the governments of the Member States for a period of six years, with partial replacement every three years. As the independent Community judiciary, the Court has a vital role in ensuring that Community law is uniformly interpreted and applied throughout the entire territory of the internal market, and that the institutions respect the provisions of the Treaties and the general principles of the law common to the Member States, particularly as regards the protection of individual rights.

The Economic and Social Committee

Based very much on the French model of a 'Conseil Economique et Social', the Committee was created in the founding Treaties as a consultative body grouping together 'representatives of the various categories of economic and social activity' and with 'advisory status' (Art. 193 EEC).

The 189 members of the Committee are appointed every four years by the governments of the Member States and sit in three main groups, representing employers, unions and other interest groups such as consumers, farmers and co-operatives. The Committee must be consulted and issue an opinion on a wide range of EC legislative activity (Art. 198 EEC), although its opinions are purely advisory and often merely noted by the Council and Commission.

The Court of Auditors

This EC institution, governed by Article 206 of the EEC Treaty, is responsible for the external auditing of all revenue and expenditure in the EC budget. It consists of 12 members appointed for a six-year term by the Council. Situated in Luxembourg, it has substantial investigative powers, and produces a weighty annual report as well as special reports on individual issues such as the payment of food aid to developing countries.

The European Investment Bank (EIB)

This is an autonomous public financial institution, based in Luxembourg, and set up by the Treaty of Rome with the task 'to contribute, by having recourse to the capital market and utilising its own resources, to the balanced and steady development of the common market' (Art. 130 EEC). The EIB's capital is entirely subscribed by the Member States; in order to fulfil its tasks of granting loans and giving guarantees in a wide range of EC activities, such as projects for developing less-favoured regions, and projects of common interest to several Member States, the Bank normally borrows on the capital markets and relends on a non-profit-making basis.

33

EC law and the legislative process

There are three principal sources of EC law: Treaty provisions; primary legislation adopted by the Council and Commission acting under Treaty provisions;
and secondary legislation adopted by the institutions, normally the Commission,
to implement primary legislation. The first source of the EC law, the Treaties as
amended by the SEA and possibly the TEU, covers a wide range of areas of
economic, commercial and social activites. The best examples of such primary
provisions and their direct impact on EC activity are the rules on competition
(Arts 85ff. EEC) and state aids (Arts 92ff. EEC) which are directly applied by the
Commission and, if needs be, by the Court of Justice, to ensure that there is as
little distortion of competition between industries and markets as possible.
Secondary legislation is a more complex and dynamic area, with EC legal acts
divided up into different categories: regulations, directives, decisions and recommendations.

- *Regulation*   a law which is binding and directly applicable in all Member
  States without any implementing national legislation. Both Council and
  Commission can adopt regulations, used in many areas such as the regu-
  lation of agricultural markets, transport policy and commercial policy.
- *Directive*   a law binding on Member States as regards the results to be
  achieved, but to be implemented into national legislation in the form each
  Member State sees appropriate. Most of the Single Market legislation is in
  the form of directives.
- *Decision*   an act binding entirely on those to whom it is addressed, with no
  national implementing legislation required.
- *Recommendation*   no binding effect, can be adopted by Council and
  Commission.

The first two categories are the most important and widespread of EC secondary
legislation and are adopted in accordance with the various procedures laid down
in the reform of the Treaties through the SEA, which also defined the areas in
which the co-operation and assent procedures should be used. Figure 2.1
illustrates the two procedures for the adoption of EC legislation.

THE EC BUDGET

The budget of the EC must above all be seen in proportion to the GDP of
individual Member States. The total 1992 EC budget, 65.6 billion ECU, was
only approximately 1 per cent of total Community GDP. When the wide range of
activities and the ambitious goals of the EC are borne in mind, it becomes
apparent that there remains a great doubt as to the extent to which the EC can
meet even its short-term commitments with the resources it has available. The
sources of revenues for the EC budget and the destination of expenditure are
shown in Figure 2.2 and discussed below.

EEC legislation from start to finish
(Directives and regulations)

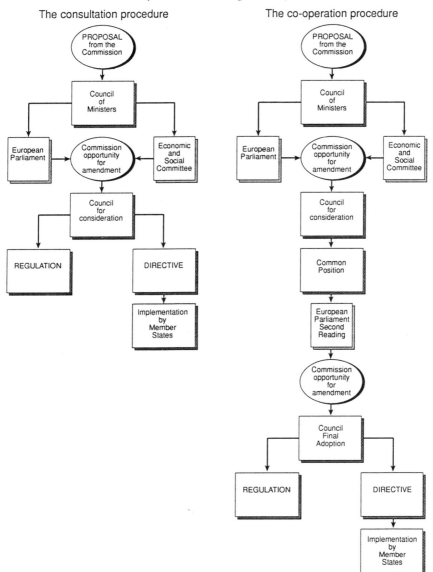

Figure 2.1 The legislation procedures of the European Community

Source: based on a diagram used in the EC Commission

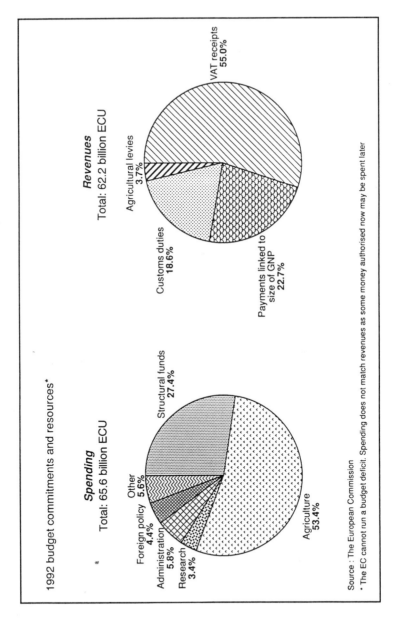

1992 budget commitments and resources*

Spending
Total: 65.6 billion ECU

Structural funds
27.4%

Other 5.6%
Foreign policy 4.4%
Administration 5.8%
Research 3.4%

Agriculture 53.4%

Source : The European Commission
* The EC cannot run a budget deficit. Spending does not match revenues as some money authorised now may be spent later

Revenues
Total: 62.2 billion ECU

VAT receipts 55.0%

Agricultural levies 3.7%

Customs duties 18.6%

Payments linked to size of GNP 22.7%

Figure 2.2 Revenue and expenditure of the EC budget 1992

Source: *The Economist,* 8 Feb. 1992, p. 56

Income

The EC is financed by its own resources, which are made available to it in the amounts and under the conditions laid down in a series of decisions of the Council, subsequently ratified by the Member States. The difference between income (62.2 billion ECU) and expenditure (65.6 billion ECU) is explained by the fact that the EC may commit itself to expenditure to be financed later. The income comes from the sources shown in Table 2.1

- *VAT* a proportion of the VAT base of each Member State, set at 1.4 per cent for the period 1985–92, with a ceiling of 55 per cent of GNP on the VAT base in order not to penalise those countries in which private consumption represents a relatively high proportion of national wealth (Portugal, Greece, Ireland and the UK). In addition, there were compensatory measures for Spain and Portugal in force until 1991 for a transitional period following their accession, as it has taken some time for them to obtain full benefit from membership.
- *Customs duties* on products imported from outside the EC, since there are no duties intra-EC, and a common tariff on imports.
- *Agricultural levies* import levies charged at the external frontiers of the EC in order to bring the price of imported foodstuffs up to the higher EC price level: sugar and isoglucose levies, levies on producers in the EC aimed at limiting surplus production.
- *GNP resource* the 'fourth resource', made up of contributions from Member States based on their GNP at a rate set in the annual budget.
- *Miscellaneous* other minor sources of income include Community taxes on the income of EC staff, who are exempt from paying national income tax, the revenue from fines imposed for breaches of competition law, and from the activities of the Office for Official Publications.

Expenditure

In terms of expenditure, the EC budget has been dominated by spending on the Common Agricultural Policy. It can be seen from the 1992 estimates in Table 2.2 that this continues to be the case, severely limiting expenditure on other crucial

Table 2.1 Sources of income of the 1992 EC budget

Source	Amount (1991) in billions of ECU	% of budget
VAT	34.21	55.0
Customs duties	11.57	18.6
Agricultural levies	2.3	3.7
GNP resource	14.12	22.7
Total	62.2	100

Table 2.2 Main sectors of expenditure of the EC budget, 1992

Area	Amount in billions of ECU	% of budget
1 EAGGF Guarantee	35.03	53.4
2 Structural Funds	17.97	27.4
3 Multi-annual programmes	2.23	3.4
4 Other policies	2.88	4.4
5 Miscellaneous	3.8	5.8
6 Other	3.69	5.6
Total	65.6	100.0

policy areas and regional development. Some major categories of expenditure are as follows.

- *EAGGF Guarantee* is the section of the European Agricultural Guidance and Guarantee Fund which pays for guaranteed agricultural prices to EC farmers.
- *Structural funds* are those aimed at improving regional economic and social development in the EC. These include the European Regional Development Fund (ERDF), the European Social Fund (ESF) and the Guidance section of the EAGGF, specifically aimed at restructuring in the agricultural sector.
- *Research* includes the area of research and technological development (1.95 billion ECU) and the various Euratom and other energy programmes.
- *External Actions* this category includes the EC development aid actions towards Mediterranean, Asian and Latin American countries as well as special measures for the development of Eastern and Central Europe under the PHARE programme (1.1 billion ECU) and special technical assistance to the former Soviet Union (TACIS) (0.45 billion ECU). The European Development Fund, for development aid to countries under the Lomé Convention (an association agreement between the Community and certain African, Caribbean and Pacific countries), is funded directly by Member States and is not part of the EC budget.
- *Administration* this category covers the administrative costs of running the EC and its institutions, 30 per cent of which are related to the fact that there are nine working languages, involving interpreters, translators and the printing of documents.

As far as net contributors and beneficiaries among the Member States are concerned, it is clear that there are substantial differences between what Member States contribute to the EC and what they receive from it. At the beginning of the 1980s the British government successfully obtained a budget rebate under the abatement mechanism, which is currently under review. Figures are available from various sources, and Table 2.3 provides a comparison of net contributions

Table 2.3 Contributions to and receipts from the EC budget, 1983 and 1989

	Millions of pounds in 1983				Millions of ECU in 1989				Agriculture budget in 1989 ECU	
	Contribution	Receipt	R – C	Gain or loss £ per head	Contribution	Receipt	R – C	Gain or loss ECU per head[1]	millions	per head[1]
FRG	3,296	2,136	-1,160	-19	11,110	4,580	-6,530	-106	3,700	60
France	2,587	2,587[2]	0	0	8,623	5,677	-2,946	-53	4,606	82
Italy	1,653	2,523	+870	+15	7,606	6,177	-1,429	-25	4,506	78
Netherlands	901	1,075	+174	+12	2,700	3,830	+1,130	+76	3,469	233
Belgium	527	712	+185	+19	1,807	683	-1,124	-114	546	55
Luxembourg	15	160	+145	+363	73	8	-65	-163	2	5
UK	2,956	1,796	-1,160	-21	6,568	3,214	-3,354	-59	1,797	32
Ireland	114	520	+406	+116	371	1,712	+1,341	+383	1,072	306
Denmark	243	417	+174	+34	871	1,045	+174	+34	977	192
Greece	229	637	+408	+42	566	2,565	+1,999	+200	1,701	170
Spain	—	—	—	—	3,575	3,544	-31	-1	1,850	47
Portugal	—	—	—	—	458	946	+488	+47	174	17
Unattributable[3]	—	—	—	—	—	10,348	+10,348	—	—	—
EC	12,521	12,563	—	—	44,329	44,329	—	—	24,403	75

Sources: for 1983 data see Clough 1983, for 1989 data see Gardner 1991
Notes: 1 per head of total population
2 estimate
3 includes overseas aid

and receipts between 1983 and 1989. In addition, Table 2.4 provides estimates for net contributors and recipients for the 1992 budget, both including and excluding the UK rebate.

It is interesting to note that Germany remains the largest net contributor, in spite of the increased burden of German unification. As agricultural expenditure falls as a proportion of the total budget, the Netherlands is expected to become a net contributor, having benefited from CAP spending to a large extent in the 1980s. Denmark, another of the richer Member States, however, is forecast to remain a net recipient, continuing to profit from its productive agricultural sector.

The increased spending under structural funds is of some benefit to Spain and Greece, in particular, although the sums involved are relatively small. In more general terms, it is clear that there must be great increases in structural funds and the provision of additional transfers, possibly in the form of the proposed Cohesion Fund, for the poorer Member States to make substantial gains in financial terms from membership of the EC. Table 2.5 shows the financial perspective for 1997 as proposed by the Commission in its assessment and forecast for Community spending following the Maastricht Agreement. If this is not done, the ambitions of the founding fathers to promote regional equilibrium between richer and poorer areas of the EC will remain largely unfulfilled. It proposes a 35 per cent increase in the EC budget by 1997, well in excess of any projected growth in GNP, in order to meet the economic and social objectives set out in the Treaty of European Union.

Table 2.4 1992 EC budget in billions of ECU

	After UK rebate	Before UK rebate
Net contributors		
Germany	9.0	8.5
UK	3.0	5.0
France	1.5	0.9
Netherlands	0.1	0.0
Net recipients		
Denmark	0.5	0.5
Italy	0.6	1.1
Luxembourg	0.7	0.7
Portugal	1.1	1.2
Belgium	1.6	1.7
Ireland	2.4	2.4
Spain	2.9	3.2
Greece	3.9	3.9

Source: Gardner 1992

Table 2.5 EC financial perspectives, 1987–97

Commitment appropriations (billion ECU 1992)	1987	1992	1997
Common Agricultural Policy	32.7	35.3	39.6
Structural operations (including the Cohesion Fund)	9.1	18.6	29.3
Internal policies (other than structural operations)	1.9	4.0	6.9
External action	1.4	3.6	6.3
Administrative expenditure	5.9	4.0	4.0
Reserves	0	1.0	1.4
Total	51.0	66.5	87.5
Payment appropriations requires	49.4	63.2	83.2
as % of GNP	1.05	1.15	1.34
Own resources ceiling as % of GNP	(none) (except VAT = 1.40%)	1.20	1.37

Source: COM 92-2000, 1992: 39
Note: Average annual GNP growth:
　　　1987–92 (actual)　　3.1%
　　　1992–7　(projected)　2.5%

CURRENT AND FUTURE ISSUES IN THE EC

1993 and the Completion of the Single Market

The adoption of the Single European Act in 1986 and the Commission White Paper on the Completion of the Single Market with its deadline of 31 December 1992 gave the required boost to an EC that had become bogged down in its attempts to create the common market, one of the fundamental objectives of the Treaty of Rome. The economic costs of having national markets effectively divided from one another were assessed and were estimated to be 3 per cent of the total GNP of the Member States of the EC by Paolo Cecchini in his report on the 'Cost of non-Europe' written in 1988 (see Cecchini 1988). By July 1991, over 200 of the 272 directives in the White Paper had been adopted, and efforts have been increasing to remove the remaining obstacles to the realisation of the freedom of movement of people, capital, goods and services by the beginning of 1993.

The White Paper (CEC 1985) placed proposals in three main groups:

- the removal of physical barriers, such as border checks on people and goods;
- the removal of technical barriers, including technical standards and specifications, rules on the awarding of public contracts, and laws governing services, capital movements and industrial co-operation;
- the removal of fiscal barriers (VAT and excise duties).

41

The speeding up of the legislative process through the introduction of qualified majority voting in the Council and the use of directives based on minimum harmonisation and mutual recognition rather than comprehensive harmonisation of national provisions has had a substantial impact on the development of the internal market, yet the obstacles that remain are considerable, since they are rooted in national interest and tradition. In addition, those directives already adopted have not all yet been transposed into national law and are often infringed by Member States.

Physical barriers

As islands, the UK and Ireland have strict controls at their frontiers and a relatively lax system for the identification of people within the countries. Other Member States require all people to carry identification, with a photograph; moreover these States conduct strict procedures for the registration of places of work and residence. The removal of frontier controls for the free movement of people is therefore a major source of concern for the British government, which wishes to continue to rely on border controls for the prevention of terrorism, drugs trafficking and crime in general, and illegal immigration. In spite of the signing of the Schengen Agreement in 1990 between France, Germany and the Benelux countries, joined later by Spain, Portugal and Italy, for a frontier-free area, there are still difficulties hindering the complete removal of border controls between the signatories.

Technical barriers

- *Transport*   there are still many areas of the market for transport which have to be opened up to freer competition, including rail, air and sea.
- *Financial services*   regulations concerning the provision of services in the banking and insurance sectors have recently undergone a 'communitarising' process; once this process is complete there will be very few such barriers left.
- *Public procurement*   there are still major areas of national public services exempted from competition from abroad and, in some cases, even at the national level.

Fiscal barriers

Indirect taxation: VAT rates and excise duties still vary substantially between Member States. For example, a packet of cigarettes costs ten times as much in Denmark as in Greece. Denmark and Ireland receive a substantial amount of state revenue through high indirect taxes, whereas Luxembourg benefits from much tourist traffic as a result of its low rates. In a completely open market, such differences are bound to distort trade, in particular in border areas, but attempts to bring rates closer together, which requires the unanimous agreement of Member States, are meeting with limited success.

Plates 4, 5 Examples of twinning in Western Europe. Here two places in the former county of Rutland (now part of Leicestershire) in the UK advertise their links: in the case of Whitwell, with a fair degree of self-importance

It can be seen that the objectives and deadline of 1992 have served to hasten the development of the Internal Market in a wide range of areas, but the prospect of achieving a complete and fully open market in the short term still remains poor. National traditions and differences are a distinct feature of the EC and are likely to predominate over harmonisation and integration.

Economic and Monetary Union

In order to benefit more fully from the Internal Market, it is generally agreed that a single European currency would be far more economical than the present situation with 11 national currencies (the Belgian and Luxembourg francs are already in a monetary union with fixed parity). Proposals to develop economic and monetary union in the EC date back to the 1960s, and the SEA contains explicit reference to 'the convergence of economic and monetary policies which is necessary for the further development of the Community'.

There has been closer co-operation in monetary terms within the European Monetary System (EMS), and most EC currencies now fluctuate against one another only to a very restricted extent, thanks to its Exchange Rate Mechanism (ERM). The more widespread use of the European Currency Unit (ECU), a currency based on a basket of all 11 EC currencies, has contributed to awareness of the usefulness of an EC-wide unit. As far as economic co-operation is concerned, this has been based very much on co-ordination and mutual information rather than on any specific policies aimed at convergence. It was only with the publication of the report of the Delors Committee in 1989 that concrete proposals were advanced for a move to full economic and monetary union in three phases.

- *Phase 1* convergence of economic performance through stronger economic and monetary coordination; free movement of capital and liberalisation of financial services in the internal market; all EC currencies in the ERM.
- *Phase 2* the establishment of a European system of Central Banks, decision-making on monetary affairs shifted to EC level, and a narrowing of the fluctuation bands of the ERM towards zero.
- *Phase 3* the irrevocable fixing of exchange rates, binding EC-level rules in the area of macro-economic and budgetary policy, and the Central Banks responsible for monetary policy and currency reserves in the EC.

In the Treaty of Maastricht it was decided to set the deadline of 1999 for the introduction of the single currency, although there are conditions to be met by participating Member States. The UK has decided to 'wait and see', using an opt-out clause grudgingly allowed by the other 11 countries. In spite of the clear advantages of economic and monetary union in terms of the removal of transaction costs and greater transparency in pricing and costs in the internal market, several Member States fear the loss of national sovereignty and the obligation for governments with tight control of public spending to co-ordinate policy with those following more inflationary policies. The eventual outcome for EMU is still far from clear.

Political union

The Treaty of Maastricht, signed following just over one year of negotiations in Intergovernmental Conferences and remaining to be ratified by national parliaments or in referenda in the course of 1992, marked a watershed in the development of the EC. In addition to Economic and Monetary Union, referred to above, the draft Treaty on European Union contains a range of new powers and orientations for the EC of the 1990s. These can broadly be summarised under the following headings:

- common foreign and security policy;
- common immigration/visa policy;
- new EC powers;
- social policy;
- cohesion.

Common foreign and security policy

The implementation of a common foreign and security policy which shall include the framing of a common defence policy

(Art. B TEU)

The objectives of such a common policy are to enable the EC to go beyond mere 'co-operation' on foreign policy, as has been the case until the end of 1992 under the EPC (European Political Co-operation) procedure in operation since the 1970s and formalised in the SEA. Although there is provision for qualified majority voting on the action to be taken, any actual decision of policy or principle must be taken unanimously, effectively giving any Member State a right to veto. The recognition of republics in Yugoslavia was an indication of the need for a common foreign policy, since without it, Germany overrode the more cautious views of other Member States by recognising Croatia and Slovenia.

As far as defence is concerned, 'the policy of the Union shall respect the obligations of certain Member States under the North Atlantic Treaty' (Art. D.4 TEU), which effectively means that there may be moves towards a European Defence Identity, under the WEU (Western European Union) but still respecting NATO.

Common immigration/visa policy

This area is regarded as important, but still subject to opposition from the UK, whose geographical position as an island, it argues, makes it important for unilateral policy to be applied. Nevertheless, there is provision for a policy, with decisions taken by unanimity.

New EC powers

The powers of the EC have been extended in new chapters, including consumer protection, education, health and trans-European networks (see Chapter 8), for which qualified majority voting rules will apply, in addition to certain areas of environmental policy (see Chapter 9).

Social policy

The most controversial area is increased Community powers. The Treaty contains a protocol, signed by 11 Member States without the UK, extending EC powers to a wide range of social policy areas.

Cohesion

There is a commitment in a protocol to set up a 'cohesion' fund to assist poorer countries, such as Spain and Portugal (TEU Annex I).

Overall, the Treaty represents an important development in the further integration of the EC, with key areas remaining, nevertheless, in the hands of Member States, and all governed by the principle of subsidiarity. As far as the legal effect of the Treaty is concerned, it remains to be ratified by national parliaments, several of which may require a referendum of their respective populations. There is also a legal dispute over the validity of the protocol on social policy, since it excludes the territory of the UK, although it is geographically part of the Single Market.

Enlargement

The Treaty of Rome states in Article 237 that 'any European State may apply to become a member of the Community'. Member States must however be democracies and have economic systems that are compatible with the common market, i.e. market economies. These criteria have been used to argue that Turkey and Morocco are not eligible for membership and that ex-CMEA countries have a long way to go before their economies are compatible. As far as EFTA and certain other applicants are concerned, however, there are few obstacles to their accession in the course of the 1990s. The subject of new members is dealt with in detail in Chapter 11.

The EFTA countries have maintained close commercial ties with the EC and the negotiations for the creation of a European Economic Area in 1990/1 have paved the way for speedier accession negotiations for those EFTA members that apply individually. Moreover, the accession of countries such as Sweden and Austria, both with prosperous economies, would not have the same regional impact as the accession of countries such as Portugal or Greece, and the former countries would be net contributors to the EC budget. Administrative complications can be expected with the accession of new members, in terms of EC staffing policies and the provision of additional language services. On the other hand, there are many who feel that the EC has an obligation to accept eligible new members.

The future of the EC

The beginning of the 1990s represents a watershed in the future of the European Communities. Events in Central and Eastern Europe, German unification, and a greater awareness of the need for enhanced co-operation through the Gulf Crisis, have created a new sense of urgency in the further development and integration of the EC. There has been much talk of deepening and widening, with the more ambitious tendency arguing that the EC needs to become more integrated before admitting new members, countered by the expansionists, who wish to see more members and a 'watering down' of EC powers in a Community based more on co-operation.

The first 40 years of the EC's history have shown that ambitious ideals of European Union, with sharing of sovereignty in centralised institutions, have foundered due to lack of commitment and through practical difficulties in the Member States themselves. A Community based on the respect of individual national identities and traditions can develop only at the speed of the slowest member in terms of enthusiasm for the European dream. The future development of the EC remains, therefore, firmly in the hands of the governments of the Member States, and the extent to which they desire integration. It remains unlikely that they, or the populations who elect them, are going to be willing to surrender so much national history into a United States of Europe for many decades to come.

THE REGIONAL STRUCTURE OF THE EC

So far, the organisation of the EC has been considered as a single entity composed of 12 Member States. In practice, it is necessary, for various purposes, including the application of regional policies, to subdivide the EC into regions at a number of different levels. Each of the 12 Member States of the EC has various subdivisions of its own for purposes of administration. With the establishment of the EC, however, a system of regions and subregions has been created for the use of the supranational bodies of the Community. Statistical data are collected and analysed at subnational level, and decisions regarding the allocation of funds from the EC budget may be influenced by the regional structure.

According to COM 90-609 (1991), Annex 0.1 (p. 5):

> The Nomenclature of Territorial Units for Statistics (NUTS) was established by the Statistical Office of the European Communities, in co-operation with the Commission's other departments, to provide a single uniform breakdown of territorial units for the production of Community regional statistics.

In Table 2.6, the number of regions in each of three NUTS levels, 1, 2 and 3, is shown for each Member State. Two complications must be noted: first the former GDR is not counted under Germany (but see notes 2 and 3 in Table 2.6)

47

Table 2.6 Correspondence between NUTS levels and national administrative divisions in the Community

Member State	NUTS 1		NUTS 2		NUTS 3	
Belgique/Belgie	Regions	3	Provinces	9	Arrondissements	43
Danmark[1]	–	1	–	1	Amter	15
BR Deutschland[2]	Länder	11	Regierungsbezirke[3]	31	Kreise	328
Ellas	Groups of development regions[4]	4	Development regions	13	Nomoi	51
España	Agrupación de comunidades autónomas	7	Comunidades autónomas + Ceuta y Melilla	18	Provincias	52
France	Zeat	8	Regions	22	Départements	96
	+ DOM	1	+ DOM	4	+ DOM	4
Ireland	–	1	–	1	Planning regions	9
Italia	Gruppi di regioni[4]	11	Regioni	20	Provincie	95
G.D. Luxembourg	–	1	–	1	–	1
Nederland	Landsdelen	4	Provincies	12	C.O.R.O.P.-Regios	40
Portugal	Continente + Regiões autonomas	3	Comissões de coordenação regional + Regiões autonomas	7	Grupos de Concelhos	30
United Kingdom	Standard regions	11	Groups of counties[4]	35	Counties/Local authority regions[4]	65
EUR 12		66		174		829

Source: COM 1990
Notes: 1 a breakdown of Denmark into three regions is given in most of the tables and maps
2 regions of the former GDR not yet included (5 Länder, 15 Bezirke, 218 Kreise)
3 26 Regierungsbezirke + 5 Länder not subdivided into Regierungsbezirke
4 grouping for Community purposes

and, second, some of the extra-European territories of France, Spain and Portugal are included in the EC. These are described either as 'non-continental' or as 'overseas'.

- France has four overseas territories (*Départements d'outremer*): Guadeloupe and Martinique in the Caribbean, Guyane on the mainland of South America and Réunion in the Indian Ocean.
- Spain has three non-continental units, Islas Baleares in the Mediterranean, Las Palmas and Santa Cruz de Tenerife in the Atlantic, each equal in status to the provinces of the mainland, plus two small territories, Ceuta and Melilla, on the coast of Morocco.
- Portugal has two non-continental units in the Atlantic, the Açores and Madeira.
- Finally, it must be noted that the Isle of Man and the Channel Islands are not in the EC.

In most tables in this book, data for the former GDR have been shown separately from those for the FRG unless they relate to the post-unification situation. The smaller overseas territories of the EC are omitted from most data sets.

As many new states of the USA came into existence after the Declaration of Independence, they were mostly formed in a virtual vacuum, with the US Land Survey having considerable power in shaping them on territory purchased or conquered from France, Russia (Alaska), Spain or the Indians. The Statistical Office of the European Communities (hereafter Eurostat) has been faced with a completely different situation. Each Member State took with it into the Community a complex, long-established set of major and minor civil divisions. One of the advantages of the continued use of existing regions over the creation of a completely new system is that data sets for past periods can be related to current data much more easily and precisely. On the other hand, great disparities in both area and population size are found at each level, both within and between countries.

At all levels in the hierarchy of units, a number of considerations can be expected to carry weight when a system of regions is being created. To avoid friction, protest and possibly even conflict, existing divisions should be used as far as convenient. For example, national groups such as the Welsh and the Basques have been recognised implicitly in the EC system. Administrative units at any level and of any size should, if possible, be reasonably compact rather than elongated or fragmented. Several regions within the EC are unavoidably fragmented because they consist of groups of islands. At any level in the hierarchy, units should for convenience be broadly comparable in area, population and total GDP. These latter criteria are in practice mutually exclusive, except in a hypothetical area with a uniform distribution of population and an identical level of economic development throughout. Perhaps the most important consideration is comparability of population size.

For simplicity, the regionalisation of the EC will be discussed in turn at four levels, starting with the sovereign state level. The criteria that could be used for creating a system of regions will be related to the levels. The location of NUTS 1 level regions is shown in Figure 2.3. It should be appreciated that not all regions at a given level in the hierarchy are subdivided at the next level below (see Figure 2.4).

Sovereign state level

There is a great imbalance in population size. Germany has almost 80 million inhabitants, Luxembourg fewer than 400,000. Blake (1991) alludes to the inconvenience of allowing Luxembourg full status in the EC: a 'luxury' of having a NUTS 3 level region at the top level, likely to be repeated if Malta, Cyprus and Iceland join the Community.

Figure 2.3 The location of the 68 regions of the European Community at NUTS 1 level. In this and in other maps (as in the text), the English version is used for the names of Member States but the names of the regions are as represented in appropriate languages. Greek names are transliterated into the Latin alphabet

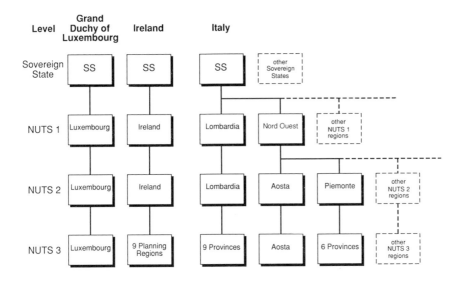

Figure 2.4 The relationship of the NUTS levels 1–3 of the European Community. Luxembourg, Ireland and parts of Italy are used to illustrate the situation

NUTS 1 level

Three countries – Denmark, Luxembourg and Ireland – are not subdivided at this level. In Germany there are great disparities in size between the 11 Länder of former West Germany, less between the five Länder of former East Germany. The principle applied to the regionalisation of Germany was the retention of the federal structure in the new EC system. In the UK, Scotland, Wales and Northern Ireland are distinct cultural entities, but the eight standard regions of England are no more than convenient groups of counties. Since the Second World War, France, Italy and Spain have reduced the high degree of centralism in their political and administrative organisation and have recognised the aspirations of some of their regions to the achievement of regional autonomy. To some extent, then, the NUTS 1 level regions of the EC take into account traditional features largely overlooked or suppressed in some countries, when each was dominated by a strong centralised administration. In the view of Le Bras and Todd (1981), the appearance of uniformity was largely illusory in the case of France. In Chapter 11 it will be argued that the development of the supranational EC could actually give new life to 'subnations' in Western Europe, just as the breakup of Yugoslavia and the USSR has been doing in those countries, but for a different reason.

NUTS 2 level

At this level, some NUTS 1 level units, such as Lombardia in Italy, Ile-de-France in France, and Hamburg in Germany, are not subdivided. Ireland, Denmark and Luxembourg are still not subdivided. The UK is divided into groups of counties (e.g. Derbyshire and Nottinghamshire) or single counties (e.g. Lincolnshire).

NUTS 3 level

France (*départements*), Spain and Italy (provinces) and the UK (countries/regions) are represented by the basic subdivisions with 50–100 units, but the FRG is much more finely subdivided, with over 300 Kreise, to which may be added over 200 Kreise from the GDR.

The regional system of the EC has considerable limitations. In any study of data based upon it, variations in size within each level, and relationships between levels, must be looked at carefully. Whatever the region, it should be remembered that its population is an aggregate of individuals, each with a particular type of employment, level of income, and aspirations. Any process of aggregation, whether spatially based on regions or class based, loses details of individuals and produces averages that cannot do full justice to the complex situation on the ground.

FURTHER READING

Barnes, I. and Preston, J. (1990) *The European Community: Key Issues*, London: Longman.

Cecchini, P. (1988) *The European Challenge 1992*, Aldershot: Wildwood House.

European Parliament (1991) *Fact sheets on the European Parliament and the Activities of the European Community*, Directorate-General for Research, Luxembourg.

Hudson, R., Rhind, D. and Mounsey, H. (1984) *An Atlas of EEC Affairs*, London: Methuen.

Jacobs, F. and Corbett, R. (1990) *The European Parliament*, Harlow: Longman.

Owen, R. and Dynes, M. (1989) *The Times Guide to 1992*, London: Times Books.

3

POPULATION

STRUCTURE AND DISTRIBUTION

For at least two centuries, Europe experienced fast population growth through natural increase. Thanks to considerable net out-migration from various parts of the continent to the rest of the world over long periods and to high mortality rates of infants and children (see Langer 1972), even when growth was fastest it was usually only between 1 and 2 per cent per year, in contrast to the much faster rates of growth that are now experienced in many developing countries, mostly in the range of 2–4 per cent per year. Greatly increased yields in agriculture, widespread industrialisation, increased literacy, emigration, and customs such as late marriage or inheritance laws favouring the oldest son, are considered to have contributed to the reduction in the rate of population growth this century in Europe. The increasing acceptance and use of contraceptive methods has also been an influence. The annual increase of population in the EC is now very small and, as a result, the share of total world population in the Community is declining, and will continue to do so for many decades.

In order to illustrate the stable nature of the population of the EC and EFTA, a selection of countries is compared in Figure 3.1 to show the proportion of young and elderly in their total population. The population of a country is conventionally divided according to age into three main groups. The middle group, those aged 15–64 inclusive, consists largely of the working population, while the other two groups are defined as 'dependent', whether they are children under 15 years of age or elderly citizens over 64 years of age. The proportion in the middle group varies considerably from country to country, but the youngest and oldest groups have the biggest variations. The FRG and Kenya are near the extremes in the world of contrast in age structure, with children representing 15 per cent and over 50 per cent of total population respectively, and the elderly 15 per cent compared with 2 per cent.

In greater detail, and closer to home from the point of view of the EC, Figure 3.2 shows the striking difference in age structure between the populations of the FRG (before unification) and Turkey. The effect of the Second World War on males over 60 years of age in 1985 shows clearly in the German population,

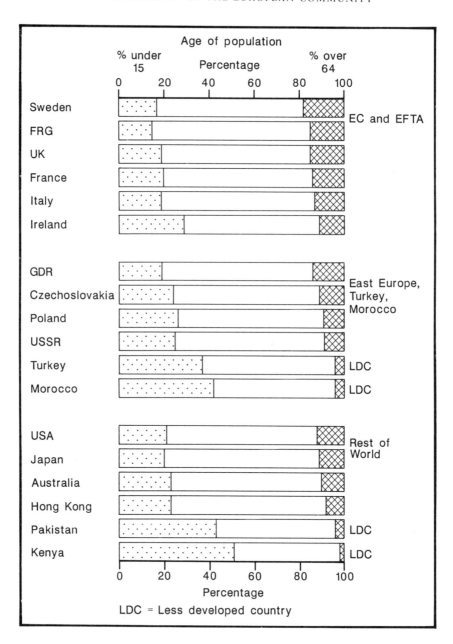

Figure 3.1 The proportions of young and elderly people in the population of selected countries of the world, 1989. Since 1989 the two Germanies have merged and the USSR has become fragmented

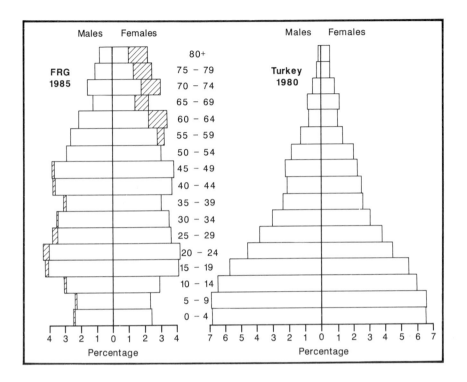

Figure 3.2 A comparison of the age–sex structure of the populations of the Federal Republic of Germany (FRG) before unification and Turkey. The latest available data have been used for each country

although almost throughout the world, male life expectancy is lower than female. The enthusiasm in the FRG for unification in 1990 may to some degree have been related to the forthcoming decline in population there, a drop from 61.5 million to 51.5 million being expected in the next 30 years. On the other hand, like the Maghreb countries of Northwest Africa (Morocco, Algeria and Tunisia), Turkey is experiencing fast growth, about 2.2 per cent per year, a rate likely to continue for some decades, with a total fertility rate (the average number of children per female) of 3.7, compared with only 1.4 in the FRG. One of the problems expected to face the EC increasingly in the future is the pressure of population growth in other parts of the world on food supply, fuel and raw materials, and on the condition of the natural environment. A more recent and immediate problem has however arisen to complicate the situation, namely the collapse of command economies in Central Europe and the USSR, and the resulting economic migration towards the more affluent countries of Western Europe.

The 1990 population of the countries of Europe is shown in Table 1.3 in Chapter 1. Since it is never possible to be entirely up to date and accurate with demographic data, it is to be expected that various sources in current use give somewhat different estimates. Disparities are not however large enough to affect broad calculations and conclusions about demographic features and problems. The US Population Reference Bureau (PRB) has for decades provided up-to-date estimates of population for all the countries of the world. Its estimates for 1990 are in column (4) of Table 1.3. Without the GDR, the EC had 328.4 million inhabitants in 1990 according to the PRB, an increase of 3.6 million over 1986–7. With the inclusion of the GDR, the EC had 344.7 million inhabitants in mid-1990 out of an estimated world total of 5,321 million, or 6.5 per cent.

In order to show the distribution of population in the EC in a way that can easily be appreciated, 100 dots are used in Figure 3.3, each proportional to 1 per cent of the population of the Community including the GDR, or 3.45 million people. This method of representation has the advantage that the number of people in a given part of the EC can be calculated quickly. Thus, for example,

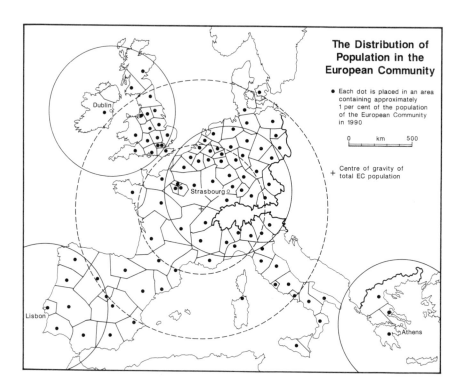

Figure 3.3 The distribution of population in the European Community shown by 100 dots, each dot representing approximately 1 per cent of the total population of the EC, about 3.45 million people. Circles with a radius of 500 km are centred on Strasbourg, Dublin, Athens and Lisbon and circles with a radius of 500 and 1,000 km are centred on the centre of gravity of the total EC population, near Dijon in France

within a straight line distance of 500 km of Lisbon in Portugal there are 8 dots: 8 per cent of the population of the EC, or about 27.5 million people. Within a similar radius of Strasbourg in France there are 42 dots: 42 per cent of the population of the EC, or about 145 million people. Different distances can be used according to whether proximity to a large local population is considered important in a given situation (e.g. for the location of Euro-Disneyland near Paris) or reasonable accessibility to a large share of the population of the EC, a consideration that could, for example, be critical for a factory producing for the whole EC market (e.g. the motor vehicle plants in the Cologne and Stuttgart areas of Germany).

URBAN POPULATION

Urbanisation in Europe was closely associated with the Industrial Revolution. Many current EC problems are related to urban centres, including run-down industrial centres, and congested large centres and conurbations (clusters of cities). The terms 'urban' and 'rural' are defined in various ways, making comparability only approximate. Three definitions of urban are used in Europe: size of settlement (e.g. nucleated centre with over 2,000 inhabitants); status of settlement (e.g. capital of a district of given status); and function of settlement (e.g. level of employment in activities other than agriculture).

In Europe, Turkey and the Maghreb there is a broad correlation between the percentage of economically active population engaged in activities other than agriculture, and the percentage defined as urban. In virtually every country, however, the proportion of rural (as opposed to urban) dwellers exceeds the proportion in agriculture, since rural settlements include many people in services and some in industry in addition to the agricultural population itself, whereas in and around modern cities and towns there are usually few people engaged in agriculture. Table 3.1 shows that in the EC the extremes in percentage of population defined as urban are 95 per cent for Belgium and 30 per cent for Portugal. A comparable range is found among other countries of Europe.

Table 3.1 Urban population as a percentage of total population in EC countries in 1991

Member State	Urban pop.	Member state	Urban pop.
Germany	90	UK	87
France	73	Ireland	56
Italy	72	Denmark	85
Netherlands	89	Greece	58
Belgium	95	Spain	91
Luxembourg	78	Portugal	30

Source: PRB, 1991 World Population Data Sheet

The 30 largest urban agglomerations of the EC are listed in Table 3.2. Much of the urban population of the Community is concentrated in a limited number of conurbations or large individual centres. The larger urban agglomerations have problems related to their sheer size and the potential for concentrated pollution and traffic congestion. Housing can be a problem, as also the deterioration of inner-city areas. Until by-passed or cut through by motorways, large cities can form obstacles to movement by road between many pairs of places beyond their limits. Thus, for example, London has been an obstacle to traffic flows between parts of the UK to its north and west and the Channel ferry ports of Kent. The M25 motorway has done less than was hoped to alleviate the problem.

Table 3.2 The 30 largest urban agglomerations in the EC in population size (in thousands)

Agglomeration	Member State	Pop. (000s)
1 Paris	France	8,707
2 Rhein–Ruhr	Germany	7,792
3 London	UK	7,678
4 Madrid	Spain	4,120
5 Berlin	Germany	3,400
6 Rome	Italy	3,094
7 Athens	Greece	3,027
8 Milan	Italy	2,877
9 Barcelona	Spain	2,701
10 Naples	Italy	2,608
11 West Midlands	UK	2,356
12 Manchester	UK	2,339
13 Hamburg	Germany	1,624
14 Turin	Italy	1,568
15 Munich	Germany	1,483
16 West Yorkshire	UK	1,478
17 Copenhagen	Denmark	1,372
18 Lisbon	Portugal	1,329
19 Brussels	Belgium	1,268
20 Lyon	France	1,221
21 Marseilles	France	1,110
22 Rotterdam	Netherlands	1,025
23 Amsterdam	Netherlands	994
24 Lille	France	936
25 Dublin	Ireland	915
26 Valencia	Spain	850
27 Genoa	Italy	827
28 Tyneside	UK	782
29 Glasgow	UK	765
30 Liverpool	UK	753

Source: Eurostat 1989b, section 7

The seven large urban agglomerations in Figure 3.4 illustrate the complexity of the urban situations and problems in the EC. Paris and London are the largest concentrations of population dominated by a single centre. Paris has a higher density of population than London but fewer secondary centres in a radius of 50–60 km. The Rhein–Ruhr area of Germany is associated with a very large coalfield and attendant heavy industrial establishments, while the main urban centres of Lancashire and Yorkshire in England combine interests in declining coal and textile industries with two major ports and heavy industry. In the

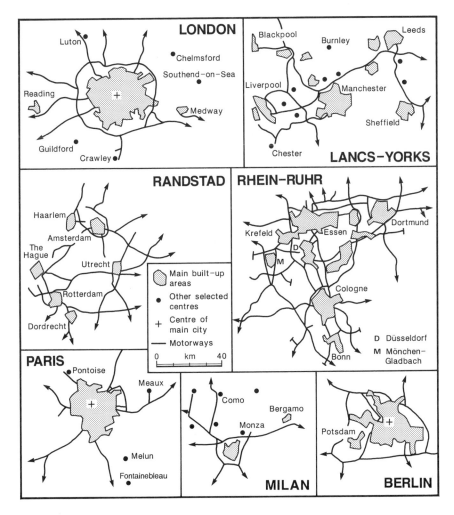

Figure 3.4 Seven major urban agglomerations of the European Community. The scale is the same for all seven maps

Netherlands the cities in Randstad (ring city) encircle an agricultural area, while the industrial area of Milan in Italy extends north from the city towards the Alps. The recently unified Berlin is likely to grow considerably in its regained role of capital of all Germany, although the effective transfer of functions from Bonn is expected to be a slow and costly process. The three largest urban concentrations, Paris, London and the Rhein–Rhur area, together have about 7 per cent of the total population of the EC and account for about 10 per cent of the EC's total Gross Domestic Product (GDP).

From Liverpool to Stuttgart, the larger cities of the EC form a loose urbanised zone, which has counterparts in the USA and Japan. All three are shown in Figure 3.5, represented on the same scale and with their longest axes parallel to facilitate comparison. The European cluster has been less cohesive than the other two through the presence of national boundaries and the English Channel, both to become less of obstacles in 1993, assuming the Channel Tunnel is operational then and the Single Market a reality.

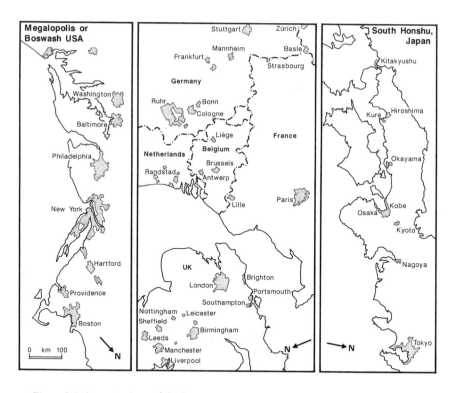

Figure 3.5 A comparison of the largest concentrations of major urban centres in the USA, the European Community and Japan. All three maps are on the same scale. The orientation of each map has been chosen to facilitate comparison by placing the longest axis of each group of cities in the same direction in the figure

POPULATION CHANGE

Natural change and total fertility rates for the countries of Europe are compared in Table 3.3. The natural change of population is the difference between the number of births and deaths in a given period (usually a year) per 1,000 inhabitants. The number of births in a given population is related to the proportion of women of child-bearing age in the total population and to the average number of children they have, conventionally measured by the total fertility rate (TFR).

As noted in the beginning of this chapter, Western Europe has the most stable population of any large region in the world. Even so, considerable differences in the rate of natural change occur between different countries and regions within the EC. Again, if the EC is to be enlarged, then relatively high rates of increase in some Central European countries may be of concern and, even more so, the fast rates of growth in Turkey and the Maghreb countries, should these areas become more closely associated.

The data for natural increase in Table 3.3 give an indication of the current rate

Table 3.3 Natural increase of population in European and other selected countries, percentage annual rate of increase, and total fertility rate, 1991

	Natural increase	Fertility		Natural increase	Fertility
EC			Former CMEA		
Germany[1]	0.0	1.5	Poland	0.5	2.1
France	0.4	1.8	Hungary	−0.2	1.8
Italy	0.1	1.3	Czechoslovakia	0.2	2.0
Netherlands	0.4	1.6	Bulgaria	0.1	2.0
Belgium	0.1	1.6	Romania	0.5	2.3
Luxembourg	0.2	1.5	USSR	0.9	2.5
UK	0.2	1.8	*Other selected*		
Ireland	0.6	2.1	Yugoslavia	0.5	1.4
Denmark	0.0	1.6	Albania	1.9	3.0
Greece	0.1	1.5	Turkey	2.2	3.7
Spain	0.2	1.3	Algeria	2.7	5.4
Portugal	0.2	1.5	Morocco	2.5	4.5
EFTA			Tunisia	2.2	4.1
Austria	0.1	1.4	USA	0.8	2.1
Switzerland	0.3	1.6	Canada	0.7	1.7
Norway	0.3	1.9	Australia	0.8	1.8
Sweden	0.2	2.1	Japan	0.3	1.5
Finland	0.3	1.7			
Iceland	1.1	2.2			

Source: PRB 1991, *1991 World Population Data Sheet*
Note: 1 FRG 0.0, 1.4; GDR 0.0, 1.7

of change of population. In Europe and the Maghreb, Hungary, with a decrease, and Germany and Denmark with no change, contrast sharply with Algeria, with an annual increase of 2.7 per cent. The data for total fertility rate are an indication of future prospects, since the babies born in the 1990s will include many of the mothers of the 2020s and 2030s. The low indices for most of Western Europe point to a decline in total population in the not too distant future. For example, Heilig *et al.* (1990) distinguish three possible scenarios for Germany to 2050: a 'demographic revival' taking the present 80 million to more than 90 million, compared with 'extreme graying', and the continuation of current rates, both giving about 50 million. Immigration in the next decade or so could be a crucial influence. Germany's prospects are similar to those for many Western and Central European countries with comparable low fertility rates. In two Catholic countries, Italy and Spain, the fertility rates are now among the lowest in the world.

When population change in the EC is studied at regional level, even sharper contrasts are seen than at national level. The regions of the EC with the highest and lowest rates of natural increase are shown in Table 3.4. The largest area of high rates of increase in the EC extends through the southern part of the Community from Portugal, Spain and southern Italy to Greece, but also includes Ireland. There is also an area of comparatively high natural increase in northern France and the Benelux countries. In contrast, the FRG and parts of North Central Italy have several regions with actual decreases. The three German city regions, the Länder of Berlin, Hamburg and Bremen, have among the most marked negative rates of natural change in the world.

The probable demographic future of Europe, including the USSR, Turkey and the Maghreb, is shown graphically in Figure 3.6. The EC, EFTA and Central Europe have a combined population of around 500 million, expected to change very little for several decades unless some totally new demographic situation arises. In the former USSR, however, further fast growth is expected in the southern non-Slav republics of Central Asia, and in Azerbaijan. The admission of Turkey and/or any of the Maghreb countries to full membership of the EC would drastically upset any economic plans based on a stable demographic structure.

Table 3.4 Natural change of population (in per thousands) in EC regions

Highest		Lowest	
Ile-de-France	7.8	West Berlin (FRG)	−7.0
Ireland	7.8	Hamburg (FRG)	−5.4
Northern Ireland (UK)	7.7	Nord-Ouest (Italy)	−4.8
Campania (Italy)	6.8	Bremen (FRG)	−4.6
Nord-Pas-de-Calais (France)	6.7	Emilia-Romagna (Italy)	−4.4
Canaries (Spain)	6.6	Centro (Italy)	−3.2

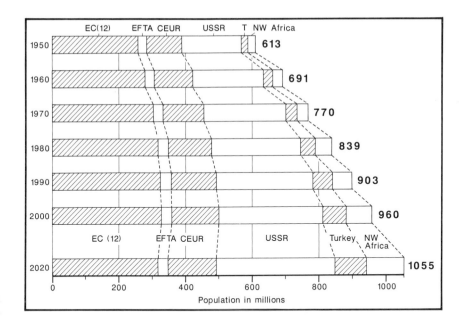

Figure 3.6 Past and possible future population changes in Europe, Turkey and Northwest Africa. EUR (Central Europe) contains all the countries not in the EC (European Community), EFTA (European Free Trade Association) or the former USSR, every part of which is included in this diagram

While the rapid growth of population is regarded as the principal demographic problem in most parts of the developing world, a major problem in the EC is the increasing proportion of the elderly. This matter will be discussed in Chapter 7 under healthcare.

MIGRATION

For the purposes of this section, three 'levels' of migration will be considered: within each of the existing 12 Member States of the EC; between pairs of these; and between the EC and countries outside the EC. It is difficult to obtain accurate up-to-date figures for migration at any level, so estimates for movement in the mid–late 1980s are mostly the best available. Migration itself is variously defined, depending among other criteria on the degree of permanency of a move. The causes of migration are numerous, and may be related both to favourably perceived economic and environmental features in places of destination, and to negative features in places of origin. The three levels referred to above will be discussed in turn.

Internal migration data for nine of the 12 EC Member States for 1986 or earlier are published in Eurostat (1990). The comparability of the results is limited on account of the differing population and area sizes of the countries and the number of regions used to show interregional movement. There is migration in both directions between every pair of regions in each country, so a more meaningful measure of interregional migration trends is that of net migration into or out of each region. Of the five largest EC countries in population, the FRG, France, Italy, the UK and Spain, mobility is greatest in the UK and least in Italy and Spain. In both the FRG and France there is a general net flow of migrants from north to south. In France there is also migration out of the Ile-de-France (Paris), some of it into immediately adjoining regions, and from the older industrial regions of Nord-Pas-de-Calais and Lorraine; the Mediterranean region has the largest gains. In the FRG a considerable movement has taken place out of Nordrhein-Westfalen, while Bayern and Baden-Württemberg have gained. In the UK, the Southeast receives and loses roughly the same number of migrants, the older industrial regions are still the net losers, while the Southwest and East Anglia have been gaining. In Spain, Madrid is still the main focus of migration but in Italy, Emilia-Romagna and Toscana are now absorbing many immigrants, while the former pull of Rome and Milan has diminished; the regions of the South and Sicilia continue to record an outflow.

Internal migration does not affect the total population of a country, whereas international migration does. It cannot be assumed, however, that the places that attract internal migrants in each country will also be those that attract ones from other countries. Thus, for example, while older industrial regions in the northern countries have frequently experienced net out-migration of their own citizens, since the 1930s such regions have attracted foreign migrants.

Movement between the present Member States of the EC before its formation was considerable in certain directions after the Second World War, notably from Italy to the heavy industrial areas of France, Belgium and the FRG, but the influence of the EC has of course been felt more recently, as each country joined. Even now, the right to take up residence anywhere in the EC is restricted, although assured when employment is found. Tradition and cultural barriers such as language still make different parts of Western Europe much more distinct from one another than are different parts of the USA, where mobility between states is much greater.

The main trend in the EC with regard to migration is to reduce or remove obstacles to the free movement of population internally through new legislation, and to maintain and even strengthen control of external immigration into the Community as a whole. As various measures increasingly relax restrictions on residence for members of any EC country in any other one, a net flow of migration within the EC should theoretically increase from poorer and/or high unemployment regions to richer and/or low unemployment regions. A net movement from environmentally or climatically less attractive areas to more attractive ones, especially of older citizens, might also be expected. On the other hand, the considerable difference in the rate of natural increase between regions (see pp. 61–3) does not generally seem marked enough to produce obvious flows from regions with higher increases to regions with lower increases or decreases. One notable exception is Ireland, from which there is a steady flow of migrants to the UK, the exceptional influences of strong links in the past and the common language contributing to this movement.

At present, intra-EC migration is broadly concentrated in two directions. Economic migration, with differences in GDP per inhabitant and in unemployment levels, results in some net movement from Spain, Portugal and southern Italy to northern areas of the EC. Environmental migration, especially of retired citizens, produces a small movement southwards.

The EC has experienced a net inflow of migrants from non-EC countries since the Second World War, but problems of status and definition make precise comparisons between countries difficult. 'Disguised' immigration in the sense that it is not defined as such has affected both the UK and the FRG, the former absorbing into the population large numbers of Irish and Commonwealth citizens, the latter receiving millions of refugees from a reshaped Central Europe after the Second World War and, until 1961 (erection of the Berlin Wall), large numbers of East Germans. On the other hand, migrant workers from such countries as Yugoslavia, Turkey and Tunisia do not automatically obtain citizenship, although they may acquire it. The data in Table 3.5 show that France and the FRG have the largest number of immigrants not only absolutely (almost 7 million together) but also in relation to population. The Benelux countries, the UK, Italy and Denmark are the next most affected, while Portugal, Ireland, Spain and Greece all trail far behind. In many respects the FRG and France have been the most successful countries in the EC economically in the postwar period, while the southern countries are the least prosperous at present. Linguistic problems may be another of many possible factors that influence migration.

In the late 1980s, migration was small in scale both within the EC and between the EC and the rest of the world, compared with some periods in the past. The situation can be expected to change in the 1990s for various reasons:

1   The relaxation of restrictions on emigration from the GDR resulted since

Table 3.5 Non-EC immigrants in EC countries, 1989

	Total (000s)	% of total pop.		Total (000s)	% of total pop.
France	3,630	6.5	Italy	1,300	2.5
FRG	3,190	5.2	Denmark	102	2.0
Belgium	315	3.2	Portugal	65	0.6
Netherlands	435	2.9	Ireland	17	0.5
UK	1,650	2.9	Spain	141	0.4
Luxembourg	10	2.7	Greece	31	0.3

Source: Buchan and Wyles 1990

mid-1989 in the immediate movement of several hundred thousand East Germans into West Germany. Officially this net outflow from East Germany may never be recorded as migration, but its repercussions have already been great. Murray (1992) notes that West Germany has had to absorb almost 3 million immigrants between 1986 and 1991 and can expect another 400,000 in 1992. In addition to East Germans, some 20,000 ethnic Germans from Central and Eastern Europe arrive monthly.

2   The possible entry of other European countries into the EC would also affect migration. The EFTA countries are small in total population and economically are generally at a higher level than most of the 12 EC countries, so their accession is likely to attract a small net outflow from the present EC countries (as, for example, Switzerland has attracted Italian migrants since the Second World War).

3   Should any former CMEA countries (other than the GDR) also become full members of the EC, then one could expect a substantial net inflow into the present EC, particularly of migrants from Poland, Czechoslovakia and Hungary, as job losses occur in both the agricultural and industrial sectors in those countries. In contrast to official levels of near zero unemployment in Central Europe under centrally planned economies, many regions in these countries have subsequently experienced a rise in unemployment and they are also lower in GDP per inhabitant than most regions of the existing EC. It is estimated that 800,000 a year could enter the EC from Central Europe, many initially into Germany. According to White (1991): 'The Soviet Union is sending an army of up to 6 million migrant workers to fill a gap in Europe's labour market. The guest workers are being offered two-year contracts, at the end of which they will be obliged to go home.'

4   Although the empires of the Western European countries had mostly disintegrated by about 1960 (Portugal in the early 1970s), relics of the empires remain. Hong Kong is the only colony of a member of the EC with a population of more than a few hundred thousand. The agreement to restore Hong Kong to China in 1997 has led the British government to grant UK citizenship to about 5 per cent of the population of Hong Kong, about 250,000 people including dependants. Should the option be taken up by all those eligible, the impact on the UK would be enormous. Many immigrants would no doubt disperse in due course from the UK to other EC countries or move on to attractive non-European countries. The changing role and prospects for white South Africans could also produce a new movement to the UK in the course of the 1990s.

5   The developing world is on the doorstep of the EC. Walker and Comfort (1991) see 'Western Europe bracing itself for its greatest challenge of the Nineties – a surge of migrants from lands bordering the Mediterranean that threatens to dwarf the growing influx from Eastern Europe'. With growing population and lack of jobs in Turkey and Northern Africa, pressure could indeed be great from that quarter.

The EC has already taken special steps to restrict internal migration, such as the clause in the Treaty of Accession of Portugal to the EC which restricts mobility of Portuguese citizens to Luxembourg even after the Single Market is completed in 1993. Options being currently considered to confront the external problem include a tightening of migration controls into the EC, common policies on asylum and illegal immigration, and aid to improve economic conditions outside the EC, assisting, for example, in an increase in food production. With the growth of support for the far-right and anti-immigration political parties in some EC countries, there have been moves by the governments of several Member States to make immigration and its consequences a more central political issue. Steps have already been taken by individual Member States, including Italy and Albania, France and Algeria, and Belgium and Morocco, to combat problems arising from illegal immigration and urban unrest.

THE LOCATION OF POPULATION WITHIN THE EC

As the EC has grown from its original group of the six Member States in the 1950s its territorial extent has grown appreciably and distances between its extremities have also increased. The longest distance across the original EEC, that from northern Germany to Sicilia, is only about half that from northern Scotland to Crete. From Bordeaux to Munich is only about half the distance from Lisbon to Berlin. The EC now has a very irregular and fragmented territory.

The Commission of the EC has stressed the economic significance of centrality and peripherality:

> The physical distances between regions in the Community are inevitably far greater than within individual countries. The outlying areas are, in some cases, very remote from the areas in which people and economic activities are concentrated, i.e. the main centres of supply and demand. This remoteness affects the economic development potential of these regions.
>
> (COM 87-230 (1987), Annex, p. 114)

Two measures of centrality/peripherality will be described: the first a classification made for the Commission in connection with the above statement, the second a measure developed by the authors.

Every settlement, local area and larger region in the EC has a unique position in relation to all others. For example, Bourges (Ile-de-France) is centrally located in France, whereas Brest (Bretagne) and Strasbourg (Alsace) are peripheral within that country. In the whole of the EC, on the other hand, Strasbourg has a fairly central location, while Brest is still peripheral. In the EC of the late 1980s, the FRG was peripheral geographically if not economically, but the addition of the GDR has made it rather more central, while the accession of new members from EFTA and Central Europe would further increase its centrality. If a place, local area or region were entirely self-sufficient economically, then its success or failure would be related primarily to its own natural resources, to the levels of technology available, and to the ability and enterprise of its population. The more each region specialises to serve the whole EC market with the products from its agriculture and industry, or with its services, the more important becomes its accessibility with regard to the total population and market of the Community. A place near the centre of the EC will have a smaller aggregate travel to all other places in the Community than will a place near the periphery to the same set of places. In Chapter 8 the relative accessibility is shown for 20 key places in the EC.

An 'official' classification of the regions of the EC into five types according to centrality/peripherality is given in COM 87-230 (1987), Annex, pp. 119–20. They are Inner and Outer Central, Intermediate, and Inner and Outer Peripheral. These five categories are shown for the EC in Figure 3.7. Peripherality is only broadly related to distance from the centre of the EC because some weight is also given to the local distribution of population, some extra centrality being attributed to areas in or near a large local or regional concentration of people.

In Figure 3.3 the distribution of population in the EC is shown by 100 dots, each representing 1 per cent of the total population of the Community, or 3.45 million people. The mean centre ('centre of gravity') of the distribution of the 100 dots is about 40 km northeast of Dijon in France (having been pulled a small distance from its previous position near Dijon by the addition in 1990 of the GDR). As the distribution of population of the EC is uneven, with a large concentration in England, the Benelux and Germany, the centre of population does not coincide with the centre of territory. The exact location of the centre of population in a fairly thinly populated part of France is of less importance than the broad idea of such a centre. Circles with radii of 500 and 1,000 km around the centre of EC population have been drawn in Figure 3.3 to show a single measure of centrality.

Figure 3.3, already referred to in Chapter 1, can be used to make various calculations about the distribution of population in the EC and in particular about the question of centre and periphery. Other radii, larger or smaller than 500 km, can of course give different results. A circle of only 100 km radius appropriately placed on Düsseldorf (Ruhr), Paris or London would still contain several per cent of the total EC population. A circle of much larger radius would produce less differentiation between different parts of the EC. A drawback in the use of direct distance to measure centrality is that the speed of travel by land is not uniform in all directions from a given centre. In spite of the above reservations, the data in Table 3.6 illustrate clearly the general advantage with regard to access to the total EC population and market of being central in the EC rather than at the extremities.

Centre and periphery may also be thought of as relative to where the viewer is located. In Figure 3.8 four views of the EC are shown, three from places that by any definition are peripheral in an EC context, Athens, Aberdeen and Lisbon, and one Warsaw, at present outside the limits of the Community. There is no right or wrong way of looking at a map and no reason for keeping to the

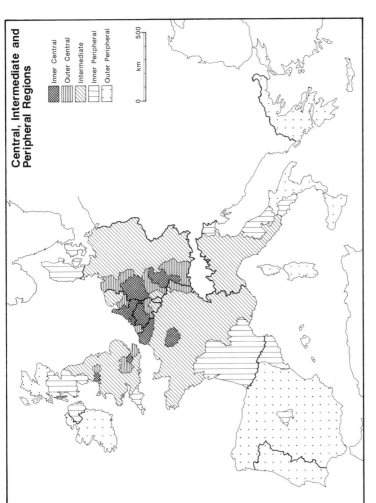

Figure 3.7 Central, Intermediate and Peripheral regions of the European Community. There are two types of Central (Inner and Outer) and two types of Peripheral (also Inner and Outer)

Source: COM 87-230 (1987: 120)

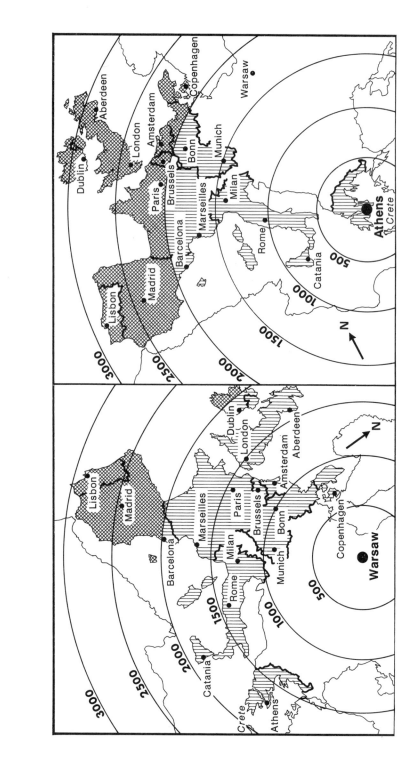

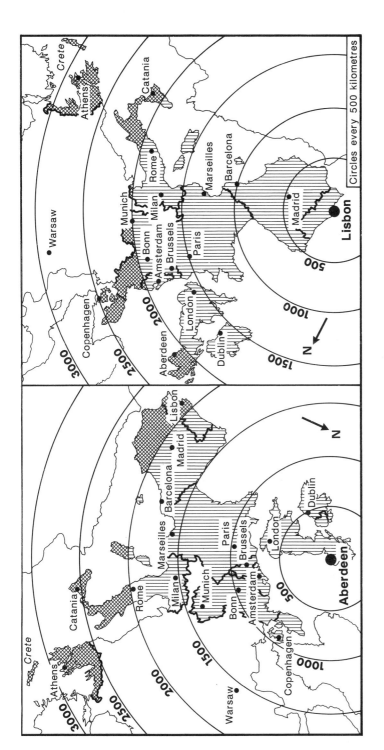

Figure 3.8 Views of the European Community from four different places in Europe on its periphery or outside it. Circles are drawn at 500 km intervals from each centre. The 12 Member States are shaded with lighter shading within 2,000 km and heavier shading beyond. The former GDR (East Germany) is not shown on these maps

Table 3.6 Percentage of the total population of the EC within radii of 250 and 500 km of selected places in the EC, and Zürich

	0– *250*	*251–* *500*	*over* *500*			*0–* *250*	*251–* *500*	*over* *500*
1 Strasbourg	7	34	59	10 Berlin		6	16	78
2 Düsseldorf	17	23	60	11 Rome		5	10	85
3 Brussels	13	26	61	12 Madrid		3	11	86
4 Luxembourg	17	21	62	13 Glasgow		3	7	90
5 EC centre of	5	32	63	14 Copenhagen		2	7	91
population				15 Lisbon		3	5	92
6 Zürich	6	30	64	16 Catania (Sicilia)		1	4	95
7 Paris	7	26	67	17 Athens		2	1	97
8 London	12	19	69	18 Crete (Greece)		1	1	98
9 Milan	6	18	76					

convention of having north at the 'top' if new insights may be gained by taking other viewpoints.

Whatever changes take place in the membership of the EC, in the distribution of population therein, and in the state of various transport links, there will always be a centre and a periphery, however defined. The overall distribution of population in the EC has changed only gradually in the last two decades, although marked local changes have taken place related, for example, to the setting up of new industrial or service activities. The main way, then, in which the less favourably located regions can be assisted is to improve their links with the more central parts of the EC. As various links in the EC are improved and land travel speeds increase, the whole Community effectively shrinks. Nevertheless, the relative advantage of central over peripheral areas in terms of accessibility to the whole Community remains broadly the same.

The conventional wisdom with regard to the centre–periphery dilemma is to improve links between central areas and remoter areas, especially islands, and indeed pressure comes from these very places for such improvements. It should not be overlooked, however, that penetration from the centre into the periphery is also made more easy. Since larger, more innovative and expanding enterprises tend to flourish in central areas, greater ease of movement in the EC as a whole could actually affect the periphery negatively.

FURTHER READING

Brunet, R. (1989) *Les villes 'européennes'*, Groupement d'Intérêt Public Reclus, DATAR, La Documentation Française, May.

Champion, A. G., Fielding, A. J. and Keeble, D. E. (1989) 'Counterurbanization in Europe', *The Geographical Journal*, vol. 155, part 1, March, pp. 52–80.

Commission of the European Communities (1991), *Employment in Europe 1991*, Com

(91), 248 final, Directorate-General Employment, Industrial Relations and Social Affairs, Luxembourg.

Eurostat (1990) *Demographic Statistics*, Brussels, Berlaymont, Bureau de Liaison.

Population Reference Bureau (various years), *World Population Data Sheet*, Washington DC.

Van da Kaa, D.J. (1987) 'Europe's Second Demographic Transition', *Population Bulletin*, 42(1).

4

AGRICULTURE, FORESTRY AND FISHERIES

THE COMMON AGRICULTURAL POLICY AND ITS REFORM

According to COM 90-609 (1991a), in 1987 the agricultural sector accounted for only 7.6 per cent of total employment in the EC. The share has been declining for many decades and seems likely to continue to do so. The contribution of the agricultural sector to the total GDP of the EC is even less than it is to employment, little more than 3 per cent in the early 1990s. It may therefore seem surprising that in the 1980s the Common Agricultural Policy (hereafter CAP) was using up over two-thirds of the total EC budget.

It is widely appreciated that in some of the EC countries, farmers have considerable influence on electoral results. It should also be remembered that more than four-fifths of the land surface of the Community is occupied by field and tree crops, natural pasture, or forest, making the sector very conspicuous in the landscape, especially now that the use of land has become the centre of concern over environmental management and conservation. In addition, the citizens of the EC spend on average around a fifth of their income on food and beverages. In view of the prominent position of agriculture in EC funding and policy-making, it is appropriate to introduce this chapter with an account of the CAP.

When the EC founding treaties were adopted in the 1950s, Western Europe was emerging from a period of war, food shortages and rationing. Agriculture was a key sector of the economy and responsible for the livelihood of a large proportion of the population in many regions. It is not surprising, therefore, that a comprehensive agricultural policy was included in the European Economic Community. The EEC Treaty lays down the following objectives:

(a) To increase agricultural productivity by promoting technical progress and by ensuring the rational development of agricultural production and the optimum utilisation of the factors of production, in particular labour;

(b) thus to ensure a fair standard of living for the agricultural community, in particular by increasing the individual earnings of persons engaged in agriculture;

(c) to stabilise markets;

(d) to assure the availability of supplies;

(e) to ensure that supplies reach consumers at reasonable prices.

(Art. 39 EEC)

The CAP was based on the principles of a Single Market, Community preference, and financial solidarity, effectively ending all national pricing and markets for agricultural production.

In order to attain the objectives set out above, a highly efficient common market organisation system was set up, based on intervention (minimum guaranteed price to producer) and external protection against cheaper imports. The levy and refund mechanism is illustrated diagrammatically in Figure 4.1 with the example of wheat. A wide range of specific price mechanisms, import levies

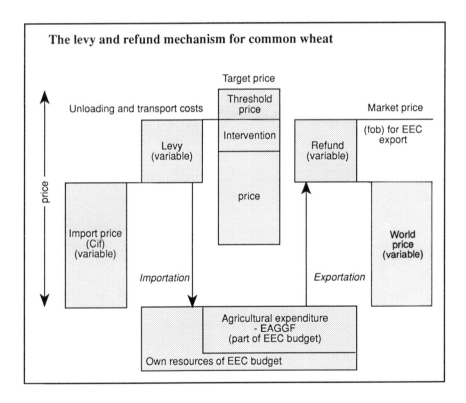

Figure 4.1 The levy and refund mechanism of the Common Agricultural Policy, illustrated with the case of common wheat

Source: European Parliament 1989, 1991, p. En/111/P/3/Anl

and export refunds have subsequently been introduced to ensure that the CAP objectives are met through the whole range of agricultural products from wheat to wine.

Unfortunately, the CAP has been too successful in achieving its objectives in most cases, and too rigid to adapt to changing market realities. Agricultural yields have increased substantially through advances in mechanisation, plant health, animal husbandry and particularly the use of fertilisers. Farmers have been encouraged to produce as much as possible in the knowledge that a guaranteed price would be paid regardless of market conditions. This policy has led to overproduction of a variety of products, with infamous mountains of butter, milk powder and beef piled up in intervention storage. This situation has not only upset public opinion, with consumers forced to pay prices higher than world prices in spite of surpluses in many product areas, but it has also been a costly burden on the EC budget, consuming more than two-thirds of the total through the 1980s (see Chapter 2; 'The EC budget') and rising from 12 billion ECU in 1980 to an estimated 35 billion ECU in 1991. In addition, the CAP has distorted world markets and soured relations with major trading partners, including the USA and the Cairns Group of agricultural exporters. Repeated efforts have been made in the 1980s to introduce reforms to the system in order to reduce surplus production and overall expenditure.

In order to combat overproduction, in particular in the dairying sector, co-responsibility levies were introduced to penalise farmers who consistently produced over certain set production quotas. Set-aside schemes have also been used as a structural means of encouraging farmers, through payment of compensation, to remove land from productive farming activities. This has led among other things to a proliferation of golf courses in certain parts of the Community. The concept of extensification has also been prevalent recently, resulting in a reduction in the intensity of farming activity in a given area. Nevertheless, in spite of the originality of these and other measures, the combination of a strong agricultural lobby and substantially varied national interests in the farming sector have rendered them largely ineffective. Increasingly, however, certain Member States have begun to call for more drastic cuts and reforms, in particular the UK and the Netherlands, and there is heavy pressure on the EC from its GATT trading partners to introduce drastic cuts in price subsidies.

In 1991 the Member States were debating another package of proposals for reform of the CAP. These were based on the Policy Paper from the Commission to Council entitled 'The Development and Future of the CAP', which emphasises that there should be a shift from price guarantees towards 'direct aid measures . . . modulated in function of factors such as size, income, regional situation' and without which 'the situation on the markets and the budget situation will become untenable' (COM 91-100 (1991b)).

Environmental considerations are also gaining ground in the reform debate on agriculture. The LUFPIG (Land Use and Food Policy Inter-Group) Report, prepared by a working group of the European Parliament and entitled 'A future for European farmers and the environment', proposes three main areas for consideration: the control of output; the environmental importance of EC agriculture; and the necessity of and a mechanism for compensation.

In a report to the Budgets Committee hearing on the reform of the CAP in the EP, Marsh identified the main issues in the reform and conversion areas:

> The process of change which is needed to bring the level of food production into line with the Community's needs and to ensure an environmentally sensitive use of resources will impose considerable change on many people who currently work in farming. Some will respond to opportunities for income flows from new activities on the farm. Some farmers, and others who work in agriculture, will find employment in other sectors, either in the rural area or elsewhere. For many, however, there may be few opportunities to offset lost farm income. The Community is likely to feel a need to help such farmers adjust.
>
> (Marsh 1991)

The LUFPIG report goes on to propose a bond scheme to provide such compensation and argues that savings of around 10 billion ECU per year would be made in the CAP by reducing intervention prices and production levels.

The proposals of the Commission, which entail price cuts of up to 35 per cent in some sectors, and radical restructuring of agricultural activities towards an income support system, are being strongly opposed by certain Member States, and by the powerful farming lobby in several countries, particularly France and Germany. It is clear, nevertheless, that there is a crisis ahead for the EC budget if drastic reforms are not undertaken. Not only would the EC flagship policy be responsible for threatening the stability of the EC as a whole, but it would also damage the chances of agreement on a range of other trade issues in the multilateral GATT talks, Uruguay Round.

NATURAL FACTORS AFFECTING AGRICULTURE IN THE EC

By world standards, the EC has a comparatively benign natural environment with regard to agricultural activities. Whereas little more than one-tenth of the world's land surface is cultivated, field and tree crops occupy more than one-third of the area of the EC. Nevertheless, before the effects on agricultural production of man-made improvements such as irrigation and the application of fertilisers can be assessed, the following four enabling factors must be considered.

1   *Thermal resources*   Each agricultural crop has different requirements, with barley or potatoes, for example, requiring more limited thermal resources than maize, vines or the sunflower. Accumulated temperatures decrease broadly northwards with latitude, and also with altitude, and the threshold

temperature at which growth starts in given plants also varies greatly. Thermal resources can be enhanced in a limited way both by providing artificial conditions such as greenhouses, common for example in the Netherlands, and by developing strains of plant that mature quickly, shortening the growing season needed. Thermal resources are adequate almost everywhere in the EC for some kind of arable farming, and indeed in the Scandinavian countries of EFTA crops are grown well north of any place in the EC. Warm temperate crops such as rice, the olive and citrus fruits are restricted to southern areas of the EC.

2   *Slope*   There is a slope limit beyond which commercial cultivation is impracticable. The terracing of steep slopes has been practised in southern Europe at least since Roman times, but for economic reasons the cultivation of field crops has now largely ceased although more permanent bush and tree crops are still grown. In general, terraces have the drawback of precluding the efficient use of agricultural machinery.

3   *Soil*   In the EC there are some local areas with soils that are inherently very fertile. Examples include the volcanic soils in Italy around Vesuvius and Etna, the drained marshlands in the Netherlands, the Fens in England, and the North Italian Lowland. In the northern part of the EC there is an extensive area of reasonably good soils formed on sedimentary rocks or on glacial deposits, extending across northern France, the southern UK, Belgium, the Netherlands and parts of Germany, into Denmark. The extent and continuity of areas of good soil is more restricted in the southern part of the Community.

4   *Moisture resources*   In the EC there are few areas where conditions are too dry for cultivation. Central and southern Spain have the areas most adversely affected by dry conditions, the long, hot, but dry summer preventing the full use of the advantageous thermal conditions without irrigation. Italy and Spain have the most extensive gravity systems of irrigation fed by rivers. Increasing use is made throughout the Community of sprinkler and drip irrigation of a more temporary nature, using local water supplies to distribute water.

In Table 4.1 the importance of irrigation in some European countries shows very clearly. Of the EC countries, Belgium, the Netherlands and Germany are the ones with the poorest prospects for water supply in the year 2000 (see Barney 1982: 156). In Central Europe, Hungary, Romania, Poland, Czechoslovakia and Bulgaria are similarly poorly endowed. Western European countries with extensive mountain areas are more generously provided.

Of the four natural factors discussed above, temperature, slope and soil are either unalterable or may be improved by artificial means. Water supply, on the other hand, can be improved through its more efficient use and by the creation of more interregional transfers. Water resources are a matter of increasing concern throughout Europe, not only to agriculture but also to industrial and domestic

Table 4.1 Water supply in selected countries of Europe

	Total withdrawal billion cubic metres	Public water supply %	Irrigation %	Industry %	Electrical cooling %
FRG	44.4	11.1	0.5	5.0	67.6
France	43.3	13.7	9.7	10.4	51.9
Italy	56.2	14.2	57.3	14.2	12.5
UK	13.2	48.6	0.3	10.8	18.8
Spain	45.8	11.6	65.5	22.9	–
Finland	4.0	10.6	0.5	37.5	3.5
Sweden	3.0	32.4	3.1	40.2	0.3
Turkey	29.6	12.8	79.1	9.8	–

Source: OECD 1991: 54, 66
Note: – negligible

users, in the production of hydro-electric power, for fishing and for navigation.

The effectiveness of precipitation (rain, snow, hail) is only broadly related to the quantity falling. Since Europe extends over 35° of latitude, from 70°N in the north to 35°N in the south, average temperature varies greatly, increasing broadly in a north–south direction. Evaporation increases with temperature, so that a given quantity of precipitation in the cooler north is more effective than the same amount in the warmer south. The season in which the precipitation comes also affects its usefulness for some purposes. In general, the period May to October is the wettest part of the year in Central and Northern Europe, whereas it is the drier half of the year in Mediterranean Europe. With the development of irrigation systems in the Mediterranean region and the emergence of great urban agglomerations throughout Europe, the need has grown to transfer water from wetter to drier areas, from mountains to plains, and from thinly populated areas to cities.

The value added per hectare of agricultural land varies greatly between regions in the EC and depends not only on the environmental constraints discussed above but also on the types of farming practised and combinations of crops and livestock found. In the report by the Commission of the EC (1992: 39), the variations are mapped. Regions with a value added per hectare more than twice the EC average include the Netherlands and Vlaams Gewest (Belgium), regions of Italy that include large areas of the North Italian Lowland, the region of Campania in the Sud of Italy, southern Greece and Crete. At the other extreme, regions with a value added per hectare less than half the EC average include Ireland, Scotland, Wales and northern England, Portugal and much of the interior of Spain, as well as Corse (France) and Sardegna (Italy).

Plates 6, 7 Making the most, agriculturally, of sloping ground. Plate 6 shows glasshouses on terraces by the Mediterranean coast, Imperia province, Italy. Plate 7 illustrates vineyards in the Moselle valley, Germany

Plate 8 Landscape in Alicante, southern Spain. This lends credence to the old saying that 'Africa begins at the Pyrenees'
Plate 9 Maximising a poor soil and a dry climate: olive trees as far as the eye can see in Andalucía, southern Spain

LAND USE AND FISHERIES

In the publications of the Food and Agriculture Organisation (FAO), four broad classes of land use are recognised: arable and tree crops; permanent pasture; forest; and other uses, including waste such as desert, and built-up land. In Table 4.2 the area occupied by each of the above uses is shown for the countries of the EC and for other selected countries or groups of countries. In the interpretation of the data shown, the great area of the USSR should be noted, almost ten times that of the EC. Before arable land is examined more closely, some aspects of the three other uses will be noted.

Permanent pasture   This varies greatly in quality between countries. In the UK and Ireland, for example, much of that in mountainous areas is of limited use. There is scope for converting some of Europe's permanent pasture into arable, should the need arise, but much of the fodder produced to raise Europe's livestock already comes from arable land.

Forest   In relation to the size of the population of the Community, the forested area of the EC is very limited. Scandinavia has a larger area under forest than the whole of the EC, with only about one-twentieth of the population. The former USSR has almost 20 times as much forest as the EC.

Other uses   In spite of the publicity given to the spread of built-up areas (domestic, industrial, transport uses), in most of the countries in Table 4.2 only a very small fraction of the residue 'other uses' land is so used. Most is waste, whether bare rocks, blown sand, swamp or Arctic waste, including 80 per cent of the area of Algeria and 70 per cent of that of Norway.

Arable land   and permanent crops include land producing field crops (mostly annuals such as wheat, sugar beet), fallow land and bush and tree crops (orchards, vineyards, olive groves). The EC has about 83 million hectares of arable land, 35 per cent of a total area of 236 million hectares. In comparison with the USA and the USSR, and in particular with Canada and Australia, the EC is poorly endowed with arable land in relation to its population size. It is, however, much better off than China, Japan and South Asia. The EC has much higher yields for comparable crops than most other parts of the world, reflecting both the presence of much good quality land and the heavy use of fertilisers.

From the data in the last column of Table 4.2 it is evident that the Netherlands, Switzerland and Belgium are the countries with the smallest amount of arable land per inhabitant in Europe, while the FRG and the UK follow. Among the larger EC countries in area, France and Spain are far more generously endowed. Turkey is also better provided than most EC countries, but its growing population will raise the number of people per 100 hectares unless new areas are brought into use to offset the increase.

Since the Second World War, the arable area of Europe has not increased greatly anywhere except in the Volga and Ural regions of the USSR, as also in West Siberia and Kazakhstan in Asiatic USSR, during the new lands campaign of the 1950s. On the other hand, the population of Europe has grown considerably.

Table 4.2 Main uses of land in the late 1980s in EC countries and in other selected countries and groups of countries

	Millions of hectares				Percentage				Total pop. per 100 ha of arable
	Total area of country	Arable	Perm. pasture	Forest	Arable	Perm. pasture	Forest	Other	
FRG	24.9	7.5	4.5	7.3	30	18	29	23	819
GDR	10.8	4.9	1.3	3.0	46	12	28	14	336
France	55.0	19.5	11.9	14.7	35	22	27	16	286
Italy	30.1	12.2	4.9	6.7	41	16	22	21	471
Netherlands	3.7	0.9	1.1	0.3	24	30	8	38	1,591
Belgium/Lux.	3.3	0.8	0.7	0.7	24	21	21	34	1,247
UK	24.5	7.0	11.6	2.3	29	47	9	15	817
Ireland	7.0	1.0	4.7	0.3	14	67	4	15	366
Denmark	4.3	2.6	0.2	0.5	60	5	12	23	196
Greece	13.2	3.9	5.3	2.6	30	40	20	10	254
Spain	50.5	20.4	10.3	15.7	40	20	31	9	190
Portugal	9.2	2.8	0.5	3.6	30	5	39	26	370
EC	236.5	83.5	57.0	57.7	35	24	24	17	413
EFTA[1]	123.7	7.9	4.4	63.8	6	4	52	38	410
Central Europe[2]	113.9	47.7	19.7	34.5	42	17	30	11	254
USSR	2,240.2	232.6	371.6	944.0	10	17	42	31	122
Turkey	77.9	27.9	8.7	20.2	36	11	26	27	188
Maghreb[3]	299.3	20.7	54.6	10.5	7	18	4	71	293
USA	937.3	188.8	242.4	291.0	20	26	31	23	132
Japan	37.7	5.2	0.4	25.0	14	1	66	19	2,369

Source: FAO Production Yearbook 1988, Table 1
Notes: 1 excludes Iceland
2 Poland, Czechoslovakia, Hungary, Romania, Bulgaria, Yugoslavia
3 Morocco, Algeria, Tunisia

In the EC itself, the total arable area in most countries has actually diminished since the 1950s, but changes in the definition of arable make comparisons difficult. The arable area for EC countries is given in Table 4.3 for selected years since 1955, the source being the FAO.

In the 1980s it became clear that the EC could satisfy many of its needs from the agriculture sector very comfortably, although it will never be able to produce commercially such crops as tea, coffee or tropical fruits. On the other hand, it can produce oilseeds and sugar, substituting imports of oilseeds from areas such as West Africa (oil palm) and of sugar cane from the Caribbean.

In spite of the current policy to reduce land under cultivation in the EC through set-aside policies, it must be remembered that the world scene changes rapidly. Conceivable futures include the possibility that significant areas of good farmland in the Community could be flooded through a rise in sea level, or that the EC will have to help to feed the growing population in the less developed countries. Under these circumstances it could be advantageous both environmentally and politically to use existing land less intensively in terms of the application of fertilisers, while maintaining or actually increasing the area cultivated, rather than letting existing arable land disappear irrevocably from use. Under current EC guidelines for set-aside procedures, individual farmers are, however, more likely if the choice arises to take the less productive land out of use in their farms rather than the more productive land.

In the remaining sections of this chapter, attention will be focused on agriculture. Before the subject of farming is resumed, the other two main sources of bioclimatic products, forestry and fisheries, will be discussed.

Table 4.3 Area of arable land plus permanent crops 1955–88 in EC countries

	Millions of hectares								
	1955	1960	1966	1971	1976	1981	1986	1988	*Irrigated*
Germany[1]	13.8	13.6	13.2	12.4	12.5	12.5	12.5	12.4	0.48
France	21.3[2]	21.5	20.5	18.7	18.7	18.6	19.0	19.5	1.37
Italy	15.8	15.8	15.3	12.4[3]	12.4	12.4	12.2	12.2	3.08
Benelux	2.1	2.0	1.9	1.7	1.7	1.7	1.7	1.7	0.55
UK/Ireland/Denmark	11.0	11.5	11.4	11.0	10.7	10.6	10.4	10.6	0.58
Greece, Spain,									
Portugal	26.9	28.3	28.9	28.1	27.5	27.3	27.1	27.1	5.13
EC	90.9	92.7	91.2	84.3	83.5	83.1	82.9	83.5	11.19

Source: FAO *Production Yearbooks*, various years
Notes: 1 Includes both Germanies throughout
     2 1953
     3 apparent change in definition between 1966 and 1971

Forestry

Very few people are directly employed in forestry in the EC, although forests cover about one-quarter of the total area of the Community and are valued for both their products and their recreational and aesthetic functions. Table 4.4 shows that since the early 1960s the forested area in all the countries listed except Austria has increased, in some cases considerably. Nevertheless, with some 55 million hectares of forest and woodland altogether, the EC has a mere 1.2 per cent of the world total.

It can be seen in Table 4.4 that the area of forest to population varies markedly among the countries listed. Spain has about 10 times as much forest per 1,000 inhabitants as the UK, while Finland has over 100 times more. EC policy favours the maintenance of the forests of the Community and even some extension of their area. There could be opposition to afforestation projects in some areas, however, both from farmers wishing to retain arable and pasture land, and from conservationists wishing to protect natural habitats from forestry development.

At present the forests in most regions of the EC supply only negligible quantities of fuelwood, while the Community as a whole produces only half of its needs of wood for construction purposes and as a raw material. The UK, the FRG and Italy account for over two-thirds of EC imports of roundwood, while only Portugal has a surplus. The UK produces only about one-tenth of its total needs. Unless drastic changes take place in the use of wood, the EC will not

Table 4.4 The area of forest and forest products in selected countries of the EC and EFTA

	Area of forest (millions of hectares)			Hectares per 1,000 pop. 1988	Products used (millions cubic metres)	
	1961–5	1975	1988		Roundwood	Fuelwood
FRG	7.1	7.2	7.4	121	34	3.7
France	11.9	14.6	14.7	259	41	10.4
Italy	6.0	6.3	6.7	116	9	4.4
UK	1.8	2.0	2.4	42	5	0.2
Greece	2.5	2.6	2.6	257	3	2.3
Spain	13.2	14.9	15.7	403	18	2.3
Portugal	3.2	3.6	3.6	346	9	0.6
Austria	3.2	3.3	3.2	416	14	1.4
Norway	6.9	8.3	8.3	1,930	11	2.4
Sweden	26.2	26.4	28.0	3,256	53	12.1
Finland	21.8	22.6	23.2	4,640	42	3.8

Sources: FAO *Production Yearbooks* 1960 (vol. 14), 1976 (vol. 30), 1989 (vol. 43) Table 1; *1988 Energy Statistics Yearbook of the United Nations*, New York

approach self-sufficiency. The entry of the EFTA countries would change that situation radically, while closer association with the former USSR, especially the Russian Republic, could benefit that country, especially if and when new areas in Siberia are exploited.

The map of EC forests (Commission of the EC 1987), shows in great detail the distribution of trees of all kinds. The proportions of coniferous and non-coniferous species vary greatly between countries and regions, with coniferous species generally in the more northerly parts of the Community, at higher altitudes, and often on areas of sandy soil. Broadleaf deciduous species are common in central regions and in higher areas in Southern Europe, while ever-green species, often of limited size due to dry summer conditions and poor soils, are common in the Mediterranean coastlands. Each type has its own advantages and disadvantages, particular products, and scenic values. The future of the forests is one of the less sensitive and urgent issues facing EC policy-makers, but the damage to European forests attributed to acid rain has now become a problem.

Fishing

The EC Common Fisheries Policy (CFP) has resolved much of the conflict over rights to fish in particular sea areas, and over the quotas permitted to be caught. Like forestry, fishing only employs directly a small proportion of the total labour force in the agricultural sector and a mere 0.2 per cent of all employment in the EC. As with forestry, however, large areas are affected by fishing, and the industry has a high profile.

A 200-mile offshore zone, in which each country with a coastline has its adjacent portion, is now recognised in the world. The combined coastal zone of the EC extends clockwise from Greece in the eastern Mediterranean through Italy and Spain to the Straits of Gibraltar, along the Atlantic and North Sea shores mainly of Spain, France and the UK, and into the Baltic, where Germany and Denmark have coastlines. Some of the world's most productive fishing grounds are located in these sea areas, but over-fishing and pollution have caused concern in the EC for at least two decades. One of the issues related to the possible entry of two of the Member States of EFTA, Iceland and Norway, is the importance to these two countries of their fishing industries.

Almost 93 million tonnes of fish were caught in the world in 1987. The EC accounted for about 7 per cent of that total. Denmark (about 2 million tonnes a year) has the largest catch in the Community, but much is used for industrial purposes. Spain follows (about 1.3 million) and then the UK and France. Norway (about 2 million), Iceland (about 1.6 million) and The Faeroes (350,000), with a combined population of less than 5 million, account for 3–4 per cent of the total fish catch of the world. If Iceland and/or Norway join the EC, they stand to lose some of their fishing rights and quotas unless some agreement is reached to safeguard their positions. Changes in the size of catch in the seven EC and EFTA countries referred to above have not been great in the

1980s. At the same time, however, conservation of stocks is becoming a more serious issue, and if the EC fishing fleets are to increase their catches in the future they will have to follow the practice of Japan and Eastern Europe and move further afield, especially to other parts of the Atlantic Ocean

EMPLOYMENT IN AGRICULTURE

The decline of employment in agriculture has been a feature of most European countries for many decades now. The process started much earlier in some countries than in others and has proceeded much further. The pacesetter by a long way was Great Britain, which as far back as 1840 only had 25 per cent of its employed population in agriculture, a level not reached in Germany until 1940, in France and Italy until around 1960, and in Greece until the late 1980s. Regional variations in the proportion of total economically active population engaged in agriculture are shown for the 68 NUTS 1 level regions of the EC in Figure 4.2. In view of the growing interest shown by many non-EC countries of

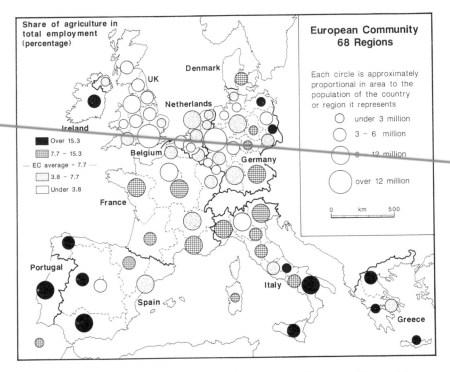

Figure 4.2 Employment in the agricultural sector at NUTS 1 regional level of the European Community in 1987

Source: COM-90-609 (1991), Table A of Statistical Annex
Note: See Figure 2.3 for the names of the regions

Europe in joining or becoming associated with the EC, frequent reference is made in this section to the situation in Europe as a whole.

Almost all the countries of Europe are still experiencing a substantial decline in employment in the agricultural sector, and it can be expected that the trend will continue for several decades in many regions of the EC as well as in parts of EFTA, in Central Europe and the USSR, and in Turkey and the Maghreb countries. The data in Table 4.5 are a guide to the countries in which the agricultural sector is likely to reduce its labour force appreciably. As will be shown in Chapter 10, Objective 1 regions of the EC, the main targets for EC regional development funds in the early 1990s, are mainly the ones most dependent on agriculture for employment.

In looking at future prospects for employment in the agricultural sector in Europe, it is important to distinguish relative and absolute change, as the following example shows. In the UK, the labour force in agriculture dropped from 960,000 in 1965 to 600,000 in 1987. In relation to the total labour force in all sectors of the economy the 360,000 'lost' was only about 1.5 per cent. In Greece, in contrast, between 1965 and 1987, the drop was from 1,935,000 to 1,010,000, a matter of almost a million jobs, equivalent to over 20 per cent of the total

Table 4.5 Employment in the agricultural sector in 1988 and expected in 2000 and 2010 (population in thousands)

	(1) Total 1988	(2) % 1988	(3) % 2000	(4) % 2010	(5) Total by 2000	(6) Total by 2010	(7) Total shed by 2000	(8) Total shed by 2010
FRG	1,220	4.1	3.0	2.0	890	595	330	625
GDR	815	8.6	6.0	4.0	570	380	245	435
France	1,520	6.1	4.0	2.5	1,000	625	520	895
Italy	1,910	8.3	6.0	4.0	1,380	920	530	990
Netherlands	250	4.2	3.0	2.0	180	120	70	130
Belgium/Lux.	90	2.1	1.9	1.7	80	70	10	20
UK	605	2.2	2.0	1.8	550	495	55	110
Ireland	205	14.9	12.0	9.0	165	125	40	80
Denmark	150	5.4	4.0	2.5	110	70	40	80
Greece	1,010	26.1	20.0	14.0	770	540	240	470
Spain	1,750	12.4	8.5	6.0	1,200	850	550	900
EC	10,360	7.6	5.7	4.3	7,585	5,340	2,775	5,020
EFTA[1]	890	5.9	4.4	3.3	660	470	230	420
Central Europe[2]	11,435	17.3	13.0	9.7	12,230	8,460	4,350	8,090
USSR	20,400	14.2	12.0	10.0	17,240	14,365	3,160	5,360
Turkey	11,720	50.1	37.0	25.0	8,655	5,850	3,065	5,870

Source: FAO *Production Yearbook 1989* (1990); Table 3 for 1988 data
Notes: 1 excludes Iceland, where fishing is prominent in the 'agricultural' sector
    2 Poland, Hungary, Czechoslovakia, Bulgaria, Romania, Yugoslavia

labour force. There is little room for further job losses from agriculture in the UK, whereas another half-million jobs could disappear in Greece in the next two to three decades.

In the projections in Table 4.5, it is assumed that between 1988 and the year 2000 the agricultural sector in all the countries and groups of countries included will lose 25 per cent of its 1988 employment. In the EC there could be about 200,000 job losses a year, spread very unevenly among the regions. EFTA would follow a similar path, but only about 20,000 a year would be involved. With a total population only about one-third that of the EC, the five former CMEA countries of Central Europe together with Yugoslavia could also be expected to lose about 200,000 jobs a year, with a much greater impact on their economies. They would thus lose about 5 million jobs from the agricultural sector by the year 2010, a major problem for the EC if it is enlarged to include these countries. The number involved in Turkey would assume massive proportions. With a total population only about one-sixth of that of the EC, Turkey actually has a larger labour force in agriculture than the whole Community, and by 2010 could lose about 5 million jobs from the sector, while the Maghreb countries could lose about 2 million. Although trends in the former USSR may not be of immediate concern to the EC, yet the whole of Europe, the USSR, Turkey and the Maghreb together face the prospect of a combined decline in the agricultural labour force from about 50 million in 1990 to about 25 million in 2010. The impact on employment structures throughout the continent over the longer term is therefore far-reaching in scope and extent, in particular in terms of migration.

In the larger and more diversified countries of the EC, great regional contrasts exist in employment in agriculture. It can be seen in Figure 4.2 that the regions that depend most highly on agriculture are in the southern part of the EC. At NUTS 2 level (see Table 4.6) the extremes within the larger countries are a long way apart, with large urban centres in small territories at one end, and

Table 4.6 Percentage share of the agricultural sector in total employment in 1987 in extreme NUTS 2 level regions of the EC

		Highest and lowest at NUTS 2 level			
Germany	4.5	Oberpfalz	12.8	Bremen	0.3
France	7.2	Limousin	16.4	Ile-de-France	0.5
Italy	9.8	Molise	26.9	Lombardia	3.6
Netherlands	4.9	Flevoland	11.3	Utrecht	3.0
Belgium	3.2	Luxembourg (Belg.)	9.9	Brussels	0.2
UK	2.4	Lincolnshire	9.0	Greater London	0.0
Greece	26.6	Peloponnisos	51.7	Attiki	1.6
Spain	14.3	Galicia	39.3	Madrid	1.4
Portugal	21.2	Centro	35.7	Lisbon	10.1

Source: COM 90-609 (1991), Table A

89

comparatively rural areas, not necessarily with unfavourable conditions for agriculture, at the other. At a still more local level, great variations can be found even in the UK, in spite of its very small total labour force in the sector. There is virtually no employment in agriculture in Greater London or in many other highly urbanised districts, but almost a quarter of employment in the district of South Holland, Lincolnshire. These great regional variations are of special signifi-cance to the EC since so much of its budget is devoted to the assistance of agri-culture, with the result that some regions, both affluent and poor, receive far greater subsidies than others, depending on the prominence of the agricultural sector.

MECHANISATION AND FARM SIZE

The continuing mechanisation of agriculture in the EC and elsewhere in Europe has had a profound effect on employment, farm and field size, and production. While the spectacular increases in yields since the Second World War can be attributed mainly to the use of fertilisers and to plant quality and protection, the drastic decline in total employment in agriculture is closely related to the expansion of mechanisation on a cultivated area that has changed little. Although many different types of machinery contribute to the mechanisation of farming, tractors can be used to give a broad representation of the process. Even with tractors, however, the effectiveness of a machine depends on local features such as quality of the land, terrain (especially slope), land ownership, and size of field.

Three relationships are shown in Table 4.7: arable land to economically active population in agriculture (column (7)) and to tractors (column (8)), and economically active population to tractors (column (6)). The change in the number of tractors in use between 1960 and 1988 is shown in column (3) (see also Figure 4.3). Great variations have occurred in the rate of mechanisation of agriculture in the last three decades, but some countries, in particular Sweden, the UK and Denmark, were already highly mechanised by 1960, so would not be expected to show a large increase in tractor numbers. In the EC the increase has been most marked in the four southern countries, Italy, Spain, Greece and Portugal, all following the path of the northern countries. In Central Europe, Poland and Yugoslavia have progressed rapidly while Hungary, Czechoslovakia and Romania have shown little change. Outside Europe, Turkey has made enormous progress recently, the Maghreb countries less.

A guide to the productivity of labour in agriculture with regard to the land worked is given by the data in column (7) in Table 4.7. In the EC, Denmark, France, the UK and Spain score highest in this respect but the relatively high score for Spain must be set against appreciably lower yields from the same area. Greece and Portugal, together with Yugoslavia, Turkey and Morocco, have particularly large labour forces in relation to arable land, but even these are far more productive than agricultural labour in China, where each hectare is worked on average by between three and four people.

Table 4.7 Mechanisation and the productivity of labour in agriculture in countries of the EC and other regions in 1988

	(1) Tractors in use (000s) 1960	(2) 1988	(3) Tractors 1988 1960–1	(4) Arable land (000 ha) 1988	(5) Agric. workers (000s) 1988	(6) Tractors per 100 workers 1988	(7) Hectares per agric. worker 1988	(8) Hectares per tractor 1988
FRG	857	1,460	1.7	7,466	1,172	125	6.4	5.1
GDR	71	168	2.4	4,924	816	21	6.0	29.3
France	680	1,518	2.2	19,547	1,459	104	13.4	12.9
Italy	249	1,363	5.5	12,149	1,823	75	6.7	8.9
Netherlands	82	194	2.4	931	242	80	3.8	4.8
Belgium–Lux.	51	117	2.3	820	84	139	9.8	7.0
UK	427	518	1.2	6,988	594	87	11.8	13.5
Ireland	44	164	3.7	963	196	84	4.9	5.9
Denmark	111	168	1.5	2,570	145	116	17.7	15.3
Greece	21	187	8.9	3,929	986	19	4.0	21.0
Spain	52	720	13.9	20,380	1,687	43	21.1	28.3
Portugal	10	77	7.7	2,750	811	9	3.4	35.7
EC	2,655	6,554	2.5	83,417	10,015	65	8.3	12.7
EFTA	431	1,007	2.3	8,157	895	113	9.1	8.1
Six Central Europe	323	2,598	8.0	47,786	11,438	23	4.2	18.4
USSR	1,122	2,692	2.4	232,426	20,401	13	11.4	86.3
Turkey	42	654	15.6	27,730	11,719	6	2.4	42.4
Three Maghreb	53	150	2.8	21,186	4,827	3	4.4	141.2
USA	4,700	4,670	1.0	189,915	3,058	153	62.1	40.7
Japan	9	1,985	220.5	4,681	4,427	45	1.1	2.4

Source: Various years of the FAO Production Yearbooks

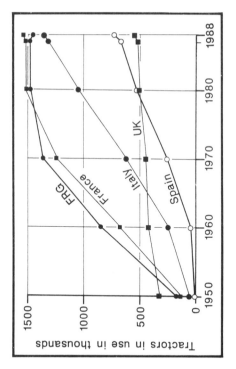

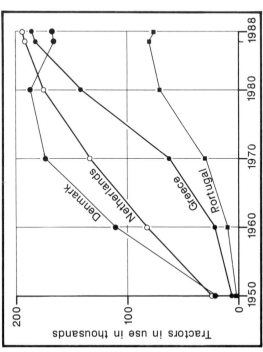

Figure 4.3 Tractors in use in selected countries of the European Community, 1950–88

Source: various years of UN FAO Production Yearbook

If it is assumed that all but the four southern EC countries have virtually reached a limit to the number of tractors needed on the farms, then the FRG and the Netherlands used about three times as many tractors per unit of arable land as Denmark, the UK or France (see column (8) in Table 4.7). The disparity is largely the result of small farm and presumably field size in the FRG and the very intensive nature of cultivation in the Netherlands. On the other hand, the large number of hectares cultivated per tractor in Spain, Greece and Portugal results from a lower level of mechanisation overall. The EFTA countries are highly mechanised, but in most of Central Europe levels are still generally low, while in Turkey, and still more in the Maghreb countries, the process has not gone very far yet.

All the EC countries except Greece, Spain and Portugal, have very roughly a ratio of one tractor per person engaged in agriculture (see column (6) in Table 4.7), a situation found also in North America and Australia. The EFTA countries are similarly placed. In all such countries it seems unlikely that further mechanisation will greatly reduce the labour force in agriculture.

Increasing mechanisation is both a cause and a consequence of increasing farm size. Since the Second World War the average size of farm has gradually grown in most regions of the EC and the total number has decreased. With some exceptions, including very large farm units characteristic of a few regions, including southern Italy and southern Spain, the family farm has been typical in much of the EC, as it was in the USA. In 1970 there were 10.6 million farms in what is now the EC, in 1990 about 8.6 million. As a result of amalgamation of enterprises and concentration, the average size, still very small compared with that in North America and Australia, increased from 12 hectares in 1960 to 14 hectares in 1985.

The smallest farms in the EC are mostly in the southern Mediterranean regions, while the largest are in the UK. The average utilised agricultural area per farm ranges between about 4 hectares in Greece and Portugal and over 50 in the UK (about 30 in Denmark and France). Farm size is not only related to the level of mechanisation but also to the fertility of the land and to the terrain, as well as to the type of crop grown (e.g. vegetables, tree crops) and to the livestock (e.g. pigs and poultry) kept. More efficient management, especially regarding the use of means of production and professional accounting, are regarded as beneficial results of economies of scale, but experience in the former USSR and its CMEA partners has shown that farm 'giantism', achieved through large collective and state farms, does not necessarily result in efficiency and high yields.

AGRICULTURAL PRODUCTION

In order to achieve a comparison of yields between various parts of the EC and between the EC and the rest of Europe, attention in this section focuses on cereal and livestock farming, both of them practised throughout the Community.

Cereals

Cereals are grown on more than half of the arable area of the EC. Wheat and barley are grown in considerable quantities in most regions of Europe, as well as in Turkey and the Maghreb. A study of the area cultivated, the yields and the production of cereals allows a broad comparison of the productivity of agricultural land among countries and regions. Since both the total arable area of the EC and the area under cereals have changed only slightly in the last two decades and seem unlikely to change much in the 1990s, attention will focus on yields, and particularly on the application of the principal chemical fertilisers, nitrogenous, phosphate and potash. It is appreciated that the use of various insecticides and fungicides, of high-quality seeds, and deeper ploughing through the use of mechanical means, also contribute to increases in yield.

The relationship between the area cultivated, yield and production is shown in Table 4.8 for the EC countries during 1979–81 and 1987–9. In Western Europe (EC with EFTA but not the GDR) during the 1980s the area under cereals diminished by 5 per cent, yields increased by nearly 20 per cent, and production by 13 per cent. Although in some countries yields are approaching a limit beyond which diminishing returns on inputs of means of production become very marked, some regions in the EC and many in the rest of Europe should be

Table 4.8 Area, yield and production of cereals in EC countries

	1979–81			1987–9		
	Area (million ha)	Yield tonnes per ha	Production (million tonnes)	Area (million ha)	Yield tonnes per ha	Production (million tonnes)
FRG	5.2	4.4	22.9	4.7	5.5	25.7
GDR	2.5	3.6	9.1	2.4	4.3	10.6
France	9.8	4.7	46.1	9.3	5.9	55.5
Italy	5.1	3.5	18.0	4.6	3.8	17.6
Netherlands	0.2	5.7	1.3	0.2	6.4	1.2
Belgium/Lux.	0.4	4.9	2.1	0.4	5.9	2.2
UK	3.9	4.8	18.8	3.9	5.6	21.7
Ireland	0.4	4.6	2.0	0.3	6.1	2.1
Denmark	1.8	4.0	7.3	1.6	5.2	8.0
Greece	1.6	3.1	5.0	1.4	3.4	4.8
Spain	7.4	2.0	14.7	7.8	2.7	21.3
Portugal	1.1	1.1	1.2	1.0	1.6	1.7
EC	39.4	3.9[1]	148.5	37.8	4.4[1]	172.4
Western Europe[2]	45.6	3.7	169.7	43.5	4.4	192.6

Source: FAO *Production Yearbook*, various years
Notes: 1 unweighted mean, therefore not used to calculate total production
        2 includes EFTA but excludes GDR

capable of achieving much higher yields than at present. For example, the fact that in the late 1980s cereal yields in the Netherlands were four times as high as in Portugal can only partly be attributed to natural qualities of the land and climate. The broad correlation between the quantity of chemical fertilisers applied per hectare and wheat yields shows clearly in Figure 4.4.

The calculation of average yields over periods of several years smooths out to some extent fluctuations due to yearly variations in weather conditions. The quantity and reliability of rainfall, extreme temperatures, soil and slope differ both within and between countries. For example, only a small area of Norway can be used for cultivation on account of lack of good soil and to some extent low temperatures, while much of Switzerland is too rugged to cultivate commercially. In the northern part of European Russia, large areas are ill-drained, while some areas are adversely affected by permanently frozen subsoil. In the Maghreb, south of the North African coastlands, dry conditions prevail, keeping yields low.

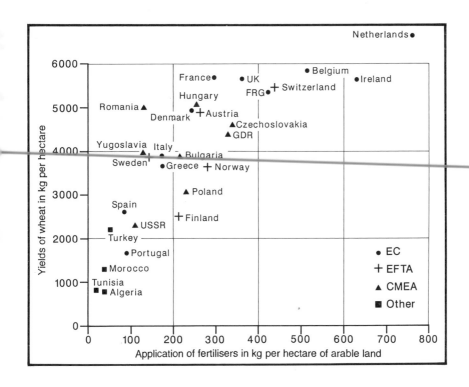

Figure 4.4 The relationship between the use of fertilisers and yields of wheat in the countries of Europe in 1987

Source: FAOPY 1988

In the last three decades, wheat and barley yields have increased in all the countries included in Table 4.8 (see also Figure 4.5). The area under these cereals has not changed much during that time whereas production has risen greatly. Even within the EC there are marked differences, a result of the more intensive use of fertilisers, as well as of the quality of land. The Netherlands, Denmark and the UK were the countries with the highest yields in the 1960s. Details of yields are available for various crops in EC regions at NUTS 1 and NUTS 2 level in Eurostat (1990: 114–21). Although local thermal and moisture conditions may vary from region to region in a given year, some contrasts in wheat yields in 1987 illustrate the regional differences: among the highest were 7,400 kg in Schleswig-Holstein and 6,900 in Niedersachsen in northern Germany, compared with 2,200

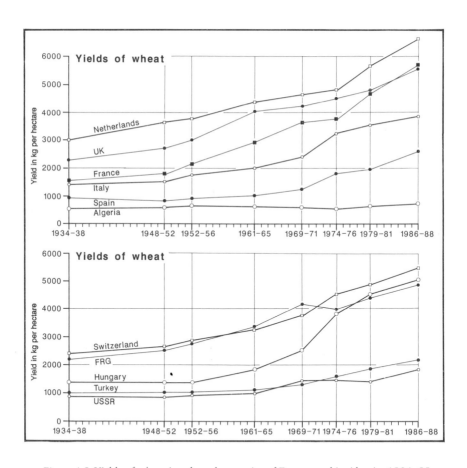

Figure 4.5 Yields of wheat in selected countries of Europe and in Algeria, 1934–88

Source: FAOPY (various years)

in the Centro region of Spain and 1,800 in the Sud of Italy. In the countries of EFTA, yields are being pushed to the limit in Switzerland, but in Sweden and Finland less use is made of fertilisers, while cool conditions limit the growing season.

In Central Europe, impressive increases have been achieved in cereal yields, but in comparison with the most successful EC countries there is scope for improvement in Poland, Bulgaria and Yugoslavia. Organisational constraints have contributed to keep cereal yields low in the former USSR compared with those in the rest of Europe and climatically much of the arable area in Russia resembles that in Canada, where yields are in general lower than in the USA and Western Europe. The impressive increase in yields in Turkey has been largely offset by a large increase in population.

The present performance of cereal cultivators in the EC points to a potential increase of 20–30 per cent in production if yields are raised in Italy, Greece, Spain and Portugal, even if the area under cereals diminishes a little. In view of the small area under cereals in the EFTA countries, a possible modest increase there would have little effect on total EC/EFTA production. On the other hand, a substantial increase in cereal production could still be achieved in Central Europe, and would threaten to increase surpluses in the EC should any of these countries become more closely associated. At present, the USSR is a net importer of cereals, but a successful restructuring of agriculture could overcome some of the organisational problems that hold production down, including the mis-application of fertilisers, poor equipment for harvesting and transporting produce, and limited storage facilities. Eventually a surplus of agricultural products, achieved in Russia before 1917, and hoped for throughout the Soviet period, could create another region of surplus on the doorstep of the EC.

The livestock sector

In the livestock sector of the EC, a large increase has been achieved since the 1950s in the amount of meat and other products obtained from each animal raised. The total number of livestock units, like the arable area, has changed little in the last decade. Indeed, the number of cattle kept has declined slightly in the EC, but the number of pigs and particularly of sheep has risen. The weight of mutton, lamb and pig-meat per sheep and pig has changed little in the 1980s, but that of beef and veal per animal has continued to rise, while milk yields per animal increased by 50 per cent between the early 1960s and the late 1980s (see Table 4.9).

Variations among the Member States of the EC in meat yields per animal are considerable, but are not nearly so marked as the extremes in cereal yields. Milk yields, on the other hand, do vary greatly, with each dairy cow kept in Denmark giving more than three times as much milk as each one in Greece. The level of provision of fodder crops and the quality of pastures produce a marked difference between the northern and southern regions of the EC in the dairying sector. As

Table 4.9 Annual yield of milk in kilograms per cow

				Change		
	Average *1961–5*	*Average* *1979–81*	*Average* *1987–9*	*61–5* *79–81*	*79–81* *87–9*	*61–5* *87–9*
FRG	3,520	4,480	4,790	127	107	136
GDR	2,660	3,890	4,610	146	119	173
France	2,550	2,630	2,900	103	110	114
Italy	2,730	3,480	3,580	127	103	131
Netherlands	4,180	5,030	5,830	120	116	139
Belgium/Lux.	3,720	3,880	4,170	104	107	112
UK	3,480	4,760	4,780	137	100	137
Ireland	2,340	3,270	3,880	140	119	166
Denmark	3,740	4,920	6,120	132	124	164
Greece	940	1,870	1,860	199	99	198
Spain	2,100	3,260	3,340	155	102	159
Portugal	1,800	2,120	3,270	118	154	182

Sources: FAO *Production Yearbook*, vol. 30, 1976, Table 90; vol. 43, 1989, Table 99

with cereals, there seems to be some slack to be taken up in the livestock sector if standards in lagging regions are brought up to those in the regions with the highest yields in the Community.

CONCLUSION

At first sight agriculture appears to form only a small part of the economic life of the EC, but it is likely to maintain a prominent position in EC funding and debate. It is therefore appropriate to discuss some further issues regarding the agricultural sector.

Fertilisers

The increasing use of synthetic fertilisers has contributed fundamentally to the increase in yield of various crops, including fodder for livestock. The EC lacks reserves of phosphates, but Germany and France have sources of potash. The USSR has abundant reserves of both phosphates and potash, while Morocco has the largest reserves of phosphates in the world; both these countries are well located to supply the EC. The harmful effect of the application of fertilisers is, however, increasingly being felt in many parts of the EC, in particular the long-term harm caused to water supplies. A reduction in the use of fertilisers may become necessary. Adverse effects of the excessive use of fertilisers and the beginnings of organic farming are referred to in Chapter 9.

The efficiency of the agricultural sector

The success of the agricultural sector in relation to industry and services in a given country or region cannot be measured comprehensively and objectively by one single index. Yields per area cultivated, already referred to, can be taken as a broad measure of success. Alternatively the level of mechanisation might be used. It may not be long before 'points' are awarded or deducted according to appropriate indicators of damage to the land and soil. A comparison of the share of the total labour force in agriculture in a given country or region with the share of total GDP accounted for by the agricultural sector is an index used here to measure efficiency according to the productivity of labour in the same way that yields measure the efficiency of the use of land. Appropriate data are provided in COM 87-230 (1987) and Eurostat (1989a: 56–64).

The share of agriculture in total employment is shown for NUTS 1 level regions of the EC in Figure 4.2. If the contribution of agriculture to GDP and to employment are compared, an index can be calculated to measure the relative strength of agriculture relative to the other two sectors of the economy in each region. Since GDP per inhabitant varies greatly between regions, the share can only be compared relatively, not absolutely. The method of calculation is shown in Table 4.10. In the country list, for example, the agricultural sector in Denmark accounts for 6.7 per cent of employment but only 5.7 per cent of GDP. The 'efficiency' of the agricultural sector in each region is calculated by dividing the percentage of the GDP of that region accounted for by agriculture, by the percentage of employment in agriculture and then multiplying by 100 (e.g. in the case of Denmark, 5.7 per cent/6.7 per cent $\times$ 100 = 85). A surprising feature of the ratio at country level is the position of the FRG beside Spain and Portugal at the bottom of the efficiency scale. On the other hand, the position of Denmark and the Netherlands at the top can be expected.

At NUTS 1 level, parity is achieved in the region of Zuid-Nederland, giving it an index of 100 (see Figure 4.6). This is the only EC region in which agriculture can hold its own against industry and services. Of the eight most efficient regions, scoring 80 or above, apart from Denmark, all are in the Netherlands or the UK (East Anglia 83, Wales 82, Northern Ireland 80) except Ile-de-France (the Paris area, 80). The lowest scoring regions are all in Spain or the FRG, but the reasons for such low scores clearly vary. Baden-Württemberg is not particularly fertile agriculturally, while it has a very large and successful industrial sector. In Bremen and West Berlin, like Madrid, agriculture is overshadowed by a successful service sector. In the Noroeste of Spain, agriculture is very backward, while the industrial and service sectors, although not outstanding in comparison with those in the EC as a whole, are more successful.

In the view of the authors, the index explained above is a useful general guide to the agricultural health of different parts of the EC. Whether assistance to the agricultural sector should go to raising efficiency in the regions with a low index (so long as changes could be guaranteed to improve standards) or to

Table 4.10 Measuring the efficiency of agriculture

By country	% emplt	% gdp	ratio (emplt = 100)	By NUTS 1 level region: Rank	% emplt	% gdp	ratio (emplt = 100)
FRG	5.2	1.7	33	1 Zuid-Nederland	5.5	5.5	100
France	8.1	4.0	49	2 Oost-Nederland	6.9	6.1	88
Italy	11.0	5.2	47	3 Denmark	6.7	5.7	85
Netherlands	5.2	4.5	87	4 West-Nederland	3.9	3.3	85
Belgium/Lux.	3.6	2.5	69	5 West Midlands (UK)	1.9	1.6	84
UK	2.3	1.4	61				
Ireland	16.5	10.6	64	56 Bremen (FRG)	1.2	0.3	25
Denmark	6.7	5.7	85	57 Baden-Württemberg (FRG)	6.4	1.4	22
Greece	28.9	18.4	64	58 West Berlin (FRG)	0.9	0.2	22
Spain	17.9	6.0	34	59 Madrid (Spain)	1.4	0.3	21
Portugal	23.9	7.7	32	60 Noroeste (Spain)	39.1	8.0	20

Sources: COM 87-230 (1987) and Eurostat 1989a

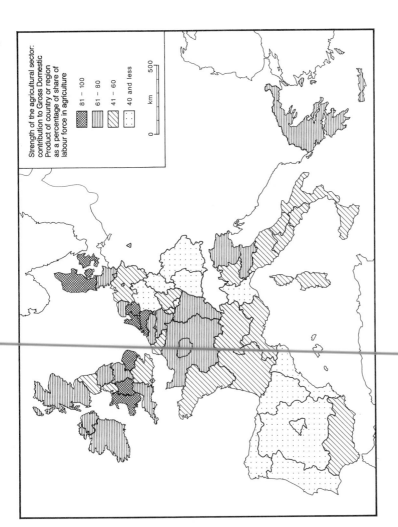

Strength of the agricultural sector:
contribution to Gross Domestic
Product of country or region
as a percentage of share of
labour force in agriculture

81 – 100

61 – 80

41 – 60

40 and less

0   km   500

Figure 4.6 Efficiency in the agricultural sector. The index is measured by dividing the share of the total GDP of each region contributed by the agricultural sector, by the share of total employment in the region accounted for by agriculture; the result is multiplied by 100. The index is 100 if the two shares are equal. Comparable data for the former GDR are not available

phasing out agriculture where further investment would be wasted, must be a consideration in applying the CAP. The NUTS 1 or even the NUTS 2 levels of regions would not, however, form a detailed enough base for the application of some policies without further refinements, given the variations in practices and performance between quite small areas in Western Europe.

A somewhat different measure of productivity in the agricultural sector is the agricultural value added per work unit, showing labour productivity. Commission of the EC (1992: 38) includes a map of labour productivity at NUTS 2 level of regions. The distribution of high and low productivity is broadly similar to that in Figure 4.6. The highest labour productivity is found in Denmark, the Netherlands, northeast France and northern Germany; the lowest in Portugal, northern Spain and western Greece. The former areas have a level of labour productivity at least four times as high (at over twice the EC average) as the latter areas (with under half) – further evidence of the great gap in economic conditions between various parts of the EC.

Trade in agricultural products

Since the sixteenth century, Western Europe has traditionally been an importer of agricultural products from other continents, for example, sugar and beverages from Latin America, cereals, cotton and tobacco from North America, livestock products from Australia and New Zealand, and various tropical fruits. In the 1930s, British policy was to encourage trade within the empire, but Germany and Italy, anticipating war and a possible blockade, were even then concerned with self-sufficiency in food. Kuczynski cites the Germany Institute for Business Research (23 May 1939):

> The struggle for an expansion of the German foodstuff productive capacity has entered on a new and decisive stage since the assumption of power by the present German government. All efforts are being made to make a greater acreage available and to secure from the present acreage the greatest possible yield.
>
> (Kuczynski 1939: 28)

According to Kuczynski, Germany was 83 per cent self-sufficient in foodstuffs, Great Britain only 25 per cent, while Italy managed 95 per cent. Could experiences in the 1930s help to account for concern over food supply in the young EEC of the 1950s?

Whereas Western Europe was a net importer of most agricultural products before the Second World War, it has largely become self-sufficient in those items that can be produced in cool and warm temperate climatic conditions. On the other hand, it still has to import tropical beverages (coffee, tea, cocoa), tropical fruits (bananas), tropical raw materials such as cotton, and more esoteric items such as spices. The data in Table 4.11 show how each EC country stands with regard to trade in agricultural products. The figures include a large amount of

102

Table 4.11 Average annual value of imports and exports of agricultural products 1986–8

	Imports	Exports	Balance
	(billion dollars)		of trade
FRG	29.0	15.0	−14.0
GDR	2.1	0.5	−1.6
France	17.5	23.6	+6.1
Italy	19.1	7.8	−11.3
Netherlands	14.7	22.4	+7.7
Belgium/Lux.	9.7	8.6	−1.1
UK	18.3	9.6	−8.7
Ireland	1.8	4.2	+2.4
Denmark	2.7	6.5	+3.8
Greece	2.4	2.0	−0.4
Spain	5.4	5.6	+0.2
Portugal	1.8	0.6	−1.2
EC	124.5	106.4	−18.1
Europe[1]	143.3	118.6	−24.7

Source: FAO *Trade Yearbook 1988*, Table 7, Rome 1990
Note: 1 excluding USSR

intra-EC trade. Of the 11 EC countries included in the table, five are net exporters of agricultural products, six are net importers. Germany, Italy and the UK are the largest importers, not only in absolute terms but also in relation to population.

The EC cannot isolate itself entirely from the rest of the world with regard to the production of and trade in agricultural products. The population of the present developing countries of the world is expected to increase from about 4.1 billion in 1990 to 7.2 billion in 2025, almost an additional 100 million people per year. The area under cultivation cannot grow that fast, while increases in yields will depend on great improvements in the quantity and quality of means of production. Indeed, from being a net importer from many less developed countries, the EC may find itself politically persuaded or forced to sell or even give food to various parts of the developing world in the future.

Climatic change and European agriculture

While future trends in agriculture in the EC will be affected by as yet unknown policy and practical decisions at all levels from the EC Commission to the individual farmer, there is also growing uncertainty over possible changes in climate related to the rapidly increasing emissions and accumulation of greenhouse gases in the atmosphere. Parry (1990) discusses various models and forecasts related particularly to the general circulation of the atmosphere. The effects of various possible future rises in the level of temperature are considered in relation to agriculture. Increases in temperature would probably change precipitation in different parts of the world in ways that are difficult to anticipate and, if some of the ice at present in glaciers and ice caps were to melt, a small rise in sea level could be expected, bringing serious consequences in some low-lying areas.

Parry (1990: 65) shows, for example, that various models agree that a doubling of carbon dioxide in the atmosphere could shift the thermal limit of the successful commercial cultivation of grain maize in Europe some 200–350 km north. The limit at present runs roughly eastwards from the northern extremity of France across central Germany and Poland to the Ukraine. Much of the UK, Denmark, southern Scandinavia and the rest of European USSR could become suitable for maize cultivation depending, however, on adequate precipitation in the right season.

The broad conclusion is that increased global temperature could substantially benefit Northern Europe, whereas Southern Europe could suffer through decreases in soil moisture in the summer due to a reduction of summer rainfall. Such a change could decrease the biomass potential in Italy by 5 per cent and in Greece by 35 per cent. According to Parry (1990: 83) 'This implies an important northward shift of the balance of agricultural resources in the EC.'

Outside Europe, some expected changes could also affect the EC. Grain production is expected to be reduced by 10–20 per cent in the USA and to fall also in Canada, as well as in the Ukraine and other agricultural areas of southern USSR. The current surplus of grain from North America could be reduced or eliminated. Of most immediate concern to the EC is the prospect that the Maghreb countries will become even hotter and drier than they are now, with even greater pressure on the growing population to seek employment in Western Europe.

FURTHER READING

Commission of the European Communities (1992) *The Agricultural Situation in the Community 1991 Report*, Luxembourg: Office for Official Publications of the European Communities.

European Documentation (1989) *A Common Agricultural Policy for the 1990s*, Luxembourg: Office for Official Publications of the European Communities.

5

ENERGY

ENERGY ISSUES AND POLICY

The energy sector accounts for only about 1.5 per cent of total employment in the EC but produces about 6.5 of the GDP of the Community. In the mid-1980s (Eurostat 1989a: 118–19) the extraction and processing of coal employed about 450,000 workers, the extraction of oil and natural gas about 60,000, and oil refining about 120,000. The production and distribution of electricity and gas employed about 1,150,000 people. On average, each person in the energy sector contributes about eight times as much to the GDP of the EC as each person employed in agriculture. Within the energy sector itself, workers in the oil and gas industry extract about 10 times as much in energy equivalent as workers in the coal industry.

Although job losses in the coal mining industry have been considerable since the Second World War, severely affecting certain regions of the EC, in the Community as a whole the absolute number leaving the industry has been far smaller than that leaving the agricultural sector. Some regions in the UK, Germany and Belgium have been seriously affected. In the UK the labour force in British Coal was only 74,000 in 1991 compared with almost 300,000 in 1980 (Bassett 1991) while in West Germany, there are only 130,000 left in coal-mining (Paterson 1991b).

EC energy policy has principally been concerned with reserves and supplies since the EC relies on non-EC countries for almost half of all the energy it consumes. The relative costs and prices of different types of energy, its more efficient use, environmental concerns, and safety, particularly in the area of nuclear energy, have all been prominent issues in the 1980s.

Before 1973, the six founding Member States of the EC, together with the remaining countries of Western Europe, were expanding their consumption of energy rapidly, mainly on the basis of cheap imported oil, although the Suez Crisis in 1956 and the Six Day War in 1967 caused alarm over Middle Eastern oil supplies. When the UK joined the EC in 1973 it added large coal reserves to those of the existing Community, a new natural gas industry, the promise of oil in the North Sea, and at that time the most comprehensive nuclear energy industry in Western Europe. At the same time, the natural gas industry of the Netherlands was developing. Another war involving Israel and the Arab states was accompanied by the first major rise in oil prices (1973–4), suddenly reducing the attractiveness of oil compared with other sources of energy. Concern over the 'limits to growth', and the finite nature of non-renewable natural resources, including the reserves of fossil fuels, especially oil, led to concern over energy conservation. A more gradual awareness, gathering strength in the 1980s, that fossil fuels are one of the main polluters of the environment and the main source of greenhouse gases (see Chapter 9) added to the complexity of the situation. By the late 1980s, a number of policy issues were set out.

Initially, energy policy in the European Communities was shared between the ECSC Treaty (objectives, production and prices in the coal industry), the EAEA (Euratom) Treaty (investment, joint undertakings and supplies in the nuclear sector) and the EEC Treaty (general matters of energy). In 1986, policy objectives up to the year 1995 were established to ensure convergence of the policies of Member States. Since 1986 the nuclear option has become highly controversial as a result of the disaster at Chernobyl, while the Iraqi invasion of Kuwait in 1990 demonstrated yet again the precarious nature of Middle Eastern oil supplies. The conditions governing EC energy supplies are therefore constantly changing. Indeed, some of the goals for 1995 have already been modified as a result of German unification and could be further affected if and when other countries, especially Norway, join the EC.

A number of statements of intent have been proposed in the EC policy documents. Energy should be used more efficiently, a process reflected in the ratio of final energy demand to total GDP, which has been improving during the late 1980s and should be improved by about 20 per cent between then and 1995. Dependence on oil should be controlled so that it should make up only 40 per cent of all energy used in the EC by 1995. EC sources of solid fuel should continue to be used but production needs to be more competitive, in view of the fact that the price of imported coal is on average only about half that of EC coal. Only 15 per cent of electricity should be generated from hydro-carbons (oil and natural gas), the rest from solid fuels, hydro- and nuclear power. Finally, the development of new and renewable energy sources should also be encouraged.

EC activities in the 1990s will be concentrated primarily in the THERMIE programme to promote energy efficiency and to stimulate the development of existing and new renewable sources of energy. The recent successes in the nuclear fusion programme in the Joint European Torus (JET), funded by the Community, hold out longer-term hopes of a new, clean, abundant source of energy. The environmental impact of energy consumption is also likely to become more topical, with proposals now being considered to impose a 'green' tax on energy consumption, to be used to fund environmental protection: a tax of 8 ECU per barrel of oil equivalent is being proposed. Such a scheme would have to be implemented by national governments, since the EC itself has no powers to levy taxes. One effect would be to favour the countries that depend heavily on nuclear energy, France, for example, benefiting relative to Italy and the UK.

Table 5.1 contains basic data for the energy industry of the 12 Member States of the EC. The data are for the mid- to late 1980s, are in some cases estimates of the authors, and are the best available from EC data sources at the time of writing. More recent and consistent data are available for reserves, production and consumption, and are used in the sections that follow. In the rest of this chapter the EC and EFTA are considered together since the oil and gas deposits of the North Sea and the hydro-electric power of the Alps are both used by Member States of the two groups, while Norway is a major source of oil and natural gas for various Western European countries.

RECENT AND CURRENT ENERGY CONSUMPTION

The fossil fuels coal, lignite, oil and natural gas accounted for 87.5 per cent of the primary commercial energy used in the world in 1990, nuclear and hydro-power for the remainder. Non-commercial sources, of particular importance in the developing countries, include animate sources (human, animal) as well as fuelwood and dung. The comparative contributions of the commercial sources to total world consumption of energy are shown in Table 5.2. Per capita energy consumption in Western Europe is more than twice the world average. Its share is, however, gradually declining because consumption per inhabitant has changed little in most countries of the EC since the early 1970s, whereas growth has been considerable in many parts of the developing world owing to population growth and to an increase in the amount used per inhabitant.

Energy consumption trends from 1937 to 1987 are shown for the countries of the EC and EFTA and for other selected countries in Table 5.3. Trends in selected countries are shown graphically in Figure 5.1. Coal equivalent is used because it is the conversion used in the United Nations data source. Given the increasing interdependence of all the countries of Europe, EC energy production and consumption should be seen in a general European context. In the five EFTA countries included in Table 5.3, the trends are confused by the change in definition of the coal equivalent of hydro-electric power because in all five hydro-electric power is a major source of electricity. In general, however, the trends compare with those in the northern EC countries. In the former CMEA partners of the USSR, great emphasis was placed on the development of heavy industry after 1945. The consumption of energy per inhabitant grew particularly fast in Poland and Czechoslovakia, which share one of the biggest coalfields in Europe, but it has risen sharply throughout the region since about 1960. Soviet oil and natural gas production expanded into the 1980s but the export of these energy sources at favourable prices to its six European CMEA partners, at the expense of the long-suffering citizens of the USSR itself, was a concession dropped early in 1991. Turkey has modest coal deposits and production while of the three Maghreb countries, Algeria has the largest oil and gas deposits, of particular interest to France.

Table 5.1 Basic energy data for EC countries, late 1980s

	(1) Production (millions of ECU)	(2)	(3) % energy of total	(4)	(5) numbers employed (000s)	(6)	(7)	(8) % dependence on imported energy 1987
	All GDP	Energy		Coal	Oil and gas	Oil ref.	Elec. gas	
FRG	763	40	5.2	186	9	26	254	54.0
France	630	34	5.4	41	11	23	209	56.0
Italy	531	26	4.8	2	7	26	157	84.9
Netherlands	152	19	12.5	–	7	8	46	15.6
Belgium/Lux.	92	5	5.5	17	1	4	32	72.6
UK	555	63	11.4	160	26	14	287	−15.2
Ireland	22	1.0*	4.6	–	–	–	14	67.0
Denmark	69	1.6	2.3	–	–	3	17	66.7
Greece	39	1.7	4.3	4	–	8	35	66.8
Spain	212	13	6.1	45	2	9	78	61.0
Portugal	27	1	3.7	2*	–	–	25*	96.5
EC	3,092	205	6.6	457	63	121	1,154	44.9

Sources: Eurostat (1990), columns (1)–(3), pp. 88–91
Eurostat (1989a), columns (4)–(7), pp. 118–19
European Parliament (1989), EN III/S/1 Table 2

Notes: * estimate
– none or negligible

Table 5.2 World consumption of primary energy in millions of tonnes of oil equivalent in 1980 and 1990

	1980	1990	Change 1980–90 (1980=100)	% 1980	% 1990
Coal	1,815	2,192	121	27.0	27.3
Oil	3,024	3,101	103	44.9	38.7
Natural gas	1,286	1,738	135	19.1	21.6
Nuclear power	172	461	268	2.6	5.7
Hydro-electric power	432	541	125	6.4	6.7
World total	6,729	8,033	119	100.0	100.0
Western Europe	1,330	1,407	106	19.8	17.5

Source: British Petroleum 1991

In Table 5.4, the production and consumption of each of the three fossil fuels, together with nuclear and hydro-power output, are shown for the countries of Western Europe and for other selected areas. The main sources of energy are given in Table 5.5. In Table 5.6 total energy production and consumption are given and the balance for each country is shown. Comparisons can be made with the USA and Japan. To make different sources comparable, coal and natural gas are given in terms of oil equivalent, while primary sources of electricity, as opposed to electricity generated from fossil fuels, are expressed in terms of the amount of fossil fuels that would be needed to generate an equivalent amount of electricity in thermal power stations. The countries included in the tables vary enormously in population size, so absolute amounts of energy should be related to size of population.

From the early decades of the Industrial Revolution, the coalfields of France, Belgium and Germany, like those of Great Britain, served as the basis of fuel and power in those countries, largely superseding fuelwood and water power. Figure 5.2 shows the location of the main coalfields of Europe. By 1990, Germany, the UK and Spain were the major producers in the EC. The run-down of the coal industry continues in Western Europe, with the extraction of lignite in Germany, especially in the former GDR, likely to be curtailed sharply for environmental reasons on account of the high level of impurities it produces on combustion. Employment has dropped steadily since the Second World War, leaving most of the coalfield-based industrial regions and their settlements without one of the original reasons for their existence. The EC RECHAR programme funds retraining and job creation in order to compensate for these changes.

Policy on nuclear power varies among the countries of Western Europe. In some there is a completely negative attitude (e.g. Denmark), others plan to derive most of their thermal electricity from it (e.g. France), and in others there is an ambivalent attitude. Apart from controversy over the true cost of producing

Table 5.3 Energy consumption in EC, EFTA and other selected countries in tonnes of coal equivalent per inhabitant, 1937–87

	1937	1950	1955	1960	1965	1970	1975	1980	1985	1987
European Community										
FRG	3.0	2.6	3.3	3.7	4.2	5.2	5.3	5.8	5.8	5.6
GDR	3.0[1]	n.a.	3.9	4.7	5.5	6.1	6.6	7.3	7.8	7.9
France	2.1	2.0	2.2	2.4	3.0	3.8	3.7	4.4	4.1	3.7
Italy	0.7	0.6	0.7	1.1	1.8	2.7	2.9	3.1	3.4	3.6
Netherlands	1.8	2.0	2.4	2.7	3.4	4.6	5.7	6.1	6.8	7.3
Belgium	4.0	3.5	4.1	4.0	4.7	5.6	5.5	6.0	5.7	5.6
Luxembourg[2]						17.0	14.7	13.4	11.5	11.1
UK	4.3	4.4	5.0	4.9	5.1	4.9	4.8	4.8	4.9	5.1
Ireland	1.1	1.1	1.3	1.8	2.2	2.6	2.6	3.3	3.4	3.5
Denmark	1.7	2.1	2.5	2.8	4.1	5.4	4.8	5.3	5.3	5.3
Greece	0.2	0.2	0.3	0.4	0.8	1.1	1.7	2.1	2.3	2.5
Spain	0.4	0.6	0.6	0.8	1.0	1.5	2.1	2.4	2.2	2.1
Portugal	0.2	0.3	0.3	0.4	0.5	0.7	1.0	1.2	1.4	1.3
EFTA										
Austria	1.0	1.5	1.9	2.2	2.6	3.3	3.6	4.1	4.0	4.0
Switzerland	1.8	2.1	1.4	1.9	2.7	3.2	3.3	3.6	3.8	3.8
Norway	3.4	4.4	2.3	2.8	3.6	4.5	4.9	6.5	6.5	6.8
Sweden	2.5	3.2	2.7	3.5	4.4	5.8	5.5	5.5	5.0	5.0
Finland	1.0	1.2	1.2	1.7	2.7	4.1	4.5	5.5	5.2	5.7
Other selected										
Poland	0.8	2.5	2.6	3.1	3.5	3.6	4.2	5.0	4.6	4.8
Czechoslovakia	1.8	3.0	3.9	4.8	5.6	5.4	6.0	6.4	6.3	6.3
USSR	n.a.	n.a.	2.2	2.8	3.6	4.1	5.0	5.6	6.2	6.6
Turkey	0.1	0.3	0.2	0.2	0.4	0.5	0.7	0.8	0.9	1.0

Sources: various numbers of *United Nations Statistical Yearbook, United Nations Energy Statistics Yearbook*
Notes: n.a. not available
1 for prewar Germany as a whole
2 Luxembourg with Belgium until 1970

nuclear electricity, the main drawbacks include the risk of a serious accident and the problem of disposing of nuclear waste. Until the Chernobyl disaster in 1986 it had been reasonable to argue that fossil fuels have at least two disadvantages compared with nuclear power. Their extraction, especially of deep-mined coal, has been the cause of numerous accidents, while their combustion produces material harmful to people and to the environment.

Hydro-electric power has been regarded as both cheap and clean. It has the disadvantage (like fossil fuel deposits) of being located only in certain areas,

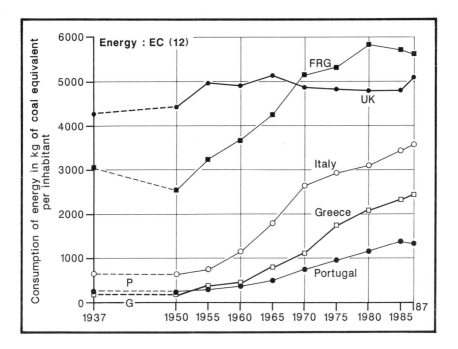

Figure 5.1 The consumption of energy in kg of coal equivalent per inhabitant in selected countries of the EC, 1937–87

Source: UNSYB (various years)

whereas thermal electric power stations can in theory be located virtually anywhere, therefore often being placed near major centres of population, an advantage because losses through the transmission of electricity increase exponentially with distance. Hydro-electric dams and reservoirs, especially very large ones, can cause environmental problems, occupying land that had other uses, interfering with river flows, and themselves silting and, in extreme cases, depriving irrigated areas downstream of nutrients for agriculture (e.g. the Aswan Dam in Egypt). On the whole, the hydro-electric stations of Western Europe are comparatively benign and are not a serious threat to the environment, although disasters through the bursting of dams, and subsequent flooding, have occurred occasionally.

Although an energy policy for the whole of the EC is gradually emerging, in terms of both output per inhabitant and level of self-sufficiency, there are marked differences in approach between Member States, each of which adapts as best it can to the fast-changing world energy scene. Imported oil accounts for almost 30 per cent of all energy consumed. In 1990 Norway was the only country in Western Europe in which energy production exceeded consumption (see Table

Table 5.4 Production and consumption of main commercial sources of energy in 1990 (millions of tonnes of oil equivalent)

	Coal		Oil		Natural gas		Primary electricity	
	Prod.	Cons.	Prod.	Cons.	Prod.	Cons.	Nucl.	Hydro-
FRG	67.9	72.8	3.9	112.5	13.4	46.9	32.6	3.6
GDR	53.5	53.7	–	13.7	–	6.3	0.4	0.1
France	7.6	18.8	3.4	88.7	2.5	25.1	61.1	11.2
Italy	0.2	15.7	4.6	92.3	15.6	39.3	–	7.7
Netherlands	–	8.9	–	34.2	54.5	30.4	0.8	–
Belgium/Lux.	1.7	9.9	–	24.1	–	8.3	9.9	0.1
UK	55.9	64.1	91.6	82.4	40.9	48.8	14.2	1.5
Ireland	–	2.1	–	4.4	–	1.4	–	0.2
Denmark	–	5.3	5.9	8.8	–	1.9	–	–
Greece	6.4	8.4	–	14.5	–	0.1	–	0.6
Spain	17.9	19.9	–	48.1	–	5.0	11.5	5.7
Portugal	–	0.8	–	11.0	–	–	–	0.8
EC	211.1	280.4	109.4	534.7	126.9	213.5	130.5	31.5
EC % of world	9.7	12.8	3.5	17.2	7.2	12.3	28.3	5.8

Austria	0.8	3.5	1.2	10.7	–	5.0	–	8.1
Switzerland	–	0.4	–	12.8	–	1.3	5.8	7.9
Norway	–	0.6	81.8	9.2	25.0	–	–	23.8
Sweden	–	1.6	–	15.0	–	0.6	15.8	17.7
Finland	–	3.3	–	10.9	–	2.3	4.5	2.7
Iceland	–	0.1	–	0.7	–	–	–	0.9
Turkey	20.3	22.1	3.7	23.8	–	0.3	–	5.1
Western Europe[1]	232.9[2]	312.0	201.9[2]	617.8	157.7[2]	223.0	156.6	97.7
Central Europe	169.8	163.5	14.9	79.4	38.4	68.5	14.5	13.8
USSR	295.5	275.5	570.0	402.6	655.9	568.0	43.5	55.9
USA	569.3	476.5	417.6	778.9	443.8	490.5	156.0	72.0
Japan	5.7	75.0	0.7	245.0	1.5	45.4	48.9	21.4
World	2,178.0	2,192.1	3,148.9	3,101.4	1,761.6	1,738.1	461.1	540.6

Source: British Petroleum 1991, various tables

Notes: – small output or none

1 includes Turkey in this definition

2 includes other countries, coal 0.7, oil 5.8, gas 5.8

Table 5.5 Main sources of energy in Western Europe[1] in 1990

Energy from	Total t.o.e. in millions	%
Coal		
Home	233	16.5
Imported	79	5.6
Oil		
Home	202	14.3
Imported	416	29.5
Natural gas		
Home	158	11.2
Imported	65	4.6
Nuclear	157	11.2
Hydro	98	7.0
Total	1,408	100.0

Note: 1 includes the former GDR and Turkey

5.6, col. (4)). The UK is close to a balance, while the Netherlands, Sweden and Germany are the only other countries producing internally over half of their needs. Like Japan, Italy produces less than 20 per cent of the energy it consumes while Portugal produces only a negligible quantity.

COAL AND LIGNITE

There are two main types of coal, hard coal (bituminous and anthracite) on the one hand, and brown coal (sub-bituminous and lignite) on the other. Currently, world coal reserves are estimated to be 1,020 billion tonnes, of which anthracite and bituminous coal account for 580 billion and sub-bituminous and lignite 440 billion. The energy value of a tonne of brown coal is, however, only about half that of a tonne of hard coal, so the former reserves must be scaled down for purposes of comparison.

The EC has 5.4 per cent of the higher-grade coal reserves of the world and about 10 per cent of the lower grade. Germany and the UK have most of the high-grade coal in the EC, while the former has large reserves of lignite, most of it in the former GDR. Poland is the only other European country apart from the former USSR with large reserves of high-grade coal. Turkey, Greece, Poland and several other European countries have reserves of lignite.

The location of the coalfields of Western and Central Europe has had a great influence on the development and present location of industrial activity. Figure 5.2 shows clearly a zone of coalfields extending from Scotland, Wales and north-central England through the extreme north of France, Belgium, the Netherlands and Germany into Poland and Czechoslovakia. Towards the end of the

Table 5.6 Energy production and consumption, 1990

	(1)	(2)	(3)	(4)	(5)	(6)
			Balance		Pop.	Cons.
	Prod.	Cons	Absolute	Relative	1990	kg per
	(millions of t.o.e.)		t.o.e.	Cons=100	(millions)	head
FRG	121.4	268.4	−147.0	45	63.2	4,250
GDR	54.0	74.2	−20.2	73	16.3	4,550
France	85.8	204.9	−119.1	42	56.4	3,630
Italy	28.1	155.0	−126.9	18	57.7	2,690
Netherlands	55.3	74.3	−19.0	74	14.9	4,990
Belgium/Lux.	11.8	52.3	−40.5	23	10.3	5,080
UK	204.1	211.0	−6.9	97	57.4	3,680
Ireland	0.2	8.1	−7.9	3	3.5	2,310
Denmark	5.9	16.0	−10.1	37	5.1	3,140
Greece	7.0	23.6	−16.6	30	10.1	2,340
Spain	35.1	90.2	−55.1	39	39.4	2,290
Portugal	0.8	12.6	−11.8	6	10.4	1,210
EC	609.4	1,190.6	−581.2	51	344.7	3,450
Austria	10.1	27.3	−17.2	37	7.6	3,590
Switzerland	13.7	28.2	−14.5	49	6.7	4,210
Norway	130.6	33.6	+97.0	389	4.2	8,000
Sweden	33.5	50.7	−17.2	66	8.5	5,960
Finland	7.2	23.7	−16.5	30	5.0	4,740
Iceland	0.9	1.7	−0.8	53	0.3	5,760
Turkey	29.1	51.3	−22.2	57	56.7	900
Western Europe	834.5	1,407.1	−560.3	60	433.7	3,240
Central Europe	251.4	339.7	−88.3	74	127.0	2,670
USSR	1,620.8	1,345.5	+275.3	120	291.0	4,620
USA	1,658.7	1,973.9	−315.2	84	251.4	7,850
Japan	78.2	435.7	−357.5	18	123.6	3,530
World	8,090.2	8,033.3			5,321.0	1,510

Source: British Petroleum 1991, various tables

nineteenth century, hydro-electric power also stimulated industrial development. In Figure 5.2, the distribution of present industrial areas is shown in relation to coalfields, hydro-electric sources and iron ore, the last now largely exhausted or superseded by imported high-grade ore.

The EC has enough high-grade coal to last for about a century and a half at present rates of production. In 1990, 195 million tonnes of such coal were extracted in the Community, from some 34 billion tonnes of reserves, almost all located in West Germany and the UK. Reserves of sub-bituminous coal and lignite, mostly in Germany (East and West) and Greece, would last about two centuries at present rates of extraction. In Table 5.7, European coal and lignite reserves are shown alongside those of the other main reserves in the world, now

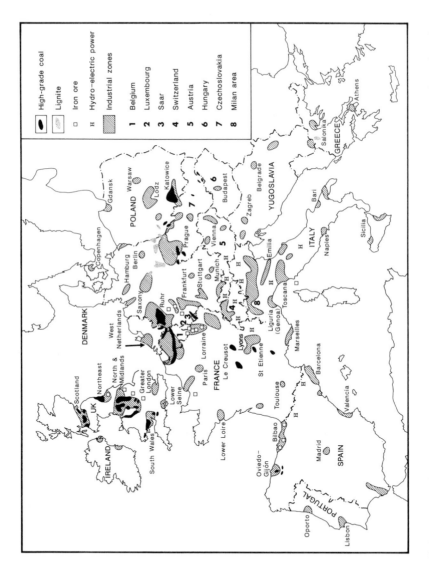

Figure 5.2 Coalfields, sources of hydro-electric power and industrial zones in the European Community and in other selected countries of Europe

Table 5.7 Coal and lignite reserves and production in 1990 in the EC and other selected countries

	(1)	(2)	(3)	(4)	(5)
	Reserves		*Percentage*	*Production*	
	Anthracite and Bituminous	*Sub-bituminous and Lignite*	*of*	*Coal*	*Lignite*
	(billions of tonnes)		*(1) + (2)*	*(millions of tonnes)*	
EC countries					
FRG	23.7	34.8	5.4	70.2	107.2
GDR	–	20.1	1.9	–	250.0
France	0.2	–	–	11.3	0.5
UK	8.6	0.5	0.8	91.8	–
Greece	–	2.9	–	–	46.5
Spain	0.3	0.3	0.1	19.6	17.6
Other selected countries					
Poland	28.2	11.5	3.7	147.6	67.6
USSR	102.5	136.5	22.1	478.0	151.8
Japan	0.8	–	0.3	8.6	–
USA	129.5	130.8	24.1	647.0	305.7
Australia	44.9	45.5	8.4	161.8	48.1
South Africa	54.8	–	5.1	182.2*	–
China	152.8	13.3	15.4	916.2	81.5
India	60.1	1.9	5.7	184.9	8.5
World	636.7	442.0	100.0	3,121.6	1,417.0

Source: British Petroleum 1991
Note: * includes Zimbabwe

of direct concern to Western Europe since imports from various non-EC countries seem likely to increase in the 1990s. Outside Europe, hard coal reserves are concentrated as follows (percentages of world total): China (26–7), USA (22–3), former USSR (18–19), South Africa (10), Australia (5), India (2). Excluding China, the remaining developing countries of the world, with over 40 per cent of the population of the world, have only a few per cent of the world's coal reserves. The EC and Japan import increasing quantities of coal as their own mining activities decline. Although very unevenly distributed globally, coal reserves would not be exhausted at present rates of production at least until the twenty-second century and, indeed, most could stay in the ground forever if the two main disadvantages of burning coal and lignite, pollution and greenhouse-gas emissions, are to be controlled.

Table 5.8 and Figure 5.3 show the decline of the Western European coal industry since the Second World War. Production of high-grade coal in the present EC countries dropped from 478 million tonnes in 1953 to 195 million tonnes in 1990. As a result of the increase in mechanisation and the closure of

Plate 10 The dirtiest fuel of all: shovelling lignite bricks into a coal cellar in Zwickau, former GDR

Plate 11 Natural gas centre at Groningen, north Netherlands: a far cleaner fuel than coal

Table 5.8 Coal and lignite production in the EC, 1953–88 (millions of tonnes)

	1953	1960	1965	1970	1975	1980	1985	1990
Anthracite and bituminous coal								
West Germany	142.1	143.3	135.5	111.4	94.5	88.3	83.0	70.2
France	52.6	56.0	51.3	37.4	23.6	20.2	17.1	11.3
Netherlands	12.3	12.5	11.4	4.3	–	–	0.1	–
Belgium	30.1	22.5	19.8	11.4	6.8	5.8	5.7	2.3
UK	227.8	196.7	190.5	144.6	106.6	108.6	76.8	91.8
Spain	12.2	13.8	12.9	10.8	9.2	9.9	12.7	19.6
Portugal	0.5	0.4	0.4	0.3	0.2	0.2	0.2	–
Sub-bituminous coal and lignite								
West Germany				107.8	37.0	37.9	34.5	107.2
East Germany								250.0
Italy	0.8	0.8	1.0	1.4	0.4	0.7	0.5	1.5
Greece	0.4	2.6	5.1	7.8	3.5	4.3	6.9	46.5
Spain	1.8	1.8	2.8	2.8	1.8	4.6	8.3	17.6

Source: *United Nations Statistical Yearbooks*; British Petroleum 1991
Note: no production from Luxembourg, Ireland or Denmark

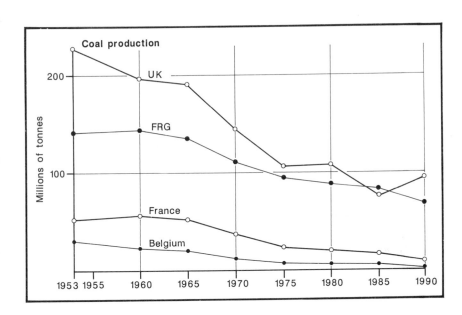

Figure 5.3 Coal production in selected EC countries, 1953–90

Source: various years of UNSYB, British Petroleum 1991

many of the mines that were less productive in terms of output per man-shift, the total labour force in the industry has declined to about a fifth of its size in the early 1950s. In view of the high level of impurities in much European coal, the particularly bad image of lignite, and the competitive prices of non-EC coal, even after the cost of transport from other continents, it seems likely that the decline of the industry will continue. Given the proximity to the coast of most of the centres of population and industry in the EC, low-cost, high-quality coal from such distant countries as Australia (high labour productivity in coastal mines) and China (low labour cost and increasing mechanisation) can compete, not forgetting Polish coal much nearer to home. Such competition is a further threat to domestic coal production, which is often more costly, yet the provider of employment in sensitive areas of the Community.

OIL AND NATURAL GAS

Oil

At present rates of production, the proved oil reserves of the world would last much less time than those of natural gas or coal. In the decade before 1973, oil consumption was increasing fast, and in that year it accounted for almost half of all commercial primary sources of energy used in the world. The low cost of production of oil, especially in the Middle East, its versatility as a fuel and as a source of material for final products, and the ease with which it can be transported, made it very attractive in the industrial countries of the world. By 1990, however, oil accounted for less than 40 per cent of the total world commercial energy consumption.

Western European countries were almost entirely dependent for their needs on imports of oil from outside the region until the development of North Sea deposits. Norway still has several decades of reserves at present rates of production, but the UK has extracted more per year than Norway, from smaller reserves. The reserves of the Middle East are about 30 times as large as all those of Western Europe, including the UK and Norway. The main oil and gas fields of Europe are shown in Figure 6.2. Their direct influence on industrial location and development has been much less than that of the coal fields.

In spite of price rises, Western Europe continues to import large quantities of oil. It only has 1.5 per cent of world oil reserves (end of 1990), has 6.5 per cent of world production, mainly from Norway and the UK, but accounts for about 20 per cent of world oil consumption. If Western Europe continues to consume oil in the quantities used at present, then it will depend increasingly on the Middle East, where five countries alone have over 60 per cent of the world's oil reserves: Abu Dhabi, Iran, Iraq, Kuwait and, above all, Saudi Arabia. In contrast, the former USSR has only about 6 per cent and North Africa only about 4 per cent. On the other hand, a drastic cutback in the use of oil in the more developed countries, either for environmental reasons, or through a switch to alternative sources, could leave the oil-rich countries with an unwanted resource, which they themselves would not use up for a long time, and from which most developing countries could not derive any great benefit at current prices.

Most of the oil products consumed in Western Europe are refined in the region from crude oil shipped from several parts of the world. In 1990, 483 million tonnes were imported into Western Europe, including 199 from the Middle East, 102 from North Africa and 95 from the USSR. Of the total, 414 million tonnes were crude, 69 refined. The decline in refining capacity of all the major importers of oil in Western Europe, together with the UK, has been sharper than the decline in oil consumption (see Table 5.9). In the 1960s, the establishment of oil refineries in a number of less industrialised regions in the six original EC Member States was intended to provide employment, an energy base and, most importantly, a catalyst for further development around such poles. Examples include those at Brindisi in the Sud region of Italy and Augusta in Sicilia.

The future of oil consumption in the EC is less predictable than that of the coal industry, but conflicting prospects mark the beginning of the 1990s. Road networks are to be improved and extended, and the number of motor vehicles in use is expected to rise, but motor vehicles account for about 20 per cent of carbon dioxide emissions in Western Europe. Motor vehicles with engines that are both more economical and cleaner than most on the roads now could make the two prospects more compatible and not too damaging to the oil and motor vehicle industries.

Since the notoriously politically unstable Middle East has such a large proportion of the world's oil reserves, there is considerable uncertainty about

Table 5.9 The oil industry in the EC and EFTA in 1990

	(1)	(2)	(3)	(4)	(5)	(6)
					Refining capacity	
	Reserves	Production	Consumption	Consumption	1980	1990
		(millions of tonnes)			(barrels a day (000s))	
Germany	–	3.9	126.2	2,690	3,575	2,025
France	–	3.4	88.7	1,875	3,320	1,700
Italy	–	4.6	92.3	1,900	4,140	2,300
Netherlands	–	–	34.2	745	1,775	1,395
Belgium	–	–	24.1	495	1,020	705
UK	500	91.6	82.4	1,745	2,460	1,825
Denmark	–	5.9	8.8	180	–	–
Spain	–	–	15.0	1,040	1,425	1,420
Norway	1,000	81.8	9.2	200	–	–

Source: British Petroleum 1991

supplies. The Middle East producers export to all the developed regions of the world as well as to many developing countries. A return to the high price levels of the early 1980s would have serious consequences for the developed market economies and also, to some extent, for Central Europe. As a net exporter of oil, the former USSR could benefit, but the failure to discover large new deposits to match those of the Volga–Ural fields, developed in the 1940s, and of West Siberia, developed in the 1960s, means that their oil exports may continue to decline; indeed, in 1990–1 total production itself fell. During the 1970s and 1980s so many unexpected changes in price and supply occurred in the world that past trends are a poor guide to the future. Price fluctuations, conflicts in the Middle East and pressure from environmentalists may well continue to influence the fortunes of Western Europe's oil industry. Large new deposits of oil may indeed be discovered somewhere in the world, but almost certainly not in Western or Central Europe. Possible areas include the Arctic coastlands and continental shelf of Russia, and the interior of China.

Natural gas

The consumption of natural gas in the world, apart from the USSR, has increased somewhat in absolute terms in the last 20 years, but it has declined relatively from 22 to 18 per cent of all primary energy. Its importance is likely to grow in the next decade or two since it is 'cleaner' than coal, while its reserves are roughly equivalent to those of oil, yet are being used up only half as quickly. The EC's share of the world's natural gas reserves is about 2.5 per cent (the Netherlands 1.5, UK 0.5, Germany 0.2). Apart from the former USSR, Norway is the only non-EC country in Europe that is well placed, having 2.1 per cent of the total world reserves. Western Europe therefore has about 4 per cent of the proved natural gas reserves of the world (see Table 5.10), but produces almost 9 per cent of the world total, and consumes about 13 per cent. It is therefore using its reserves at a faster rate than the world average, and must also import part of its consumption.

The concentration of 38 per cent of the world's natural gas reserves in the former USSR, mostly in the western half of the Russian Republic, and in the Middle East (Iran has 14 per cent of the world total) results in a very uneven distribution according to population. India and China, with about 40 per cent of the total population of the world, have only 1.5 per cent of proved natural gas reserves. The USA has less than 5 per cent of the world's reserves, but produces nearly 30 per cent of the world total, from reserves that would barely last to the end of the 1990s, and actually consumes slightly more than it produces. Japan has negligible reserves, but its imports make up only about 2 per cent of the world total.

Intra-Western European trade in natural gas consists almost entirely of exports from the Netherlands and Norway, to Germany, France and Belgium, while the Netherlands also exports to Italy, and Norway to the UK. The former USSR supplies several Western European countries, in particular Germany, Italy

Table 5.10 Natural gas in Western Europe, 1990

	Reserves (trillions of cubic metres)	% of world reserves	Life of reserves at present levels of production in years	Production	Consumption
				(millions of t.o.e.)	
Western Europe	5.0	4.1	28	158	223
Netherlands	1.7	1.4	29	55	30
Norway	1.7	1.4	62	25	0
UK	0.6	0.5	12	41	49
Germany	0.4	0.3	24	13	53
Italy	–	–	–	16	39
France	–	–	–	3	25
USSR	45.3	38.0	56	656	568
Middle East	37.6	31.5	> 100	93	90
World	119.4	100.0	58	1,762	1,738

Source: British Petroleum 1991

and France, all served by pipeline. It has also been the only supplier of consequence to its former CMEA partners of Central Europe. Algeria supplies
liquefied natural gas to Belgium, France and Spain.

Given the great decline in the value of Soviet oil exports to Western Europe in
the late 1980s and stagnation in the industry itself, it is of great importance to the
Russian economy to increase the supply of natural gas. Soviet natural gas
production expanded fast throughout the 1980s, with a 2.4 per cent rise from
1989 to 1990. In 1990 Soviet proved natural gas reserves had a life of 56 years at
current rates of production, but proved oil reserves had a life of only 13–14
years.

HYDRO-ELECTRICITY AND NUCLEAR POWER

When the output of hydro- and nuclear generated electricity in Western Europe is
expressed in terms of the amount of fossil fuel that would be needed to generate
the same amount, it is clear that these two sources of primary energy make a
major contribution to the energy supplies of the region. In 1990 they accounted
for 7 and 11 per cent respectively of all the primary energy consumed in Western
Europe. There has hardly been any change in the amount of hydro-electric power
produced in Western Europe in the 1980s but the consumption of nuclear power
has grown three times during the decade (see Figure 5.4 and Table 5.11).

By 1980, most of the commercial hydro-electric potential of Western Europe
had already been brought into use, so there is now little scope for creating further
generating capacity in this sector. Norway and Sweden together accounted for 42
per cent of the output of hydro-electricity in 1990; France, Italy, Switzerland and

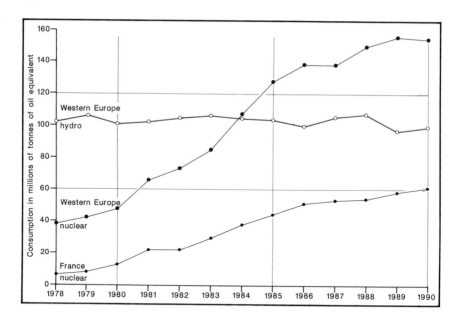

Figure 5.4 Consumption of hydro-electric and nuclear power in Western Europe (the EC and EFTA) 1978–90. The electricity consumed is expressed in the oil equivalent of kWH

Source: British Petroleum 1991

Table 5.11 Consumption of nuclear power in Western European countries, 1980 and 1990, in millions of tonnes of oil equivalent

	1980	1990	% share of all primary energy 1990
France	12.8	61.1	30
Germany	10.9	33.0	10
Sweden	6.5	15.8	31
UK	7.8	14.2	7
Spain	1.1	11.5	13
Belgium/Lux.	2.7	9.9	19
Switzerland	3.5	5.8	21
Finland	1.7	4.5	19
Netherlands	1.0	0.8	1
Western Europe	49.3	156.6	11

Source: British Petroleum 1991
Note: No nuclear power in 1990: Austria, Denmark, Greece, Iceland, Ireland, Italy (negligible), Norway, Portugal, Turkey. Italy 1.3 in 1980

Plate 12 The first hydro-electric power station in Italy: Vizzola Ticino, near Milan. This represented the beginnings of modern, clean energy. Most hydro-electric power has now been harnessed

Austria for about 35 per cent, principally from the Alps. Other mountain areas such as the Pyrenees (Spain and France) and the Apennines (Italy) provided smaller quantities.

Nuclear fuel is mainly obtained from uranium. In Western Europe, only France, with about 5 per cent of the world's reserves, has an appreciable amount. France is also involved in the extraction of uranium in its former colonies of Gabon and Niger. Outside the former CMEA bloc, the USA, Canada, Australia, South Africa and Namibia have the largest reserves of uranium in the world; all these countries have strong links with Western Europe.

Although the UK pioneered the use of nuclear power in Western Europe in the 1960s, it has now been overtaken in the absolute amount consumed by France, Germany and Sweden, and in the share contributed to total national energy consumption also by Spain, Belgium and Luxembourg, Switzerland and Finland. Nine out of 18 Western European countries have a nuclear power industry, nine do not. On the basis of size, apart from Iceland, none of the countries without a nuclear power industry is actually too small, or too backward technically, to have at least one commercial nuclear power station. The choice not to do so may be economic, but in some cases, as with Denmark, it is for reasons of safety and environmental policy. Ironically, in nuclear-free Denmark, Copenhagen is located only a few kilometres across the Øresund from Barsebaeck, one of Sweden's nuclear power stations, built deliberately by the Swedes at some distance from any large concentrations of (Swedish) population.

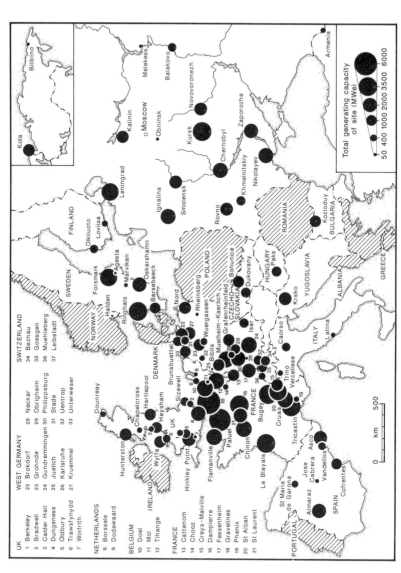

Figure 5.5 The location of nuclear power stations in Europe

Source: Mounfield 1991, maps on pp. 101 and 133 combined, with the permission of the author

Note: Countries with no nuclear stations are shaded

Plate 13 Power on the River Loire, Middle Ages style: the château at Saumur, north central France

Plate 14 Power on the River Loire, twentieth-century style: nuclear power station at Chinon, France

In Central Europe and the former USSR, safety considerations will force the closure of some of the existing capacity. Stations in the former GDR were shut down as soon as unification took place. In contrast, according to Kadlec (1991), the rapid expansion of nuclear power capacity is regarded as vital in the new Czechoslovakia. In Bulgaria, on the other hand, there is pressure to close the key station at Kozloduy, although this supplies much of Bulgaria's electricity needs.

Whatever developments take place in nuclear power in Western Europe, fossil fuels will remain the largest source of power in Western Europe's electricity industry for some time, but the burning of coal, especially lignite, is increasingly regarded as undesirable environmentally, while oil is needed for other energy uses, especially transport, and as a raw material. In the 1990s, natural gas is likely to grow in relative importance. On the other hand, it is widely appreciated that wind, wave, tidal and solar generated electricity cannot be developed quickly enough, in large enough quantities, to supply more than a small proportion of the expected electricity needs of Western Europe in the next two decades at least. Indeed, only comparatively modest funds are available for research and development in this area of environmentally relatively clean electricity sources.

FURTHER READING

British Petroleum (BP) (1991) *Statistical Review of World Energy*, yearly, BP Corporate Communications Service.
Mounfield P. R. (1991) *World Nuclear Power*, London: Routledge.

6

INDUSTRY

INDUSTRIAL POLICY

Of the three sectors into which economic activity is conventionally subdivided, industry accounted for 33.2 per cent of all employment in the EC in 1987 (agriculture 7.6, services 59.2) and produced 36.5 per cent of total GDP. In all 12 Member States of the EC, the share of production of industry exceeded the share of employment in the sector (see Table 6.1). The definition of industry varies from one context and source to another, extractive industry often being separated, for example, from manufacturing industry. Unfortunately, therefore, values for such aspects as production and employment vary from one source to another. According to the Commission of the EC (1990), in 1987 Fuel and Power employed 1,750,000 persons, Manufacturing 29,200,000 and Building and Construction 8,450,000.

Since industry accounts for by far the largest share of the exports of the EC to countries outside the Community, its high performance in relation to industry in other regions of the world is crucial to the future of the Community. From North America and Japan, competition comes from industries based on high technology, sophisticated organisation, and the backing of very large internal markets. From many parts of the developing world, competition comes from countries in which labour is much cheaper than in the EC. It may seem surprising, therefore, that the EC does not have an explicit overall policy for industry. Article 130f of the Treaty of Rome as amended by the SEA states that: 'The Community's aim shall be to strengthen the scientific and technological basis of European industry and to encourage it to become more competitive.' It can also be said that such measures as the rules governing competition, the dumping of products below world market prices, and state aids (Arts 85ff., 91 and 92 of the Treaty of Rome), are aimed to enable EC industry to develop in a fair and open market of stability and free competition. The Single Market programme itself, with its emphasis on EC industry and goods, is another aspect of policies aimed at promoting the fortunes of EC industry with a view to improving its competitiveness. Nevertheless, specific measures aimed at key industrial sectors are much more limited and focused, as on assistance to

129

Table 6.1 Employment in industry in the EC

	(1) % in industry (1987)	(2) % of gross value added (1985)	(3) Relative productivity of industry
FRG	40.5	41.5	102
GDR	47.0[1]		
France	30.0	32.3	108
Italy	32.2	34.7	108
Netherlands	26.5	34.4	130
Belgium	31.4	31.9	102
Luxembourg	29.2	34.1	117
UK	32.8	38.1	116
Ireland	28.7	36.4	127
Denmark	27.1	28.1	104
Greece	25.4	29.4	116
Spain	32.6	37.3	114
Portugal	34.6	39.0	113
EC	33.2	36.5	110

Source: Col (1) COM 90-609 (1991), Annex Table A
    Col (2) Eurostat 1989a: 41
Note: 1 in 1989

restructuring and retraining in the iron and steel and shipbuilding sectors, specific trade agreements such as restrictions on the importation of competing motor vehicles from the Far East, and the funding of primary and applied research in new technology areas.

Some regions of the EC are much more highly industrialised than others, while some have declining industries, others have industries in the ascendant. The Community supplies some direct aid to industry from the European Regional Development Fund, the ECSC gives loans to the coal and steel sector, the European Investment Bank provides investment for various needs, ESPRIT is concerned with information technologies, and the New Community Instrument (NCI) has been created to assist small and medium sized enterprises. The total finance available for industry amounts however to less than 10 per cent of the EC budget, whereas agriculture receives more than 50 per cent. Yet industry employs about five times as many people as agriculture and accounts for about ten times as much of the total Community GDP.

The competitiveness of EC industry in traditional industrial sectors such as textiles and motor vehicles is weak against imports from the Far East, and even the EC high-technology industries find it difficult to compete with Japanese and US producers. There is therefore increasing pressure from EC industry on governments to introduce protection in a variety of sectors, the kind of measure outlawed by the free competition and open market principles of the EC. It is clear that if the EC is going to continue to defend its founding principles, yet ensure that its industries develop successfully, there is a need for new initiatives in an overall industrial strategy for the Community in the future.

INDUSTRIAL RAW MATERIALS IN EUROPE

In the late eighteenth and early nineteenth centuries, before the era of railways and steam navigation, modern industry in Europe was based (with some exceptions, such as cotton) on local resources. These resources included falling water and coal for providing power to drive machinery, metallic minerals, and products from agriculture and forestry. As coking coal replaced charcoal for the smelting of iron ore, and as coal also replaced water power for driving machinery, locations in coalfield areas became particularly attractive to industrialists. Rivers and canals were widely used, but compared with the railways that followed, had very limited capacity to move raw materials and finished products.

As population grew and industrial development in Western Europe expanded rapidly, many parts of the region could no longer produce enough food or raw materials for their needs. The development of the steamship made it economically realistic to transport increasing quantities of food and raw materials from other continents over great distances. In the later nineteenth century, for example, guano, nitrates and copper were exported from Peru and Chile to Europe. Iron ore, on the other hand, was still mainly obtained from local ores of comparatively low grade, or from northern Sweden. The movement of high-grade iron ore from other continents to Western Europe developed on a large scale only after the Second World War. Some non-fuel minerals, including bauxite, have been used commercially only in the twentieth century. Coal, on the other hand, was widely available, and production adequate to supply almost all of the energy needs of Western Europe well into the twentieth century. Railways and shipping services could move coal easily from coalfields such as those of South Wales and the Ruhr to other parts of Europe, such as Switzerland and Italy, with no coalfields. Since the Second World War, the EC has become largely self-sufficient in foodstuffs, but it imports about half of its energy needs, and about 90 per cent of its non-fuel mineral needs, the most important of which are shown in Table 6.2. It should be appreciated that Japan is even more dependent on the rest of the world for its food, fuel and raw materials.

The EC has about 6 per cent of the total population of the world but it consumes about 20 per cent of the non-fuel minerals used. In relation to both consumption and population, its share of the reserves of most of the world's non-fuel minerals is very limited. The countries with the largest reserves of 11 of the most widely used non-fuel minerals are shown in Table 6.2, together with the reserves, if more than negligible, located in Western and Central Europe. While there has been concern in the Western industrial countries over the location of some mineral reserves of world significance in regions regarded as unstable (e.g.

Table 6.2 The location in the world in 1985 of the estimated reserves of 11 major non-fuel minerals (metallic content of 1–9)

	Largest reserves (% of world total)	*Europe, excl. USSR*
1 Iron ore	USSR 35, Brazil 15, Australia 14, India 7	Sweden 2 France 1
2 Chromite	South Africa 78, USSR 12	–
3 Manganese ore	South Africa 41, USSR 37, Australia 8, India, Brazil, China, 2 each	–
4 Nickel ore	Cuba 34, Canada 14, USSR 13, Indonesia 7	Greece 4
5 Bauxite	Guinea 27, Australia 21, Brazil 11, Jamaica 10	Greece 3 Yugoslavia 2 Hungary 2
6 Copper	Chile 23, USA 17, Zambia 9, Zaïre 8	–
7 Lead	USA 22, USSR 13, Canada 13	Yugoslavia 4 Bulgaria 3 Spain 2
8 Tin	Malaysia 36, Indonesia 22, Thailand 9, Bolivia 5	UK 3
9 Zinc	Canada 15, USA 13, USSR 6, South Africa 6	Spain 4 Ireland 3 Poland 2
10 Phosphates	Morocco 49, South Africa 19, USA 10, USSR 9	–
11 Potash	Canada 48, USSR 33	Germany 14

Source: Bureau of Mines 1985

southern Africa) or unfriendly (e.g. the former USSR), as can be seen in Table 6.2, enough of the reserves are in regions that are unlikely to cut off exports of primary products to Western Europe, the USA or Japan in the event of a conflict or of political discord. The break-up of the USSR means that its large reserves of eight out of the 11 minerals in Table 6.2 could be of greatly increased importance to the EC.

Raw materials are being used increasingly efficiently and sparingly in the developed industrial countries as time passes (Larson *et al.* 1986), and substitutes and synthetic materials are giving increasing flexibility and choice (Clark and Flemings 1986) in the use of various non-fuel minerals. The supply situation for non-fuel minerals should therefore be of less concern in the EC than energy, but there is no reason for complacency. Another trend is the increasing proportion of the processing of non-fuel minerals to be carried out in the countries in which they are extracted. Such a trend benefits developing countries in a limited way by adding value to the products they export, but it also means that pollution is 'exported' from Europe to them.

THE DISTRIBUTION OF INDUSTRIAL ACTIVITY

The great difference in the level of industrialisation among the countries of the EC can be seen in Table 6.3. Columns (1) and (2) show the percentage of total EC population and of industrial output. The score in column (3) is calculated by dividing the industrial share by the share of population, the EC average being set at 100, thus removing the effect of population size. The FRG is the most highly industrialised country according to this measure while Greece is the least, the 'gap' being roughly three to one. France, the UK and the Netherlands are the other countries with above average scores. If Italy were subdivided into north and south, the north would achieve a high score, while the south would join the relatively less industrialised countries, Greece, Spain and Portugal.

The level of industrialisation varies greatly also within countries. Figure 6.1 shows the share of the economically active population in industry in the NUTS 1 level regions of the Community (see Figure 2.3 for the names of the regions):

The most highly industrialised (more than 20 per cent above the EC average):
- FRG: Nordrhein-Westfalen (heavy industry)
  Baden-Württemberg (engineering)
  Saarland (coal)
- Italy: Lombardia (engineering, textiles)
- UK: East and West Midlands (coal, engineering, textiles)
- Spain: Este (light industry)
- GDR: all the newly created Länder (wide variety but outdated)

Table 6.3 Distribution of EC industrial output by country

	(1) Share total population 1985	(2) Share of EC industrial output 1985	(3) Industry/ population 1985	(4) Change 1985–90 (1985 = 100)
FRG	18.8	24.3	129	118
France	17.2	18.6	108	113
Italy	17.7	17.1	97	118
Netherlands	4.5	4.7	104	109
Belgium/Lux.	3.2	2.7	84	115
UK	17.6	18.9	107	109
Ireland	1.1	0.9	82	144
Denmark	1.6	1.2	75	107
Greece	3.1	1.2	39	103
Spain	12.0	8.2	68	116
Portugal	3.2	1.5	47	135
EC	100.0	100.0	100	

Source: Eurostat 1991a (7): 46, 52, 53

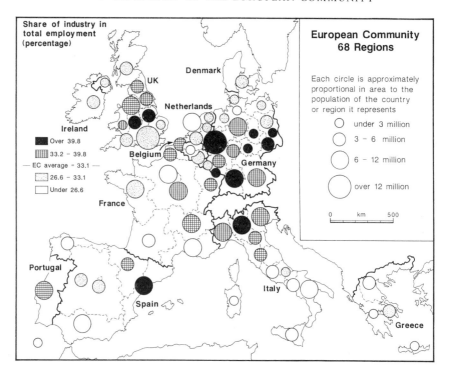

Figure 6.1 Employment in the industrial sector as a percentage of total employment at NUTS 1 level of the European Community in 1987

Source: COM 90-609 (1991), Table A of Statistical Annex

The least highly industrialised (more than 20 per cent below the EC average):

- Greece, South Italy, southern Spain (agriculture)
- Ile-de-France, Mediterranée, Brussels, West-Nederland (services)

From the distribution of industry in Figure 6.1, it is evident that the industrial heartland of the EC is a triangular area with its corners in Central Scotland, the former GDR, and North Italy. At the centre of the triangle is the older industrial region Nordrhein-Westfalen and the newer industrial region of Baden-Württemberg. In this area, also, are located the important financial centres of Frankfurt, Paris, London and Milan, as well as the 'capital' of the EC, Brussels.

Employment in industry at NUTS 2 level varies even more than at NUTS 1 level. The extremes given in Table 6.4 show that a high level of industrialisation is to be found not only in coalfield regions (Limburg in Belgium, the East Midlands in the UK) but also in regions where, earlier this century, hydro-electric power was a boost to development (Lombardia in Italy, Cataluña in Spain). In contrast there is a low level of industrialisation both in some very prosperous regions, including Hamburg (port) and Brussels (administration), and in some

Table 6.4 Employment in industry at NUTS 2 level, 1987

	Employment in industry (%)			
	Highest level		*Lowest level*	
FRG	Stuttgart	49.4	Hamburg	26.3
France	Franche-Comté	41.7	Corse	13.1
Italy	Lombardia	43.4	Calabria	16.3
Netherlands	Noord-Brabant	33.3	Noord-Holland	20.9
Belgium	Limburg	39.2	Brussels	20.2
UK (NUTS 1 level)	East Midlands	40.6	Southeast	28.1
Greece	Dytiki Makedonia	34.0	Ionia Nisia	13.1
Spain	Cataluña	44.2	Extremadura	19.4
Portugal	Norte	42.3	Algarve	20.2

Source: COM 90-609 (1991), Annex Table A

very poor regions, still with a large agricultural sector (Calabria in Italy, Extremadura in Spain).

At NUTS 3 level and below, even greater extremes in the level of industrialis- ation can be observed, as the following UK examples show (CSO 1990). The highest percentages of employment in manufacturing are recorded in the districts of Pendle, Lancashire (textiles), with 55.4 per cent, and Barrow-in-Furness, Cumbria (shipbuilding) with 55.3 per cent. The UK average for manufacturing is 23.9 per cent. At the other extreme there are many districts with under 10 per cent in manufacturing, as for example in Greater London (e.g. Kensington and Chelsea 3.3 per cent) and in rural areas (e.g. four out of the six districts in Dyfed, southwest Wales).

As with agriculture, the distribution of industry in the EC can be studied on the basis of the value of production as well as according to numbers employed in the sector. Since productivity per worker varies greatly from one region to another, the distribution of the value of production coincides only broadly with the distribution of employment. The most highly industrialised regions of the EC according to output are mainly in the western part of Germany, in central and northern England, in Wales and in North Italy. Those regions of the EC in which industry makes the smallest contribution to GDP are either still heavily agricultural (e.g. Greece, the Sur of Spain, Bretagne in France), or prominent with regard to services, the impact of which extends beyond the particular regions in which they are located (e.g. West-Nederland, the Southeast in the UK, Lazio (with Rome), Madrid).

The present uneven distribution of industry in the EC is the result of centuries of largely independent development within states of varying size and shape, some with long-running policies to foster industrial growth and some with policies based on a strategic and/or social motive for dispersing industry over the national

Plate 15 Abandoned mines in Andalucía, southern Spain

Plate 16 Older industrial constructions: pot banks in Longton, Stoke-on-Trent, England. As recently as the 1950s, hundreds of these furnaces smoked prolifically

territory reasonably evenly. Even at national level, the efforts to decentralise have often produced modest results. For example, the least highly industrialised major region of the EC is still South Italy and the Islands, in spite of massive efforts since the 1950s through the Cassa per il Mezzogiorno to place large industrial establishments such as iron and steel works, oil refineries and motor vehicle manufacturing in key centres there. Much of the development in the South and Islands actually took place when Italian industry in total was expanding fast.

In its quest for convergence and homogeneity in the EC, the Commission faces enormous problems with regard to industry. One estimate of employment in manufacturing (see Commission of the EC 1990) shows a decline in the EC workforce from 34.1 million in 1980 to 29.2 million in 1987. Employment in fuel and power plus building and construction dropped during that time from 11.7 million to 10.2 million. If the reverse trend were occurring, EC policymakers could conceivably direct new employment to regions with relatively little industry at present. As it is, the task at the moment seems to be damage limitation. The possibility that industries (presumably successful) in the most highly industrialised regions should actually be closed down and plant somehow transferred to the least industrialised regions would be economic suicide. As indicated at the beginning of this chapter (see 'Industrial policy'), the funds available to the Commission for the industrial sector are microscopic compared with the task ahead.

The future of industry in the EC is likely to be increasingly affected by the growth of contacts with EFTA countries, the countries of Central Europe and the former USSR. In Figure 6.2, seven prominent European industrial regions are indicated by the letters A to G. In regions A and C, several million people are employed in the industrial sector. Region B includes the Benelux countries, northeast France, the western side of Germany, and Switzerland. Here, altogether, about 10 million are employed in industry, with virtually every branch being represented. While regions A, B and C are of outstanding importance in the industrial life of the EC, there are many other prominent regions or individual centres, including, for example, the coastlands of northern Spain and Cataluña (Barcelona) and both Paris and London.

Region D in Figure 6.2 was the main industrial concentration in the European CMEA partners of the former USSR. Now that ideological and political considerations no longer keep Poland and Czechoslovakia apart from the EC, closer ties are developing, not least through the need to improve environmental conditions in areas close to Germany and Austria (such as Bohemia) which are large 'exporters' of pollutants. From a locational point of view, it should be noted that region D is much closer to the industrial heartland of the EC than to Moscow or the Donbass, is distant from the Urals, and is remote from the sources of primary products transported mainly by rail or pipeline from the Asiatic regions of the former USSR. In due course it may prove cheaper for the Central European countries to import some of their primary products from other continents rather than from Russia.

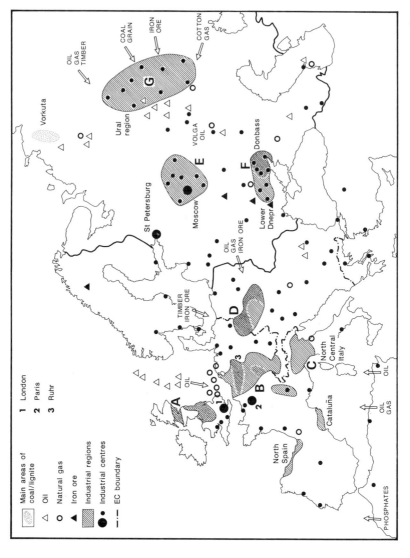

Figure 6.2 Industrial regions and centres of Europe and the location of the main deposits of fossil fuels

The main industrial regions of the European part of the former USSR currently have only limited links with the EC, exchanging few products, but they are likely to attract growing attention in the 1990s. There are three major industrial regions (letters E–G in Figure 6.2). They are all 'importers' of food, fuel and raw materials from other regions of the USSR, including the northern part (e.g. Vorkuta coal), but mainly from Siberia, Kazakhstan and Soviet Central Asia. The Central Industrial region (E) centred on Moscow, has a poor fuel and raw material base. It specialises in textiles and engineering. The Donbass coalfield (F) produces more high-grade coal than the UK or Germany, but it has high production costs. With iron ore deposits to the west (Krivoy Rog) and north (Kursk), it remains an iron and steel and heavy engineering concentration of international significance. The Ural region (G) is rich in non-fuel minerals and has an iron and steel industry modernised and greatly expanded in the 1930s. The appreciable distance of the main industrial regions of European Russia and the Ukraine from Western Europe is evident in Figure 6.2. The fact that these regions suffer from many of the problems associated with the older industrial regions of the EC and Central Europe should also be kept in mind by prospective investors in the region. In particular, if the Ukraine were to become a member of the EC, its coal and steel industries would pose a problem of massive proportions to the ECSC.

IRON AND STEEL, AND SHIPBUILDING

Iron and steel

Two of the industries of Western Europe that have suffered the greatest cuts in employment and output since the 1960s are iron and steel, and shipbuilding. They will be used to exemplify declining industrial sectors and will be discussed in turn.

The first sector of industry to be regulated by the common market, through the ECSC, was the iron and steel industry. According to the ECSC Treaty:

> The Community shall progressively bring about conditions which will of themselves assure the most natural distribution of production at the highest possible level of productivity, while safeguarding continuity of employment and taking care not to provide fundamental and persistent disturbances in the economies of Member States.

> (Art. 2 ECSC)

Objectives include the restructuring of the industry to adapt to the changing market, and to provide regional and social aid to make steel manufacturing successful. A more recent concern has been to make the industry more competitive in the face of deregulation and greater pressure from cheap products of third countries, especially some developing countries with lower wages and home supplies of high-grade iron ore (e.g. Brazil, Venezuela). An additional influence has been a drop in demand, due to the use of alternative materials and to the more efficient use of steel itself. During 1974–87, steel production in the EC dropped from 156 to 113 million tonnes, prices slumped, and jobs were reduced from about 900,000 to little more that 400,000. In 1989 alone, 260 million ECU were spent to help with closures and compensation for lost jobs. RESIDER, a programme to promote restructuring and employment in other sectors, has been set up to implement further changes.

Figure 6.3 shows the massive rise in steel production between 1950 and 1970 in all the six main steel-producing countries currently Member States of the EC.

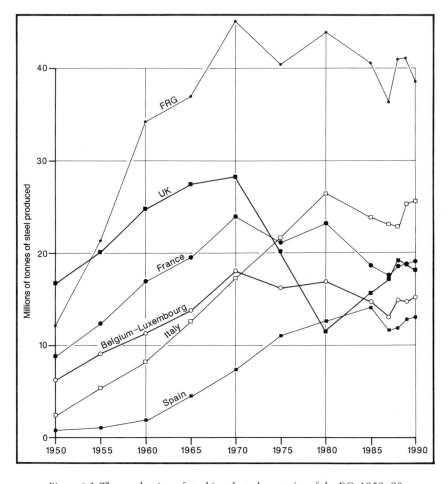

Figure 6.3 The production of steel in selected countries of the EC, 1950–90

Source: various years of UNSYB and numbers of Eurostatistics

In the 1970s the UK suffered the greatest setback, while the FRG, France and Belgium-Luxembourg retained their 1970 levels and Italy and Spain continued to increase output. Italy has been the slowest to adjust output to ECSC requirements, while Spain was not yet a member. Total EC steel production was 135.5 million tonnes in 1985, 137 million in 1990. It is expected that the slimming process has now ended and that between 1990 and 1995 output will be sustained or even rise somewhat; about 75 per cent of total capacity will be in use.

In 1989 there were almost 400 European steel works, including a few large integrated works, together with many smaller ones. Virtually every plant has been affected in some way during the 1980s and every EC country produces some steel. The data in columns (2)–(4) of Table 6.5 show that relative to their total population size, Luxembourg and Belgium are the leaders in steel production, followed by the FRG, which accounts for about 30 per cent of all EC output. Figure 6.4 shows only a selection of the many NUTS 3 level regions with problems arising from changes in the iron and steel industry. Some mills have been closed down completely and production concentrated in smaller numbers. In general, the older areas of iron- and steel-making have been the ones most affected, with the new coastal plants (e.g. near Marseilles in France, Taranto in

Table 6.5 EC production of steel and ships

	Steel					Ships
	(1) Pop. % 1990	(2) Steel million tonnes 1990	(3) Share of EC output 1990	(4) Steel/pop. 1990	(5) Change 1985–90	(6) % share of EC output 1988
FRG	18.8	40.5	29.9	159	95	30.6
France	17.2	18.6	13.7	80	102	3.9
Italy	17.7	23.9	17.6	99	107	7.3
Netherlands	4.5	5.5	4.1	91	98	9.3
Belgium	3.1	10.7	7.9	255	107	2.9
Luxembourg	0.1	3.9	2.9	2,900	90	–
UK	17.6	15.8	11.7	66	114	6.9
Ireland	1.1	0.2	0.1	9	161	–
Denmark	1.6	0.5	0.4	25	116	16.9
Greece	3.1	1.0	0.7	23	103	0.8
Spain	12.0	14.2	10.5	88	91	19.9
Portugal	3.2	0.7	0.5	16	113	1.4
EC	100.0	135.5	100.0	100	101	100.0[1]

Source: Eurostat 1991a (7): 59
Notes: 1 absolute amount 1,638,000 tonnes
   – negligible or no production

Italy) continuing thanks to their large-scale, favourable location for importing the ingredients, and their modern construction.

Shipbuilding

One of the industries of the EC that has suffered very serious contraction is shipbuilding. Table 6.5 (column (6)) shows the distribution of merchant ships launched in 1988 in the EC. In 1948, the 12 countries now in the EC accounted for more than three-quarters of world production. In 1987 the share was 17 per cent, albeit of a larger total.

The EC shipbuilding industry employed only 69,000 people at the end of 1988, compared with 105,000 as recently as 1985. It has never employed people on the scale of textiles, or iron and steel, but in some regions its decline has had serious effects. The Community objectives with regard to the industry are to rationalise it through a controlled cut-back in production capacity, as contained in the sixth directive on aid to shipbuilding. Some reserve capacity should be retained for strategic, social, economic and industrial reasons and some aid is still required for restructuring, but competition within the Community has been diffi-cult to achieve since Member States have frequently granted aid to their own domestic industries. Since the mid-1980s, EC annual production has dropped below 2 million tonnes for the first time since the late 1940s; it was 1.6 million in 1988. The decline has been sharpest in the UK, where 1988 production was less than one-tenth of that at the postwar peak years of the mid-1950s. The Italian and French industries have dropped to about a quarter, that of the FRG to about half in the same period.

Figure 6.4 shows the location of some of the major shipbuilding yards of EC countries. By their nature, shipbuilding industries have tended to be located in comparatively remote and peripheral regions in both national and EC contexts, which aggravates the problem of creating new employment in manufacturing. If recent trends continue, much of the remaining industry could be closed down by the end of the century as the share of world production accounted for by Japan (over 50 per cent) and the Republic of Korea (some 20 per cent) dominates the industry. Both these countries, in their turn, should be apprehensive at the prospect of China becoming a major producer and exporter of ships.

TEXTILES, CLOTHING, FOOTWEAR AND MOTOR VEHICLES

Textiles, clothing, footwear and motor vehicles have been chosen to represent industries that account for substantial proportions of all EC employment in industry and that, at the same time, are experiencing continual competition.

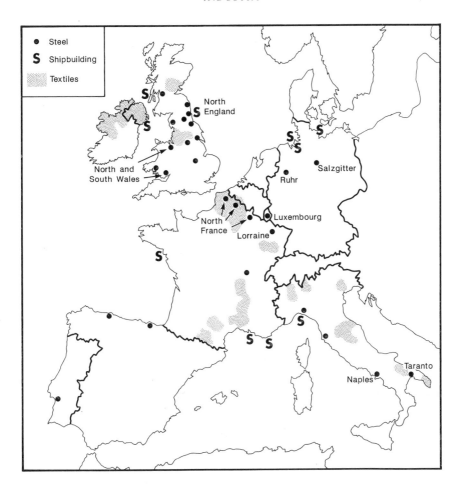

Figure 6.4 Selected areas of the European Community affected by the decline of the steel, shipbuilding and textile industries

Source: based on map in COM 87-230 (1987), map 2.2.3-B.4, p. 84 of Annex

Textiles, clothing and footwear

In 1987 these branches employed about 3.5 million people in the EC, 13 per cent of the workforce in industry, and accounted for 4 per cent of the EC's exports of finished products. Between 1979 and 1989 alone, however, 1,350,000 jobs were lost, affecting women particularly severely, since much of the industry had been located in areas with heavy industry and with few other jobs for women (e.g. Lancashire, Yorkshire, Nord-Pas-de-Calais, Nordrhein-Westfalen). EC policy on the above industries has been to ensure an internal market, encourage research

143

and development, control state aid, direct restructuring, and guide external policies.

Textiles (wool, cotton and man-made fibres) are the subject of the GATT Multifibre Agreement, dating from 1974, and subsequently updated. The aim has been to phase out restrictions on imports into the EC. Some 30 countries of Central Europe, Latin America and South and East Asia are referred to explicitly. Since 1973 there has been a greater increase in the imports of textiles than in consumption in the EC. Although some sectors of the EC textile industry have been given safeguards, output and employment have contracted. In the 1980s alone, the textile sector lost 400,000 jobs (1,950,000 to 1,560,000). In order to confront the challenge of exporters to the EC, heavy investment has taken place in textiles, with two trends to be noted: the merging of firms to produce very large enterprises, and the contracting out of some of the work to very small firms.

From a long-term perspective, the rise and decline of the textile industry in Western Europe can be seen to follow the introduction of modern methods of production in each country in the region, and the later development of the same processes elsewhere (e.g. in Russia and Japan in the nineteenth century; in countries such as India and Brazil in the twentieth). The data in Table 6.6 show a decline in output between 1935 and 1985 in the FRG and the UK. In columns (1)–(3) of Table 6.7 the situation during 1985–1990 in the EC textile industry is shown, however, to be less depressing than it was earlier, with output in the Community as a whole slightly up, although job losses continue. With over one-third of all output of textiles, Italy is the EC country that will be most affected by changes in the future.

While the distribution of the manufacture of clothing and footwear is not identical to that of textiles, the three sectors are broadly related. They are less amenable than textiles to improvements in efficiency through innovations and heavy investment, and are therefore weaker in the face of competition from the developing world. During 1985–90, not surprisingly, there was a decline in

Table 6.6 Output of cotton yarn in selected years 1935–80 in thousands of tonnes

	1935	1950	1960	1970	1980
Germany (FRG)	359[1]	282	421	239	170
(GDR)		24	73	69	131
France	250[2]	251	315	270	171
Italy	171	216	239	247	231
UK	557	433	285	184	91
Spain	31[3]	58	95	143	110

Source: Mitchell 1981: 458–9
Notes: 1 prewar Germany
2 1938
3 1933 (Civil War followed)

144

Table 6.7 Textiles, clothing and footwear output in the EC, 1985–90

	Textiles			Clothing			Footwear		
	(1) Share of EC output 1985	(2) Text/pop. 1985	(3) Change 1985–90 (1985=100)	(4) Share of EC output 1985	(5) Clothing/ pop.	(6) Change 1985–90 (1985=100)	(7) Share of EC output 1985	(8) Footwear/ pop.	(9) Change 1985–90 (1985=100)
FRG	13.1	70	100	18.0	96	87	8.9	47	69
France	16.1	94	88	17.6	102	79	16.9	98	83
Italy	33.7	190	113	30.3	171	96	45.0	254	86
Netherlands	1.8	40	104	1.2	27	91	0.7	16	78
Belgium/Lux.	3.3	103	111	2.2	69	110	0.3	9	67
UK	10.8	61	92	14.5	82	103	10.5	60	91
Ireland	0.6	55	119	0.7	64	91	0.3	27	n.a.
Denmark	0.8	50	87	0.9	56	68	0.5	31	95
Greece	4.0	129	104	1.8	58	90	1.1	35	78
Spain	9.0	75	107	9.5	79	105	11.7	98	62
Portugal	6.3	197	108	2.8	88	103	3.5	109	130
EC	100.0	100.0	102.5	100.0	100.0	80	100.0	100.0	83

Source: Eurostat 1991a, various months

Note: In columns (2), (5) and (8) the share of the EC total of the branch of industry in the country is divided by the share of the population of the country and multiplied by 100

output of 20 per cent in clothing and 17 per cent in footwear. Only the footwear industry of Portugal has expanded impressively, albeit from a modest base, thanks to Community membership and preference. With 30 per cent of clothing output of the EC and 45 per cent of footwear output, Italy will feel the contraction of the industry most severely.

Figure 6.4 shows the distribution of regions of the EC with problems of decline in textiles (see COM 87-230 (1987): 84), using as a basis NUTS 3 level regions, but has been simplified to give a general picture of the situation. The linen industry of Northern Ireland, the jute industry of Dundee, and the cotton and woollen counties of England (Lancashire, Greater Manchester and West Yorkshire) are included. North France and the Rhône valley appear, while southern Belgium is also affected. In Italy certain old textile districts in the North (woollen in Biella, Vicenza, and at one time silk in Como) and elsewhere are included. The textile industry in Spain, mainly in Cataluña (Barcelona) was not deemed to have problems, possibly because the assessment was made in the mid-1980s, when Spain was joining the EC, but the region does have high unemployment. Several of the textile regions with problems also have either an iron and steel industry or shipbuilding. Thus, for example, Northern Ireland has textiles and shipbuilding, Nord-Pas-de-Calais and southwest Belgium have textiles and steel.

Motor vehicles

In 1989 the motor vehicles industry accounted for about 7 per cent of industrial jobs and 6 per cent of manufactured value added in the Community, and in that year 13.8 million vehicles were produced (cf. USA 12.8, Japan 12.6). The production of the EC was almost 29 per cent of the 48 million motor vehicles produced in the world. The countries manufacturing passenger cars in the EC are shown in Table 6.8.

Table 6.8 The manufacture of passenger cars in the EC, 1990

	(1) Passenger cars (000s)	(2) Share of EC output (%)	(3) Cars/pop.	(4) Change 1985–90
FRG	4,166	38.0	202	112
France	2,816	25.7	149	119
Italy	1,389	12.6	71	135
Netherlands	108	1.0	22	102
Belgium	231	2.1	68	145
UK	1,049	9.5	54	124
Spain	1,230	11.1	93	140
Total EC	10,989	100.0	100	121

Source: Eurostat 1991a, various months

Registration of new passenger cars in the EC rose from 9.6 million in 1985 to 11.8 million in 1989. Cars owned per 1,000 population were 390 in 1988 but ranged from 126 in Greece and 138 in Portugal to 482 in the FRG. Even though ownership in West Germany is probably approaching saturation, there is still the prospect of considerable expansion in the number of vehicles registered elsewhere in the EC, in addition to the registration of new passenger cars needed for the replacement of existing vehicles. Wijsenbeek (1991) gives the number of cars per 1,000 inhabitants in the EC (12) as 357 in 1985 and 379 in 1990. He forecasts 463 by the year 2000 and 515 in 2010, estimates that will please the manufacturers of motor vehicles if not environmentalists.

EC motor vehicle manufacturers face the prospect of much competition, both within the Single Market and from outside the Community, and therefore need to restructure and merge further. Commission of the EC (1990: 13–13) highlights the following prospects: financial weakness of some EC companies; instability of competition between six producers; competition from Japanese transplants in Europe; competition from Japanese and US manufacturers in the USA; and the emergence of new producers in East Asia. From a completely different angle, environmental problems could result in measures to reduce the use of passenger cars, diverting people to public road transport, to rail and other means of transport, while congestion resulting from the failure to extend and improve the road network could also deter growth.

Figure 6.5 shows the location of major centres of motor vehicle manufacture, assembly and production of parts. If the industry follows the experience of textiles, iron and steel, and shipbuilding, and even if the production of vehicles actually expands, a reduction in the labour force seems inevitable. The decision as to which plants will shed labour and which, if any, will close, will largely rest with the manufacturers, since the Community has little influence on the industry.

A characteristic of the location of the industry as it expanded after the Second World War was decentralisation in several countries, notably France, Italy and the UK, to provide industrial jobs away from the older manufacturing centres. In France, 75 per cent of the workforce in motor vehicle manufacturing was in Paris in 1939 compared with 30 per cent now, to the benefit of regional centres such as Rennes in Bretagne. In Italy, Turin still dominates the industry, with Milan an important secondary centre, but decentralisation occurred here also, in accordance with Italian policy to assist the South, and factories were established in Naples.

In Germany a relatively new development has been the link-up with establishments in the former GDR, notably Volkswagen with Trabant in Zwickau, and elsewhere in Central Europe, with Skoda in Czechoslovakia. While Japanese transplants are very new (e.g. Washington in Northeast England for Nissan, Derby in the East Midlands for Toyota), the US Ford and General Motors companies have long been established near London in the UK (Dagenham, Luton) and in Germany (Nordrhein-Westfalen). While the long-established US firms in Western Europe have been accepted as part of the industrial scene, the

147

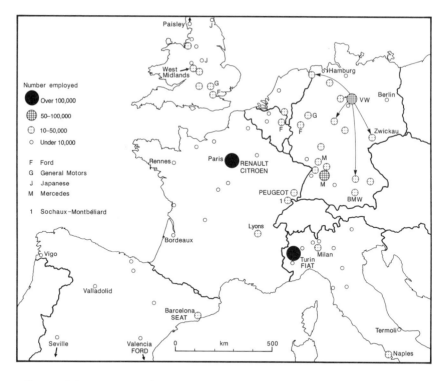

Figure 6.5 Major centres of motor vehicle manufacturing in the European Community

Main source: *Calendario Atlante de Agostini 1990* (1989)

Japanese endeavours have been criticised, especially by the French, as being springboards for Japanese penetration of the EC, basically as assembly plants, creating few jobs and limited value added.

There does not seem much scope for the development of new motor vehicle factories in the EC in the 1990s. The new factory in Portugal is an exception. Ironically it will achieve one EC goal of industrialising a backward region of the Community, but the main reason for the location, namely cheap labour, reflects another EC problem: the great divergence in income and living standards in the Community.

NEW AND EMERGING INDUSTRIES

The 1980s were characterised in terms of industrialisation by a race between the USA, Japan and Western Europe in the development and marketing of new products, in particular in the areas of consumer electronics, information technologies, robotics, telecommunications and biotechnology. The Single Market in a post-1992 EC was seen as an opportunity for some and as a fortress for others, and there has been a scramble on the part of non-EC companies in these new and emerging industrial sectors to establish a foothold and conquer markets in the EC of the 1990s. A brief analysis of the key sectors will show the extent to which the future of the industrial manufacturing base in Western Europe depends not only on the survival of more traditional industries, described in the previous sections of this chapter, but also on the extent to which EC manufacturers can compete effectively with products coming not only from the traditional competitors, but also from the so-called Newly Industrialising Countries (NICs), in particular those in East Asia.

As already explained elsewhere, the EC is characterised by the absence of a global industrial policy and by a budget that is over-stretched by the expenditure on the Common Agricultural Policy, leaving few funds for the development of new industrial sectors. The 1992 budget for the EC has set aside 1.95 billion ECU for R and TD programmes, which are governed by the Multiannual Framework Programme, as well as specific research programmes in areas such as nuclear energy. Nevertheless, this must be compared to the USA and Japan, where much more is spent on such funding than at Community level in the EC.

In the absence of a common industrial policy, the individual Member States of the EC also fund and develop their own manufacturers in these new sectors, and the EC Commission's task is to monitor such state aids and related measures to ensure that they do not distort competition or create obstacles to the free movement of goods within the new internal market. There is, therefore, a dilemma, because in over-zealous protection of free-market principles, the EC risks opening its markets to foreign competition, as it strives to stimulate competition between its own national industrial enterprises. For example, moves to protect the EC computer industry through the grouping of international activities by Siemens, Olivetti and Philips, met with criticism both in the EC and outside. Until the EC has the powers and the funding to develop and co-ordinate an overall industrial strategy in new sectors, it is likely that the emerging industries will suffer the same fate as the more traditional sectors already discussed in previous sections.

Electronics and components

A sector whose applications have an increasingly significant impact on many industrial, consumer and service-related activities, this is an area which has been identified for several years as crucial to the competitive and commercial survival of the Western European economy. The electronics sector has been characterised, above all others, by strong competition between companies in the USA, the Far East and Western Europe. Since it is responsible for supplying components to many of the expanding sectors of the manufacturing and services sectors, such as telecommunications, robotics, and banking and office automation, its significance in terms of basic industrial supply has grown astronomically over the course of the last decade. At the same time, research and development and mass-production techniques, have made it a sector that is prone to high turnovers and acute competitiveness factors, in particular with fast-growing suppliers in the Far Eastern countries.

World production of electronics components is valued at 540 billion ECU (Commission of the EC 1990), of which the EC countries account for 18 per cent. The USA and Japan in global terms are ahead of the EC, accounting for 35 per cent and 29 per cent respectively, but what is more significant is that Japan is the only major country with a trade surplus in the overall electronics area, consuming 19 per cent while producing 29 per cent. All other main blocs are net importers from Japan, in particular of products such as integrated circuits, semi-conductors, resistors, transducers and capacitors. It is significant to note that EC countries are in a negative trend as far as self-sufficiency in such products is concerned.

Since the sector itself is expanding, this trend is of major concern to EC governments, with the threat of increasing dependence on imports from non-EC suppliers, yet there is little done to co-ordinate the development of the sector at EC level owing to the desire to protect the few national producers that do exist. The ill-fated Jessi programme under the umbrella of Eureka, which failed to co-ordinate semiconductor R and D and manufacture with companies such as Philips and Siemens at European level, illustrates this lack of co-operative spirit. The share of third-country imports continues to increase in this key supply sector, as EC manufacturers see their world market share ended.

Information and industrial technologies

As in the case of the supply industry to this expanding and diversified sector, the Information Technology (IT) sector is characterised by growth dominated by the USA and Japan, with EC industry developing in an environment of sluggish R and D and reduced efficiency resulting from conflicts over standards and co-operation.

As far as the EC programmes for R and D are concerned, the ESPRIT, BRITE and EURAM programmes within the Multiannual Framework Programme (1990–4) for R and TD have contributed substantially to the development of co-operative products in IT and industrial automation fields in the EC. The 6 billion ECU allocated to the programme is valuable to the industry in the respective sectors, although this is only a small percentage of what is invested in R and D by the equivalent bodies in the USA and Japan. It is becoming increasingly difficult to envisage the IT sectors in the EC remaining competitive without substantial investment, or protection from countries that compete in terms of price and quality, often to the extent of dumping products on EC markets in order to create difficulties for local industry.

Telecommunications

Although this, too, is a growth sector, with new and diversified applications for telecom products in areas transcending the traditional office and domestic systems, the scenario at EC level is again plagued by interventionism and national barriers to competition. The European telecommunications sector, both in terms of products and services, is now moving within the framework of the 1992 Single Market Programme, with corresponding competition and reduction of state monopolies and other restrictive practices. At the same time, attempts are being made to harmonise systems and standards to facilitate the transfrontier use and sale of systems. Mobile communications and satellite transmissions are significant areas of development, which are leading to substantial restructuring of the telecom sector.

It is ironic, nevertheless, that the existence of at least three different and incompatible mobile communications systems within the EC means that it remains impossible for a British-system carphone to be used in France or for a mobile phone system originating in Denmark to be of any use in Italy. The free movement of goods and services in such a sector still needs to be improved if the EC market is to begin to resemble the US and Japanese markets. National interest continues to predominate in an area so crucial to the communicative development of the EC economy and society at large.

Aerospace

As with all industry dependent to a large extent on the defence sector for its survival, the aerospace industry in the EC faces a period of restructuring and cutbacks in government military spending, combined with added competition from the USA, where similar market phenomena prevail. In both the civil and military production in the EC aerospace industry, there is the added complication of efforts to move it from the 'excluded' sectors (Art. 223 TOR) into the open procurement markets in the post-1992 EC. The industry is becoming more open, therefore, not only to competition originating in the EC, but also to opportunist firms from outside, keen to serve a developing market in the dual (civil–military) sphere. As air transport in the EC opens up, it is likely to see stronger competition both within and outside the industrial circle of the EC.

CONCLUSION

In global terms, the emerging industries are seeing the same issues debated within the EC as outside it. The extent to which EC industries can overcome internal differences, harmonise standards, and open up their markets to each other, is vital to the survival of a crucial range of industrial sectors in terms of the future industrial base of EC Member States. It has been made clear in this chapter that there is little prospect of the creation of new jobs in traditional EC industries such

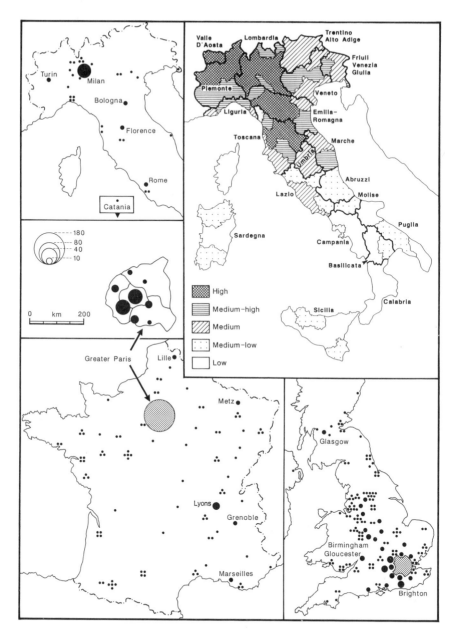

Figure 6.6 The location of a sample of new and high-technology industries in Italy, France and the UK, and the level of development of Italian provinces

Source: of data for Italian development: Carazzi, M. and Segre, A. 1989: 197
Note: The key appearing in the Paris map relates to the other maps in the figure

as textiles and heavy industry. The new industries described in this section may be expected to provide new employment opportunities in the 1990s. While they are varied in their products, they do have features in common. They do not use large quantities of energy or raw materials, and their products are not difficult or costly to deliver to markets. They mainly employ people with skills and expertise, so would be attracted to areas with existing manufacturing traditions, and educational and research facilities. Geographically, the result is disappointing for regional development in the EC (see Chapter 10) because many of the areas with a large agricultural sector and high unemployment are evidently the least attractive. Preferred locations are mostly in or near the big cities or in environmentally attractive areas such as the Mediterranean region of France. The location of a sample of high-tech industries in three major EC countries is shown in Figure 6.6. The predominance of the Southeast in the UK, the Paris area in France and the North in Italy underlines the locational advantages described.

FURTHER READING

Commission of the European Communities (1990) *European Economy, Social Europe, the Impact of the Internal Market by Industrial Sector: the Challenge for the Member States*, Brussels.

Keeble, D. and Wever, E. (1986) *New Firms and Regional Development in Europe*, London: Croom Helm.

Office of Official Publications of the European Community (1991) *Panorama of EC Industry 1991–1992*, Brussels.

153

7

SERVICES

EMPLOYMENT IN THE SERVICES SECTOR

While the definition and function of the agricultural and industrial sectors in the EC is reasonably straightforward, the tertiary or services sector consists of a wide variety of types of employment. In the USA, the first two sectors are defined as producing goods whereas the services sector is referred to as 'non-goods'. Nevertheless, many workers in such branches of services as transport and administration are directly connected with the two 'productive' sectors. Eventually the distinction between the three sectors may become so blurred that their usefulness will disappear, but at present they are widely used.

According to COM 90-609 (1991), in 1987 the services sector accounted for 59.2 per cent of total employment in the EC and in 1986 (Eurostat 1989a) produced 60.1 per cent of GDP. While there are several highly urbanised regions of the EC at NUTS 2 level with virtually no persons working in agriculture (e.g. Brussels, Greater London) and some with very few people working in industry (e.g. the Greek islands), every NUTS 2 level region has some people working in services such as local government, health, education, retailing and transport, while additionally some have functions such as administrative and financial that extend, nationally or even internationally, far beyond their limits. The lowest proportion of employment in services in any NUTS 2 level region in the EC is about one-third.

The purpose of this chapter is to draw attention to the disparities in the regional distribution of services in the EC and to identify regions in which services have a special role, such as national government, defence and the presence of major sea- and airports. In view of the great importance of the transport sector of services, this subject will be covered separately in Chapter 8. Figure 7.1 shows variations in the level of employment in services at NUTS 1 level.

With 44.1 per cent employment in services, Portugal is the lowest among the 12 Member States of the EC, contrasting with the Netherlands, which with 68.6 is the highest (see Table 7.1, col. (2)). Indeed, the Netherlands has one of the highest levels of any country in the world, but most developing countries are well below the Portuguese level. In Tables 7.2 and 7.3, the regions at NUTS 1 or 2

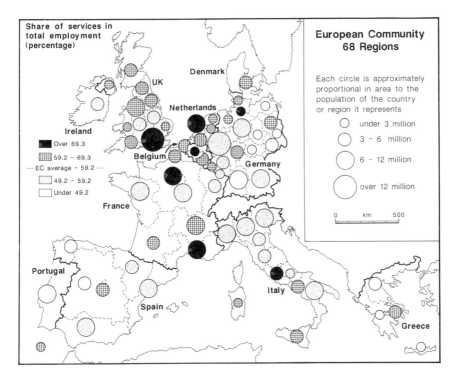

Figure 7.1 Employment in the services sector at NUTS 1 level of the European
Community in 1987

Source: COM 90-609 (1991), Table A of Statistical Annex
Note: See Figure 2.3 for the names of the regions

levels with the highest and lowest proportion of employment in services are
shown in ranked order. Those regions with a high level of employment in the
sector provide services such as national administration, transport (especially
ports), education and research for the population of large areas beyond their own
regional limits. The 12 regions with the highest scores in the EC mostly contain
national capitals (Lazio with Rome, Ile-de-France with Paris, Southeast with
London), or major ports (Zuid-Holland with Rotterdam, Liguria with Genoa and
Savona) but the impact of tourism in regions with little industry and limited
agriculture is also seen in the prominence of services in Provence and Corse in
France. The regions with the lowest proportion in services are in Portugal, Greece
and Spain. Here the high proportion in agriculture 'squeezes out' services, while
a similar feature is found in some southern regions of the FRG, but here
industrial employment is very high.

Contrasts in employment levels in services are even greater at district level
than at NUTS 2 level, as shown by examples from the UK, where services
approach and even exceed 90 per cent of all employment in some regions,

Table 7.1 Employment in services in the countries of the EC

	(1)	(2)	(3)	(4)
	Employment in services		Gross value added 1986	Value/emplt ratio
	% COM 87	% COM 90	% Eurostat	
FRG[1]	53.8	55.0	56.7	103
France	59.2	62.8	63.8	102
Italy	55.5	58.0	60.9	105
Netherlands	65.9	68.6	61.0	89
Belgium	64.5	65.5	65.8	100
Luxembourg	62.8	67.3	63.6	95
UK	61.9	64.9	60.5	93
Ireland	53.5	55.6	54.1	97
Denmark	65.2	67.1	66.6	99
Greece	45.4	48.0	53.7	112
Spain	49.1	53.2	57.4	108
Portugal	42.2	44.1	52.9	120
EC	57.2	59.2	60.1	102

Sources: COM 87-280 (1987), COM 90-609 (1990), Eurostat 1989a
Note: 1 GDR 42.2%

Table 7.2 Highest levels of employment in services, 1987

NUTS level	Region	% in services	NUTS level	Region	% in services
1, 2	Brussels	79.6	2	Zuid-Holland	73.6
2	Utrecht (Neth.)	76.1	1, 2	Ile-de-France (Paris)	73.2
2	Noord-Holland	76.0	1, 2	Hamburg	72.7
1, 2	Lazio (Rome)	75.8	2	Provence[1]	71.9
2	Corse (France)	75.0	1	Southeast (London)	70.5
2	Brabant (Belgium)	74.2	2	Liguria (Italy)	70.3

Source: COM 90-609 (1991)
Note: 1 Provence – Alpes – Côte d'Azur

including many London boroughs (e.g. Kensington and Chelsea 96.7 per cent), some coastal resorts (e.g. Brighton 91.3 per cent, Bournemouth 89.9 per cent) and some smaller cities (e.g. Exeter 91.7 per cent, Chester 89.5 per cent). Such extreme cases of dependence on services are less likely to occur outside the UK and Belgium, because nowhere else does agriculture account for such a low share of employment.

Table 7.3 Lowest levels of employment in services, 1987

NUTS level	Region	% in services	NUTS level	Region	% in services
2	Centro (Portugal)	33.4	1	Voreia Ellada (Greece)	38.3
2	Norte (Portugal)	33.9	2	Oberfranken (FRG)	41.8
1	Kentriki Ellada (Greece)	34.9	2	Niederbayern (FRG)	42.3
2	Galicia (Spain)	38.0	2	Tübigen (FRG)	43.8

Source: COM 90-609 (1991)

At present, most of the assistance to the poorer regions of the EC is targeted at regions with a large agricultural sector, the smallest employer of labour of the three sectors, and to some types of mining and industrial region. The services sector accounts for about three-fifths of all employment in the EC and includes many very poorly paid types of work, but it hardly figures at all in regional objectives.

The importance of the service sector to a region can also be measured in terms of the gross value added. At EC level the difference is small, 60.1 per cent of total value against 59.2 of all employment, but at national level there are considerable differences. A value to employment ratio can be calculated for services (see Table 7.1 col. (4)), which varies from the Netherlands, with 89 to 100, to Portugal with 120 to 100. The differences that occur at national and regional level can be explained partly by the relative efficiency of agriculture and industry in relation to services (high in the Netherlands, low in Portugal) and partly by the types of services themselves. Those providing for local and regional needs have many low-paid jobs and, it may be broadly inferred, low 'production' per employee, while those for national and international needs have many well-paid jobs and are therefore highly valued for GDP purposes.

Since employment in agriculture and industry in the EC is declining, the services sector will have to expand if unemployment is not to increase. Unfortunately, the data available for the EC on services do not give a precise indication of where new employment in the sector is needed or is likely to be created. Apart from the relocation of offices by governments or private companies, usually from the capital to the provinces, the growth of and changes in the services sector tend to be gradual. New technologies are already leading to job losses in, for example, banking, as they have done through mechanisation in agriculture and automation in industry. On the other hand, a reduction in working hours or a change in the ratio of full-time to part-time jobs could sustain employment in the industrial and services sectors in the future.

HEALTHCARE

Virtually all the administration and financing of healthcare in the EC remains in the hands of the Member States, and EC policy is therefore largely confined to the funding of programmes and information campaigns and the intra-EC recognition of medical qualifications. A precise statement about the availability and regional distribution of healthcare provision and the occurrence of illnesses and causes of death throughout the EC cannot be made because of a relative shortage of comparable data sets. In Eurostat publications there are major gaps in various aspects of healthcare, while definitions vary from country to country, and health services are organised in different ways.

Three aspects of healthcare in the Member States of the EC are shown in Table 7.4: all healthcare personnel, doctors, and hospital beds. Almost 6 million people out of a total employed population in the EC in 1987 of 145 million, or more than 4 per cent, are engaged in 'Medical and other health services, veterinary services' (Eurostat 1989a: 121). About 720,000, or 12 per cent, are defined as doctors. The ratio of doctors to total healthcare personnel (columns (1) and (3)) varies greatly from country to country, as does the availability of doctors (in per thousand, column (4)), and hospital beds, to total population. Spain and Greece are the best provided with doctors (depending on definition) but, together with Portugal, are the worst provided with regard to hospital facilities, of which beds broadly represent all aspects of healthcare hardware.

Table 7.4 Healthcare facilities in the countries of the EC

| | (1) | (2) | (3) | (4) | (5) |
| | All health personnel | | Doctors | | Hospital beds |
	Total (000s) 1987	Per 1,000 pop. 1987	Total (000s) 1986	Per 1,000 pop. 1986	per 1,000 pop.
FRG	1,232	20	165	2.7	11.0
France	1,150[1]	21	126	2.3	8.9
Italy	n.a.	–	84	1.5	7.9
Netherlands	357	24	33	2.3	11.4
Belgium/Lux.	145	14	25	2.4	6.9
UK	1,308	23	81	1.4	7.2
Ireland	63	18	5	1.5	8.5
Denmark	137	27	13	2.6	6.9
Greece	103	10	30	3.1	5.3
Spain	337	9	131	3.4	n.a.
Portugal	n.a.	–	26	2.5	3.8

Sources: Eurostat 1989a: 120–1; Eurostat 1990: 184
Notes: 1 estimated by authors
n.a. not available

If convergence in healthcare standards is to become an EC issue, then a great deal of development would be needed to bring all countries to the level of the highest. Extremes at national level are very marked, with Denmark at 3 to Portugal at 1 for all healthcare personnel to population, Spain at 3.4 to the UK at 1.4 for doctors per 1,000 population, and the Netherlands at 3 to Portugal at 1 for hospital beds. But as can be seen in Table 7.5, the availability of doctors per 1,000 total population varies greatly also within countries. In most countries, the region in which the national capital is located is the best provided. It cannot be argued convincingly that people in such places need twice as much medical attention as those in areas that are relatively 'deprived' medically, but specialists, medical schools and research centres do tend to be concentrated in the larger cities.

The quantity of medical personnel and facilities may not be related exactly to the standard of healthcare. In order to have a broad idea of standards in different regions, the level of infant mortality has been chosen. Data are good for this variable and are widely available, with records going back 200 years in Scandinavia. The data in Table 7.6 compare infant mortality rates in most of the countries of Europe and in selected non-European countries. The accompanying proportions in young and elderly age groups will be referred to below.

In spite of apparently great national and regional variations in healthcare services, infant mortality rates in the EC at national level are remarkably close. The extremes in the EC and EFTA are Portugal with 12.1 per 1,000 live births compared with 5.8 in Sweden and Finland. Levels in Central Europe and the former USSR are two to three times the EC average level of about 8 per 1,000. Turkey and the Maghreb countries are in a completely different class. The level in Algeria and Morocco is similar to that in Sweden in 1910, and to that in England and Wales around 1925. That is not to say that the two Maghreb countries would need 80 years to reach the present Swedish level, but the present gap would need decades not years to narrow appreciably. The data in Figure 7.2 are for 1987, and the indices for Denmark, Greece and Portugal all differ markedly

Table 7.5 Doctors per 1,000 population in NUTS 2 regions, 1986

Country	Region			
FRG	West Berlin	4.4	Niedersachsen	2.3
France	Ile-de-France	2.8	Champagne-Ardenne	1.6
Italy	Lazio	2.0	Basilicata	0.9
Netherlands	Utrecht	3.4	Nord-Brabant	1.2
Belgium/Lux.	Brussels	4.1	Limburg	1.6
Denmark	Hovedstadsregionen	3.3	Rest of country	2.2
Spain	Aragón	4.6	Castilla-La Mancha	2.4

Source: Eurostat 1990: 182

Table 7.6 Infant mortality rates and the proportions of young and elderly in EC and other selected countries, 1991

	(1) Inf. mort. per 1,000 births	(2) % under 15	(3) % over 64		(1) Inf. mort. per 1,000 births	(2) % under 15	(3) % over 64
Germany (all)	7.5	16	15	Austria	7.9	17	15
France	7.2	20	14	Switzerland	7.3	17	15
Italy	8.8	17	14	Norway	8.0	19	16
Netherlands	6.8	18	13	Sweden	5.8	18	18
Belgium	8.6	18	15	Finland	5.8	19	13
Luxembourg	9.9	17	13	Poland	15.9	25	10
UK	8.4	19	16	Czechoslovakia	11.3	23	12
Ireland	7.5	28	11	Hungary	15.7	21	13
Denmark	8.4	17	16	USSR	23	26	9
Greece	9.8	20	14	Turkey	62	38	4
Spain	8.3	20	13	Algeria	74	46	4
Portugal	12.1	21	13	Morocco	75	42	4

Source: PRB, *WPDS* 1991

from those for 1991 in Table 7.6. Regional variations in infant mortality rates within the main EC countries are considerable at NUTS 1 level, and black spots can be identified at NUTS 2 level, such as Thrakis in Greece with 18 per 1,000, and the Norte in Portugal with 19, about three times the lowest scores found in the EC. In practice, diminishing returns in healthcare expenditure in general and gynaecology in particular make it unlikely that infant mortality could ever drop below about 5 per 1,000.

Progress in reducing infant mortality levels in the EC may be illustrated by reference to selected Italian *regioni* (see Table 7.7). The picture is one of universal rapid decrease and also regional convergence. The decrease has come faster in the poorer regions. Even allowing for fluctuations due to small numbers of births at district level, marked disparities occur at the smallest scale of region for which data are aggregated within countries. A UK study (National Audit Office 1990) of the occurrence of perinatal deaths (still-births plus deaths in the first week of life), per 1,000 births, shows a range between 13.5 in Bradford (Yorkshire) and 6.5 in West Surrey and Northeast Hampshire.

It is generally accepted that the amount of healthcare needed per individual increases rapidly after middle age. The proportion of the population of 65 years and over in the countries of Europe (see Table 7.6) is a good indicator of the need for extra healthcare above the normal. As deaths from contagious diseases have declined in the more developed countries, deaths from causes resulting from ageing have increased. With 18 per cent, Sweden has the highest proportion of

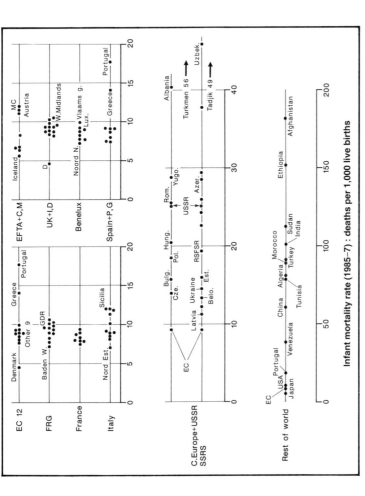

Figure 7.2 Variations in infant mortality rates at regional level in Europe and in other selected parts of the world. Abbreviations used: C – Cyprus, M – Malta, I – Ireland, D – Denmark, P – Portugal, G – Greece

Sources: CSO 1990, Table 14.1; PRB, *WPDS* (1991)

Table 7.7 Infant mortality rates in selected regions of Italy, 1961–86 (per 1,000 live births)

Region	1961	1971	1986
Lombardia (North)	35	23	8
Emilia-Romagna (North)	31	23	8
Lazio (Centre)	35	24	8
Campania (South)	55	40	11
Sicilia (Islands)	47	34	12

Source: *Annuario Statistico Italiano*, Istituto Centrale di Statistica, various years

people of 65 years of age and over in Europe. Ireland and Iceland have much lower levels. Even so, the differences among EC and EFTA countries are mostly small, and apart from Romania and Yugoslavia, Central Europe is broadly similar to the EC. On the other hand, in Turkey and the Maghreb countries, population is still growing fast and the younger cohorts are much larger than the older ones, while mortality rates are much higher among older people of given ages than in Europe. At present, healthcare for the elderly in those areas is much less a matter of concern than in the EC.

EDUCATION

As with healthcare, policy on education at Community level is limited in scope. The main influence on education at the EC level so far has been to ensure mutual recognition of examinations and qualifications between countries rather than the imposition of harmonisation and uniformity. The EC also funds training programmes through the Social Fund to assist unemployed people, vocational training, and exchange and education programmes between establishments in different Member States. As with healthcare, the availability, accuracy and recency of EC data on education are far from satisfactory.

Absolute numbers in the education sector must be seen in relation, first, to the total population size of each country (see column (1), Table 7.8) and secondly to the proportion in that population of children obliged to attend school (mostly 5–16 years), of those under 5 years of age, some of whom attend pre-school establishments, and of those up to the age of 24, potentially participants in the system of higher education.

The whole educational sector of the EC gives employment to about 8.6 million people, about 6 per cent of all employment in the Community, and accounts for 6 per cent of total GDP. Only about half of that total number are actually directly engaged in teaching, the remainder consisting of administrative, maintenance and other non-teaching staff. The total number of children and young adults in full-time education in the EC (excluding the GDR) is about 60

162

Table 7.8 Education data for the countries of the EC

	(1) % < 15 1991	(2) Education sector 1987 (000s)	(3) In education 1986/7 (000s)	(4) % of all < 25 1986/7	(5) % at Third level 1986/7	(6) % of GDP 1985	(7) PPS per head 1985	(8) Primary pupil-to-teacher ratio 1985–8	(9) Scientists 1985 (000s)	(10) Per 10,000 total pop. 1985
FRG	15	1,830*	8,961	67	26	4.6	581	17	252.7	41
France	20	1,668*	10,997	83	23	5.7	746	19	273.0	49
Italy	17	1,435*	10,029	69	20	5.0	690	14	96.8	17
Netherlands	18	344	3,154	72	21	6.8	838	17	61.4	42
Belgium/Lux.	18	278	1,896	80	23	6.0	735	15	21.6	21
UK	19	1,713	9,844	63	11	5.0	703	n.a.	163.1	29
Ireland	28	70	822	73	16	5.7	461	27	5.0	14
Denmark	17	179	1,000	73	23	6.0	934	11	19.9	39
Greece	20	158	1,904	71	20	3.4	231	23	3.5	4
Spain	20	780*	9,097	80	25	3.3	302	26	23.2	6
Portugal	21	155*	2,031	63	13	4.0	470	17	6.5	6
EC	18	8,610	59,735	72		6.1**				

Key: * Authors' estimate
** not apparently compatible with national figures
n.a. not available

Notes on Table 7.8 by column

(1) Percentage of total population under the age of 15. *Source*: PRB, *WPDS* 1991
(2) Number of people employed in the education sector in thousands. *Source*: Eurostat 1989a: 120–1
(3) Number of pupils and students in education at all levels in thousands. *Source*: Eurostat 1991b: 32
(4) Pupils and students in education as a percentage of all the population aged 5 to 24. *Source*: Eurostat 1991b: 32
(5) Percentage of all pupils and students at Third level. *Source*: Eurostat 1991b 32
(6) Public expenditure on education as a percentage of total GDP in 1985. *Source*: Eurostat 1991b 36
(7) Public expenditure per head of population in 1985 in PPS (purchasing power standard). *Source*: Eurostat 1991b 36
(8) Primary pupil-to-teacher ratio 1985–8. *Source*: UNDP 1990: 155
(9) Scientists, technicians and engineers in thousands in 1985. *Source*: UNSYB 1987, Table 49
(10) Scientists, etc. (9), per 10,000 total population.

million (see column (3), Table 7.8 for totals), which represents over 18 per cent of the total population.

Whereas full-time education is compulsory in all EC countries up to a given school-leaving age, after that age the proportion remaining in education up to the age of 24 varies greatly between countries. This fact is reflected in the percentage of pupils and students in the population aged 5–24 in column (4) of Table 7.8. At one extreme is France, with 83 per cent, at the other the UK and Portugal, each with 63 per cent. The contrast is even more strikingly shown in a comparison of the participation of students in full-time education at the Third level. In column (5) the number of students at the Third level is shown per 1,000 total population of each country (e.g. the Netherlands 312,000 students, total population 14,600,000 gives a score of 21.4). With a score of 11, the UK comes behind Portugal and Ireland, and has less than half the score found in several other EC countries. Some allowance should be made for different higher educational procedures in each country, with faster progress through the system in the UK than elsewhere. The importance of the Third level has been widely emphasised throughout the EC, since many of the more highly qualified pupils and students, regarded as vital for future economic and technological progress in the Community, pass through it.

In columns (6) and (7) of Table 7.8, expenditure on education is related to total GDP and to total population. The proportion of children and young adults to total population varies, and should be taken into consideration. Disparities at national level are evident, both in terms of percentage of total GDP spent on education (contrast the Netherlands 6.8 per cent, Spain 3.3) and, more markedly, on the amount spent per inhabitant (Denmark 934, Greece 231). Although variations are marked, all EC levels of education are well above those in most developing countries. Nevertheless, convergence and uniformity in the educational system of the EC seem a long way off.

Owing to the poor quality and limited availability of educational data for regions of the EC, information about situations and disparities at subnational level is limited. Here two data sets will be referred to: differences in the proportion of adolescents in education, and training (Eurostat 1991b: 34–5). Of the 12 EC Member States, only Italy, Greece and Spain have regional breakdowns. At national level, the FRG, the Netherlands and Denmark score highest (over 85 per cent); the UK, Ireland, Portugal and Greece the lowest (under 60 per cent). In Italy, the highest levels are in parts of the North and throughout the Centre, while Sicilia and the Alpine regions are lowest. In Spain, the northern regions and Madrid are best provided for, in Greece some northern regions and Athens.

The proportion of under-15 year olds to total population even at NUTS 1 level varies greatly, ranging from 29 per cent in Ireland to 12 per cent in Hamburg (see Table 7.9). If less needs to be spent on education in some regions than in others on account of the contrasts in numbers in young age groups, correspondingly more is needed in the healthcare sector because the proportion of elderly will be greater. If the age structure of the EC is slowly moving towards

Table 7.9 Percentage of total population under the age of 15 years at NUTS 1 level

Highest 6 in the EC		Lowest 6 in the EC	
Ireland	29.0	Emilia-Romagna (Italy)	14.4
Canarias (Spain)	26.7	Hessen (FRG)	14.5
Sur (Spain)	26.0	Saarland (FRG)	14.3
Northern Ireland (UK)	25.4	Berlin (FRG)	13.6
Campania (Italy)	24.8	Bremen (FRG)	13.0
Nord-Pas-de-Calais (France)	24.3	Hamburg (FRG)	11.9

that already found in parts of the FRG, then a gradual shift of resources from education to healthcare can be expected.

One measure of the adequacy and quality of teaching facilities is provided by data for the number of primary school children per teacher for different countries shown in Table 7.8, column (8). The average number of children per class is rather larger because teachers are not actually taking classes all the time. Variations within Europe are considerable but, once again, Turkey and the Maghreb countries fall far below Europe in the provision of this service.

The countries of EFTA have demographic structures and levels of expenditure on education broadly similar to those of the northern EC Member States. By world standards, the countries of Central Europe and the former USSR have high levels of attendance at school and in higher education. In Turkey and the Maghreb countries, in contrast, the proportion of children to total population is much higher than in the EC and attendance in educational establishments lower. If any of these latter countries were to join the EC, then there would be an unacceptably high level of disparity within the Community and the need for enormous investment in education at all levels both to make up the present deficit and to accommodate the absolute increase in the number of children for several decades to come. In contrast, any changes in Central Europe and the former USSR seem likely to be in the content and organisation of education rather than in the number of pupils and students to be taught.

FINANCIAL SERVICES

In the White Paper from the Commission to the European Council in June 1985, the precursor to the Single Market programme contained in the Single Act, the Commission made an important definition of the services sector, distinguishing in Article 99 between new service areas such as 'information marketing and audio-visual services' and 'so-called traditional (but rapidly evolving) services such as transport, banking and insurance' (Commission of the EC 1985). Transport is covered separately in Chapter 8 of this book, but of the other areas targeted by the Commission as priorities in the Single Market, the financial

Table 7.10 Primary pupil-to-teacher ratio in selected non-EC countries, 1985–8

Country	Ratio	Country	Ratio
Austria	11	Czechoslovakia	21
Norway	16	USSR	17
Sweden	16	Turkey	31
Finland	14	Morocco	26
GDR	17	Tunisia	31

Source: UNDP 1990: 155

services sector is of prime importance, in particular in the light of the need to ensure the free movement of capital.

Just as the services sector has expanded in terms of contribution to GDP in Europe, so too has the financial services sector expanded to account for more jobs and value added. As far as the Member States of the EC are concerned, the percentage contributed to GDP varies considerably, as for example in 1989 between 4.3 per cent for France and 14.9 per cent for Luxembourg, which has a long tradition of independent banking and insurance services, similar to that in Switzerland. Banking is responsible for much of the financial activity, with bank assets in the EC amounting to 6,308 billion ECU in 1989, an increase of 12 per cent over 1988, and a figure far higher than that in the USA, which stood at 4,492 billion. Japan, nevertheless, was ahead of the EC, with a figure of 6,779 billion, indicating the supremacy of the Japanese banking sector in global terms.

Financial services in the EC employed 3.5 million people in 1989: 2.3 million in banking and 1.2 million in insurance. Here again, the importance of the financial sector in Luxembourg is noteworthy, accounting for 5.7 per cent of all jobs. More recently, technological advances and economic recession have hit the sector hard, with many job losses even in the traditional financial strongholds of London and Frankfurt. It is hoped that the liberalisation of the financial service sector through the Internal Market programme will contribute to increased competition and a more thriving sector, although competition from non-EC banks, in particular Japanese ones, will continue to press EC operators.

The EC programme for the development of financial services has concentrated on key aspects of the three financial services subsectors: stock exchanges, with EC directives on capital adequacy, insider trading and mergers and acquisitions; banking, with directives covering own funds, solvency coefficients; and surveillance of consolidated banks. In the insurance sector, EC policy has also been to promote market access and freedom to provide services in both life and non-life insurance. Occurrences in the financial and commercial sectors, such as the collapse of the Bank of Credit and Commerce International, insider trading, banking scandals in Japan, and the crisis in the Maxwell empire, have increasingly drawn public attention to the risks that exist in this sector.

The extent to which financial services have become internationalised and far more complex than ever before has led individuals as well as governments to demand more transparency and scrutiny over such activities, and EC legislation is bound to lead to a tightening-up of practices. It is argued that in a freer and larger internal market, the risks of transfrontier fraud and scandal are greater, and so too must the safeguards be.

As the EC expands to take in more prosperous Member States from the EFTA area, the financial services sector will continue to grow and diversify, creating a market that will continue to have a major global presence. The move towards a single currency, discussed in Chapter 2, will further stimulate this process. At the same time, banking activities in the other direction, towards developing the economies and commercial activities of the newly democratised countries in Central and Eastern Europe, will also grow substantially. The extent to which EC banks have written off debts in Latin American and African countries in recent years has had a sobering effect, and such banking activities are bound to be more cautious in future years.

A map showing the regional distribution of employment in financial services at NUTS 1 or NUTS 2 level can be referred to in Commission of the EC (1991: 61). Regions in which employment is more than 50 per cent higher than the EC average include Ile-de-France, the Southeast (UK), Noord-Holland (Amsterdam), Copenhagen, Darmstadt (Frankfurt), Luxembourg (GD), and Madrid. Of the 12 Member States, Italy in general is the one with the lowest level of employment in financial services, although this service activity is bound to be present at a minimal level in every region.

The handling of equity investments is a major aspect of financial services and one that is highly concentrated. In Japan, by far the largest centre is Tokyo, but in Western Europe as in North America, there are several 'top' cities, as the data in Table 7.11 show. At present the dominant centres in Western Europe are London in the UK and Geneva and Zürich in Switzerland, but Tokyo is outstanding in a global context.

Table 7.11 Value of shares managed in 1990 and 1991 (billions of US dollars)

| | Western Europe | | | North America and Japan | |
	1990	1991		1990	1991
London	365	410	Tokyo	2,192	1,812
Geneva	283	266	New York	407	421
Zürich	257	247	Boston	177	165
Paris	81	142	San Francisco	112	98
Frankfurt	73	122	Toronto	86	83
Edinburgh	63	69	Philadelphia	79	76
Basle	52	52	Los Angeles	73	74
			Chicago	68	58

Source: Bennett 1991: 21

TOURISM

While the impact of tourist activity is clearly in evidence in many areas of the EC and affects the employment and income levels of numerous regions, its influence is difficult to quantify. Tourism is a subset of all leisure activities and is closely related to travel and to the availability of the transport network and the services provided on it. Conventionally, it is distinguished from home-based recreation and day trips, and involves temporary movement to places beyond the normal places of residence and work.

McMillan-Scott (1991) was the rapporteur of a Draft Report on Community Tourism Policy in which various recommendations were made. Before these are summarised, it must be appreciated that the tourist industry in total is not explicitly allocated more than very modest funds from the EC budget, although indirectly the promotion of tourism benefits from general developments in infrastructure such as the construction of roads in remoter areas and the improvement of water supply. It also benefits from rising income levels among EC Member States.

McMillan-Scott notes:

> tourism in all its components is now the largest single industry in the European economy ... and [because of] its great importance for many of the existing policies of the EC, must now receive a much higher priority in the political concerns throughout the Community.
>
> (McMillan-Scott 1991: 8)

Various reasons are given as to why tourism is important, including the major contribution it makes to international understanding and developing awareness of other cultures, languages and ways of life, its notable share in the family budgets of many Community citizens, and its dominant position in the economy and development prospects of a growing number of regions. The dangers of over-development of tourism to settlements and to the general environment in some areas are noted, and the need to monitor tourism projects is appreciated.

It is estimated that more than 6 per cent of all full-time jobs in the EC are directly created by tourism. The data in Table 7.12 came from several sources for different years but are adequate to give a general idea of the importance of tourism to various EC countries and the direction of tourist flows. Not all the activities of the catering and recreation sectors (columns (1) and (2)) are accounted for by tourism. The large numbers employed in these sectors in the UK may be due to a broader definition. Column (3) shows a marked contrast in international tourism among the EC countries, with only a small proportion of holidays being taken abroad by citizens of the four southern countries, Italy, Greece, Spain and Portugal, and also of France, intermediate in location, while citizens of Germany and the Benelux favour holidays abroad. In this respect, the UK has an intermediate position. Overall, about two-thirds of the holidays abroad by EC Member States are taken in other EC countries. In columns (5) and (6), the number of foreign visitors is shown in relation to total population. Column (7) shows that the

Table 7.12 Tourist activities in the countries of the EC

	(1) Hotels and catering (000s)	(2) Recreation services (000s)	(3) Holidays abroad %	(4) In EC %	(5) Pop. 1987 (millions)	(6) Visitors (millions)	(7) Visitors per 100 pop.	(8) % from Europe
FRG	441	180	60	34	61.0	12.9	21	71
France	439	200*	16	11	55.6	38.3	69	86
Italy	500*	250*	13	8	57.4	54.5	95	94
Netherlands	85	62	64	46	14.6	3.3	23	73
Belgium	66	33	56	47	9.9	10.6	107	87
Luxembourg	6	2	94	69	0.4	0.8	200	91
UK	1,037	480	35	21	56.8	15.3	27	64
Ireland	36	13	51	38	3.5	2.9	83	86
Denmark	50	35	44	25	5.1	7.5	147	95
Greece	160	47	7	4	10.0	7.7	77	87
Spain	319	130	8	7	39.0	51.3	132	90
Portugal	100*	50*	8	7	10.3	6.5	63	94
EC	3,239	1,482	32	20				

Sources: UNSYB 1987, Table 13c
(1), (2) Eurostat 1989/90
(3), (4) Eurostat 1991b: 126
(5) WPDS 1987
(8) calculated from original, non-rounded values
* authors' estimates

four southern countries, but especially Spain and Portugal, reach high levels. As to be expected, given the distances involved (see column (8)) it is not surprising that a high proportion of all visitors to most EC countries are 'internal'.

In Table 7.13 the flows of tourists between the five largest Member States of the EC have been separated from total flows to illustrate the strong net flow from north to south in Western Europe. In 1985 the FRG and the UK had the largest net outflows, Italy and Spain the largest inflows; France, appropriately, had an intermediate position. The pull of the sun remains one of the prime tourist attractions. Further data on tourism in the EC can be found in Eurostat (1991c), from which the data in Table 7.14 have been summarised.

While in conventional economics tourism is a bona fide contributor to gross

Table 7.13 Movement of tourists between the five largest EC countries in 1985 (in millions)

| From | Countries of destination | | | | | |
	FRG	UK	France	Italy	Spain	Out-going
FRG	–	1.5	8.7	11.7	5.6	27.5
UK	1.2	–	5.9	1.8	5.0	13.9
France	0.7	1.6	–	8.7	11.0	22.0
Italy	0.5	0.5	2.6	–	1.0	4.6
Spain	0.2	0.3	0.9	0.5	–	1.9
In-coming	2.6	3.9	18.1	22.7	22.6	69.9
Net	−24.9	−10.0	−3.9	+18.1	+20.7	

Source: UNSYB 1985, Table 151

Table 7.14 Main countries of origin of tourists visiting EC Member States, 1989 (no data for UK or Luxembourg)

Country visited	Countries of origin (% of total visitors)						
Germany	Netherlands	18	USA	13	UK	9	
France	UK	17	Germany	15	Italy	14	
Italy	Germany	42	France	8	UK	7	
Netherlands	Germany	49	UK	11	Belgium/Lux.	7	
Belgium	Netherlands	42	Germany	15	UK	10	
Ireland	UK	61	USA	14	Germany	6	
Denmark	Germany	36	Sweden	21	Norway	11	
Greece	Germany	24	UK	20	Italy	8	
Spain	UK	32	Germany	28	France	9	
Portugal	UK	31	Germany	16	Spain	10	

Source: Eurostat 1991c: 12

Table 7.15 Tourists visiting selected non-EC countries, 1987

	Pop. 1987 (millions)	Tourists 1987 (millions)	Tourists per 100 total pop.	% from Europe
Austria	7.6	16.2	213	93
Switzerland	6.6	9.2	139	76
Sweden	8.4	6.7	80	93
Czechoslovakia	15.6	24.2	155	100
Yugoslavia	23.4	8.8	38	95
Turkey	51.4	4.2	8	75
Cyprus	0.7	1.1	157	91
Morocco	24.4	2.0	8	69
Tunisia	7.6	3.4	45	49

Source: UNSYB 1987

domestic product, it is in effect a means of redistributing income and wealth. As such, its contribution to the aim of the EC to achieve greater equality among the regions in living standards is fulfilled only if a majority of the tourists going abroad, or even travelling within their own countries, on holiday, are moving from richer to poorer areas, and if the monies spent remain in the local communities themselves. Thus if, for example, more tourists from Greece or Portugal went to Switzerland or to the French Riviera than went in the reverse direction, the redistribution process would favour richer areas. Two facts, one economic and one environmental, ensure that most of the movement will be from richer to poorer areas: the citizens of the more affluent areas on the whole are better placed financially to travel greater distances, while many of the environmentally attractive areas happen to be in the poorest regions. Tourist destinations tend, however, to be concentrated quite locally, and may lead to marked regional contrasts, as for example between, on the one hand, many seaside resorts in Italy and on the Mediterranean coast of Spain that benefit in job creation from tourism and, on the other, much poorer settlements in the mountain areas behind.

The prospect for the 1990s seems to be more of the same, with faster train services, a yet more integrated motorway system, and lower air fares, all tempting people to go further afield when they go on holiday. The data in Table 7.15 show that many non-EC countries already have tourist industries of importance. Their entry into the EC could deflect some tourists from their present choices.

FURTHER READING

Eurostat (1991a) *A Social Portrait of Europe*, Luxembourg: Office for Official Publications of the European Communities.

—— (1991b) *Le Tourisme en Europe, tendances 1989*, Luxembourg: Office des publications officielles des Communautés Européennes.

8

TRANSPORT

TRANSPORT POLICY AND NETWORKS

Europe is one of the most densely populated regions of the world and also one of the most developed economically. It therefore needs a very sophisticated system of transport and communications to move people, goods and information as quickly and cheaply as possible, under given technological, organisational and geographical constraints. The emergence of the European Community and the accompanying reduction in the influence of national boundaries has made it necessary to merge and to reshape the systems of the 12 sovereign states, particularly near their common frontiers.

Although in Article 3 of the Treaty of Rome the creation of a common transport policy was one of the primary objectives for the EC, the implementation of the more detailed rules in Articles 74–84 has not led to such a policy even 35 years later. EC competition rules, and provisions governing state aid, have also been difficult to apply in a sector which is so highly characterised by the state ownership of networks, and by monopolies. The potential direct and indirect influence of the EC on the future of transport can, however, be seen in many ways. There are plans for a Community Railway Policy (see COM 89-564, 1990: 27), visions of a comprehensive motorway network linking all places of importance into an integrated system, pressure on airlines to lower fares on intra-EC flights, and proposals for new inland waterway links. The Treaty of Maastricht also introduced the concept of Trans-European networks in transport, telecommunications and energy infrastructures (EPU Title XIII). In practice, only a very small part of the EC budget is used to fund specific improvements in the transport network.

Unlike the USA and the former USSR, the EC has inherited a transport system based on the varied needs and policies of many countries. In particular, the layout of the railways and roads in the Community reflects national economic and in some cases strategic needs dating back a century or more. To be sure, even before the First World War, international trains were running. The 1930s was, however, characterised by much suspicion between some of the present EC countries, especially France and Germany, and by limited contacts. During the

172

Second World War, Germany for a time organised transport for its own needs in areas it occupied in Western and Central Europe.

Since the Second World War, the movement of goods and people between Member States of the EC has increased enormously. Even so, in a report to the European Parliament, Romera states:

> the absence of European transport infrastructure networks commensurate with users' requirements results in major costs to the European economy ... if this situation continues, the objective of completing a genuine internal market may be jeopardised because of the saturation of the infrastructure and the collapse of the different modal systems. ... the present situation, where transport infrastructure is conceived as being a national issue, means that there are no true European networks and ... it is therefore essential that the problems of continuity and compatibility between these national networks is resolved at Community level if they are to be operational at all.
>
> (Romera 1991: 5)

Attention has been drawn in a number of EC publications to neglect of the transport sector in the Member States of the EC in the last two decades. The fact that investment in land transport infrastructure fell by about 22 per cent in real terms during 1974–84 and from 1.5 to 0.9 per cent of the total GDP of the Member States is evidence of this trend. There may however have been reasons, connected for example with the oil crisis of the 1970s and an attempt to use present capacity more efficiently. Given that 90 per cent of EC trade with the rest of the world and 30 per cent of intra-Community trade is through seaports, it follows that sea transport, like land transport, should not be forgotten. Lack of funding for the transport system of the EC can be blamed among other things for a high level of accidents on the roads and for ecological damage. Delays on roads and in the flow of air traffic have been variously estimated to add around 10 per cent to transport costs in the Community.

The 1990s promise to be a period of major changes in the EC. The increasing movement of people and goods by land resulting from the completion of the Internal Market could result in an increase of about 35 per cent in traffic during 1988–2000, with traffic in the year 2000 at twice the 1975 level. The annual increase in the 1980s of 2.5 per cent per year in the movement of goods and 3.1 per cent in the movement of passengers has not been matched by improvements in infrastructure. In the 1990s an increase of about 50 per cent in the traffic between the EC and the countries of Central Europe is also expected. Meanwhile, the 1980s saw the accession to the EC of new Member States with transport infrastructures greatly inferior to those in the existing Member States. In the longer term, an overall increase of about 50 per cent in traffic is expected during 1990–2010, with road traffic growing by 74 per cent, inland waterway traffic by 8 per cent, but rail declining by 4 per cent.

In spite of the expected stagnation in the volume of rail traffic, investment in the rail system of the EC is expected to need the following amounts at 1989 prices: 1991–5, 28 billion ECU; 1996–2000, 39 billion ECU; after 2000, 17 billion ECU. The creation of a high-speed train network would cost 150 billion ECU over 20 years: 100 billion for infrastructure, 50 billion for rolling stock. The proposed Advanced Integrated Motorway System would require 25–30 billion ECU between 1990 and 2000. Altogether, land transport improvements would need an investment of 32–40 billion ECU per year. Another complication that could influence the amount of future road and rail passenger traffic is the prospect of the liberalisation of air services and the lowering of fares. This would be good news for air travellers, but likely to lead to increasing congestion in the air space over Western Europe.

At present, the EC has neither the legal nor the financial instruments to guarantee the consistency and continuity of the various types of specific local aid granted in the transport infrastructure sector. There are proposals to set up an infrastructure fund which could be financed by the revenue from a tax on energy consumption, bringing in 19 billion ECU per year. Unless a comprehensive view is taken of the transport needs of the whole Community, increased privatisation of many parts of the system could result in the neglect of links in sparsely populated and peripheral areas, where traffic is limited in scale, although vital for the existence of many settlements. The views expressed above about the transport system of the EC imply yet another shift of financial resources, power and decision-making from the 12 national governments to the EC level.

In the rest of this chapter, attention is focused on the spatial layout of the transportation system of the EC and on geographical features that will influence future policy-making and investment. With much of the territory situated in peninsulas (Italy, Iberia, Denmark) or islands (the UK, effectively Greece, Sicilia and many others), direct distances between many major centres of population are greatly extended by detours (e.g. Rome–Barcelona), while the travel time by road and rail on some journeys is increased by major sea and mountain obstacles. Selected prominent cities and clusters of cities in Western and Central Europe are shown in Figure 8.1 and 'corridors' representing the general direction of major traffic flows are indicated (rather than specific road and rail links). The main sea barriers are also shown.

Spatial aspects of the transport system are affected by two distinct sets of problems: that of integrating remote and/or peripheral areas (e.g. Ireland, Greece, Sardegna) into the Community system, and that of facilitating movement through heavily used corridors carrying long-distance or transit traffic as well as local traffic (e.g. the Rhine valley, several key Swiss and Austrian passes over the Alps, now mostly shortened by tunnels, and Kent, located between the entrance to the Channel Tunnel and London). Routes in peripheral areas have tended to be neglected because they mostly carry traffic originating in those areas and mostly terminating there, and are therefore less congested than routes in more central areas, except in particular seasons, such as the summer holiday period in some

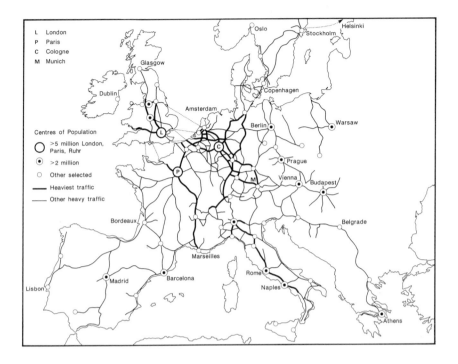

Figure 8.1 Generalised representation of main road traffic flows in Western and Central Europe. The map is based on a more detailed map in which various levels of traffic flow, from less than 1,000 vehicles per day to over 120,000 per day, are shown. The detail has been simplified to distinguish flows of over about 40,000 vehicles per day. Flows of less than about 5,000 vehicles per day have been ignored. Although the original map shows traffic on 'main international traffic arteries', most is either local or internal regional

Source: Economic Commission for Europe 1991, Map 11, Census of Motor Traffic on Main International Traffic Arteries

areas. Examples of such areas are Bretagne in France, the Southwest in the UK, northern Denmark, and Sicilia in Italy.

A study (see European Communities 1988) has been made of the islands of the EC and the problems that arise from their relative isolation through both their peripheral locations and the extra travel time needed by land traffic on journeys to or from the mainland. The Channel Tunnel and the three fixed links planned to join Sjaelland (and Copenhagen) to Sweden, mainland Denmark (via Fyn) and Germany, are the outstanding projects to speed up transit in the 1990s over sea obstacles. Greece is the most peripheral country of the EC, but the strait of Otranto is too wide ever to be crossed by a fixed link, so any substantial shortening of the travel time between Greece and the rest of the Community depends on improving the quality of the main motorway across Yugoslavia from Austria to the Greek border.

It is notoriously difficult to forecast the flow of traffic over new links in a transport system. For example, within weeks of opening in 1986, many stretches of the M25 London Orbital Motorway were carrying considerably more traffic than was forecast for 1993. The capacity of the Channel Tunnel could be tested very soon in the same way, possibly through heavier than expected 'local' traffic between Nord-Pas-de-Calais and Kent.

A rough estimate of expected traffic on different links in a system can be obtained through the use of the gravity model, according to which the expected traffic flow between a pair of places is related to their population sizes and to the distance apart (empirically, actually roughly the square of the distance). Thus London, Paris and the Rhein–Ruhr conurbation are mega-cities, relatively close to one another, and much more traffic would therefore be expected between them than, for example, between Dublin and Naples, or between Bordeaux and Hamburg, which are smaller and much further apart. Some places, however, generate more traffic than would be expected simply according to their population size and particular location, whether, for example, they are centres of heavy industry, using large quantities of fuel and raw materials, or national capitals and popular tourist areas, generating more business or holiday traffic than average.

Railways and roads serve a wide range of users, but other modes, including pipelines and electricity transmission lines, have a specialised and limited function. Specialised forms of transport, among the most notable of which are the movement of water, oil and gas by pipeline, of electricity and information by power lines and telegraph, and broadcasting, must be considered in relation to the particular sectors of the economy that they serve.

RAIL TRANSPORT

During the second half of the nineteenth century, the railways grew to prominence in Europe as the main form of land transport, leaving rivers, canals and roads with a secondary role. In Western Europe almost all cities and towns, and many villages, were on or within a short distance of a railway station. After the First World War, road and air increasingly challenged the dominance of the railways.

The rail systems of the countries of Europe are now mostly heavily subsidised and, strictly speaking, few routes would survive if rail traffic had to make a profit. According to Olins and Lorenz (1992), the level of subsidy varies greatly from one EC country to another, with the following values in millions of pound sterling per 1,000 km of line in 1989: Britain 38, France 93, the Netherlands 133, FRG 134, Belgium 217, Italy 378. While a rail company has to construct, maintain and operate the track on which it runs its services, road vehicles use public roads, to which the various taxes levied on road users contribute only a limited share. In reality, road users are therefore also subsidised. Thus, for example, long-distance coach services can generally apparently be operated far more cheaply than rail services. Another advantage to road over rail transport is its flexibility. Thanks to the enormous extent of the system of roads in Western Europe, door-to-door journeys are possible virtually between any pair of buildings, commercial or residential.

The route length of railway in each of the main countries of Europe is shown in Table 8.1, together with those for the Maghreb, the USA and Japan. In most of the EC and EFTA countries, lines have been closed in recent decades, and it may be assumed that systems are adequate for present needs. In France and the FRG, however, special new tracks have been built for high-speed passenger trains. Dependence on the railways is greater in Central Europe than in Western Europe due to the limited number of motor vehicles in use and inferior road networks, and there have been few closures of railways. In the USSR the construction of new lines continued until the end of the 1980s as new areas were opened up and short-cut links inserted in the network.

The proportion of each rail network that is electrified (see Table 8.1, col.(3)), is to some extent a measure of the sophistication of the system, but most of the countries with a large proportion of electrified track were without their own supplies of coal (e.g. Switzerland, Norway, Sweden, Italy) and had a greater incentive to convert from steam to electric traction as supplies of hydro-electric power became available. In general, the electrification of a route is only realistic if traffic is relatively heavy, even if the whole system is subsidised. Given the above

Table 8.1 Railways in European and other selected countries, mainly for 1987

	(1) Railway route in km (total)	(2) (electric)	(3) %		(1) Railway route in km (total)	(2) (electric)	(3) %
FRG	27,484	11,433	42	Sweden	11,673	7,464	64
GDR	14,008	3,092	22	Finland	5,905	1,445	24
France	34,647	11,692	34	Poland	26,824	9,978	37
Italy	19,563	10,376	53	Hungary	13,145	1,920	15
Netherlands	2,817	1,841	65	Czechoslovakia	13,102	3,715	28
Belgium/Lux.	3,888	2,069	53	Bulgaria	4,297	2,342	55
UK	16,670	4,154	25	Romania	11,275	3,411	30
Ireland	1,944	–	0	Yugoslavia	9,283	3,534	38
Denmark	2,471	199	8	USSR	145,600	50,600	35
Greece	2,479	–	0	Turkey	8,401	0	0
Spain	14,218	6,914	45	Algeria	3,761	298	8
Portugal	3,607	458	13	Morocco	1,779	869	49
Austria	5,767	3,129	54	Tunisia	2,192	0	0
Switzerland	5,016	2,969	59	USA	296,497	n.a.	n.a.
Norway	4,217	2,448	58	Japan	26,620	12,933	49

Source: Calendario Atlante De Agostini 1990, Istituto Geografico De Agostini, Novara
Note: n.a. not available

reservations about the significance of electrification, it is evident from the data that of the principal industrial countries in Western Europe, the UK lags behind the rest. As for Central Europe and the USSR, the generally smaller proportion of routes electrified reflects a slower process of modernisation. Almost everywhere in Europe, diesel traction has replaced steam traction on non-electrified routes.

The movement of freight by rail has fluctuated considerably in most European countries this century. In most countries of Western Europe, the great increase in the road haulage of freight since the Second World War has resulted in a reduction in the use of railways. Among the larger EC countries, freight traffic (in tonne/kilometres) peaked in France and the FRG in the mid-1970s. In the UK and Italy, there has been a gradual decline since a peak actually reached during the Second World War. In Spain, however, growth was considerable until the 1980s. In spite of hopes that congestion on the roads might be eased by the greater use of the railways for passenger traffic, between 1953 and 1985 the passenger/kilometres carried by rail in the EC increased by less than 20 per cent, from 153 billion to 181 billion, while that on the roads increased several times. At the other end of Europe a completely different situation is found in the former USSR. The tonne/kilometres of traffic carried by rail is far greater than that moved in the EC, and the growth of traffic has been no less massive, at least until 1990. Between 1953 and 1985 the total tonne/kilometres of goods carried increased about five times and total passenger/ kilometres over three times.

The creation of an integrated rail system for the whole of Europe, with uniform conditions throughout, may seem desirable, but even now that barriers to movement within Western Europe and between west and east are expected to be reduced, technical differences make the unimpeded fast movement of trains impossible. Spain and Portugal in the west and the former USSR in the east have different gauges of track from the rest of Europe, while variations in other dimensions, such as the height of tunnels, cause problems elsewhere. Even so, through passenger services have long been provided between various European countries (see Figure 8.2). For example, many well-known named expresses have for decades carried passengers from the northern cities of the EC to resorts on the French and Italian Rivieras and to cultural centres such as Venice, Florence and Rome. Many of these services cross Switzerland. With the addition of the six newer Member States of the EC since 1973, new problems of integration of the railway systems have arisen since all six are more peripheral than the original six countries, southern Italy excepted.

Figure 8.2 shows the lines on which international through services run. Examples are the Paris–Madrid Talgo, which takes advantage of some TGV (train à grande vitesse) track, making the journey in 12 hours, including an adjustment of wheel sets at the border; the Italia Express, Dortmund to Rome, 18 hours, via Switzerland; and the slower Simplon Express Paris–Belgrade, 25 hours. Such Euro-City and similar expresses linking major urban concentrations at some distance apart usually run overnight, and include sleeping coaches and couchettes. They tend to depart and arrive at convenient times to avoid using

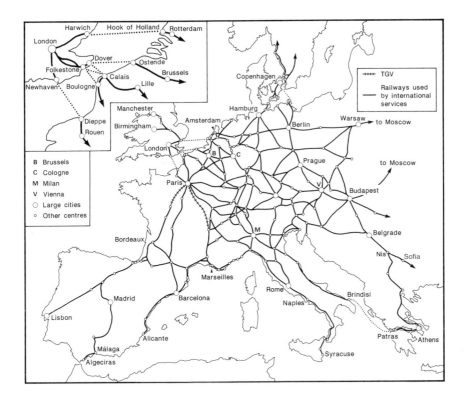

Figure 8.2 Lines used by through international train services in Western and Central Europe, and connections, 1991

Source: Thomas Cook 1991: 50–1

working hours for travel, thereby giving them the possibility of competing with journeys on the same routes in a much shorter time by air.

As will be shown later in this chapter (see 'Passenger traffic', p. 192), even to retain present levels of passenger traffic, let alone recapture medium- and longer-distance passenger travellers from road and air, the railways of the EC will have to provide much faster services on many routes. Additional subsidies will undoubtedly be required to keep down fares, already regarded in some Western European countries as too high, particularly for the quality of the second-class accommodation. The future of longer-distance rail travel in the EC may be seen in the French model. The lines carrying the TGV are Paris–Lyons and Paris–Tours. The Paris–Tours distance is 235 km in length; the 232 km from Paris to St Pierre-des-Corps just outside Tours is covered in 56 minutes, at a speed of 249 km/h (155 mph). The distance from Paris to Lyons (Part-Dieu) is 427 km, covered in 120 minutes, at a speed of 213 km/h. As with the Shinkansen services in Japan, special tracks, without the presence of slow passenger or freight trains, allow trains to travel at speeds of about twice those averaged on many conventional main lines in Western Europe.

The proposed high-speed rail network needed to serve Western Europe with a competitive rail system in the twenty-first century is shown in Figure 8.3. Its completion is estimated to need 20 years. In order to get the process moving and achieve rapid results, according to COM 89-564, the routes indicated with a heavy line in Figure 8.3 should be given priority, typically reflecting Community rather than national thinking:

> These projects, which are also interlinked by the French TGV line from Paris to Lyon, represent excellent coverage of Community territory, since nine out of the twelve Member States are involved. They also have the merit of presenting totally different geographical and economic features.
>
> (COM 89-564, 1990: 27)

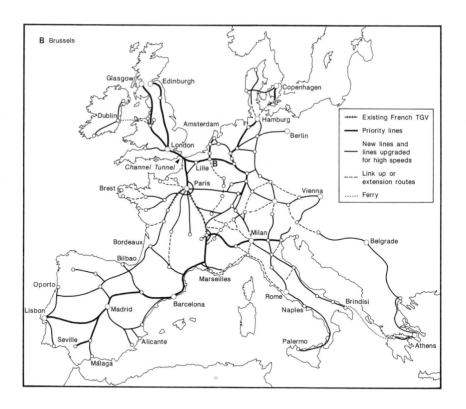

Figure 8.3 The proposed high-speed rail network for Europe

Source: COM 89-564 (1990: 31). This map has appeared in various publications, usually with differences in detail

Given the rapidity of political, economic and technological change in Europe at present, and financial constraints, the completion by 2010 of the ambitious system described above seems very ambitious. Dynes (1992) notes ominous disparities at this early stage. French high-speed trains cannot run on German tracks because the power supply is different, while German trains cannot use French tracks because they are too heavy. If the desultory progress on the transport infrastructure in the last 20 years is a guide, some drastic changes in priorities and funding are needed.

ROAD TRANSPORT

In contrast to rail transport, road transport in Western Europe has expanded enormously since the Second World War. In the former CMEA countries, expansion has also taken place, but more slowly. The rapid expansion of road transport in the present EC countries can be gauged from the tenfold growth in the number of passenger cars in use from 10,570,000 in 1955 to 108,270,000 in 1985 (see Figure 8.4). The rate of growth ranged from less than five times in the UK, to almost fifty times in Spain and Portugal, and more than sixty times in Greece. In Central Europe, the relative growth has been even faster, but the absolute number of cars in use in the 1950s was minute. The trend in the number of commercial vehicles in use throughout Europe has roughly matched that of passenger cars.

One way of measuring the level of motorisation of a region is to calculate the number of vehicles for a given number of people. In column (5) of Table 8.2 the number of passenger cars in use in each country is shown per 1,000 inhabitants. The FRG is the most highly motorised country in Europe, with 460 cars per 1,000 people, but it has some way to go to reach the US level of 560. Greece and Portugal are the least motorised countries in the EC, at not much more than a quarter of the German level. In Central Europe, car ownership is generally well below the Western European level and in Romania below that in many developing countries. In the USSR the level of car ownership is about one-tenth of that in the more affluent countries of the EC and EFTA.

In 1985 there seemed little sign of a reduction in the rate of the growth of car ownership, except in Belgium/Luxembourg. In view of the problems associated with increased road traffic in Western Europe and the greater involvement of Central Europe in the EC, it is relevant to estimate approximately the number of motor vehicles likely to be in circulation in the next two decades. The data in Table 8.2 show estimates of the number of cars in the year 2005 if the levels of car ownership per 1,000 inhabitants as follows are reached:

Column (2): 350, the UK level of the mid-1980s.
Column (3): 500, a possible ceiling for the FRG.

To reach a hypothetical saturation of 500 cars per 1,000 inhabitants by the year 2005, the number of cars in use in the EC and EFTA would have to increase from

181

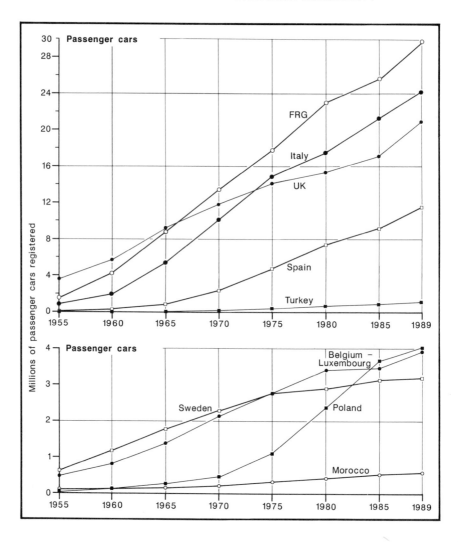

Figure 8.4 Passenger cars registered in selected countries of Europe, and Morocco, 1955–89

Source: various years of UNSYB, and Eurostat 1991: 293, for 1989 data

about 140 million in 1990 to about 190 million in the year 2005 – an increase of 36 per cent. In this scenario about 3.3 million new cars would have to be absorbed annually for the next 15 years, enough to exacerbate existing problems, always assuming that the same average distance is driven. The forecasts of Wijsenbeek (1991), referred to in Chapter 6, of 463 per 1,000 population in the EC in the early 1990s and 515 in 2010 are close to the higher estimate in Table

8.2 but are only the average, and the regional disparities will inevitably still be very marked. The picture is quite different in Central Europe, where the present 17 million cars would have to increase to about 54 million, more than a threefold increase. For the former USSR to achieve a level of car ownership of 500 per 1,000 inhabitants (with a 15 per cent increase in its total population assumed), the 13 million cars at present would have to be increased more than 14 times in the next 15 years. For Turkey and the Maghreb countries to achieve such a high level, the number of cars would have to increase (unthinkably) about 28 times. Such astronomical increases make it highly unlikely that Central Europe and the former USSR could become as highly motorised by 2005 even as Western Europe was in the 1960s.

The estimates given above show the enormous disparities in car ownership in Europe between Western Europe, Central Europe and the former USSR. Before Western European motor vehicle manufacturers begin to weigh up the potential markets in the former CMEA countries, they should question whether economic growth there is likely to sustain a substantially higher level of car ownership, whether roads and servicing facilities could be improved quickly enough to do so, and what price the former partners of the USSR will be paying for oil now that supplies will no longer be sold at favourable prices for CMEA currencies. In

Table 8.2 Possible numbers of passenger cars in circulation in the year 2005 in selected countries

	(1) Cars 1990 (millions)	(2) Millions of cars in 2005 at 350 per 1,000	(3) at 500 per 1,000	(4) Increase in millions 1990–2005	(5) Cars per 1,000 people 1990
FRG	30	< 30	33	3	460
France	24	< 24	31	7	392
Italy	25	< 25	32	7	391
Benelux	9	9	13	4	350
UK/Ireland	23	23	33	10	345
Rest of EC[1]	15	21	30	7	250
Austria/Switzerland	6	<6	8	2	380
Scandinavia	7	<7	9	2	375
GDR/Czech./Hungary	9	17.5	25	14	180
Poland/Bulgaria/Romania	5	25	36	31	70
Yugoslavia	3	9	12	9	125
USSR	13	130[2]	182[2]	174	40
Turkey	1.2	27[3]	39[3]	38	20
Maghreb	1.5	27[3]	39[3]	37	25

Notes: 1 Denmark, Greece, Spain, Portugal
2 probable increase in population allowed for
3 30% increase in population assumed

Plate 17 Example of a village ill-adapted for heavy motor vehicles. Here, in a village in Lombardia, north Italy, a tanker is emerging with difficulty through the old arch of a farmyard while a lorry manoeuvres along the narrow village street

addition, Central Europe and the former USSR already have acute environmental problems, especially of pollution in urban areas, where most of the extra vehicles would be concentrated.

In spite of great improvements in the quality of many trunk roads in the EC, especially with the construction of motorways, the actual length of road in use has not increased greatly since the 1950s. The density of vehicles per unit of road distance has therefore grown almost as quickly as the number of vehicles in use. Saturation is likely to be reached in some regions of the EC long before it is reached in other areas. Typically, perhaps, the Community imagination and vision of road transport is focused above all on upgrading and extending the present motorway system, although many schemes of a more local nature, especially to by-pass larger settlements and to assist in the integration of remote and peripheral areas, are also considered. Some new developments may, however, be prevented through increasing EC concern over the negative impact on the environment. Environmental impact assessments are now required under EC law before major projects are approved, and recent controversy has arisen in several Member States due to the failure of authorities to conduct such studies. Examples include new roads in the UK, the tunnel/bridge projects in Denmark, and various motorways in Italy and France.

The motorway map of Western and Central Europe is shown in Figure 8.5. The numerous apparent gaps are in practice all closed by main roads not of motorway status or standard. Proposed new motorways in France are indicated.

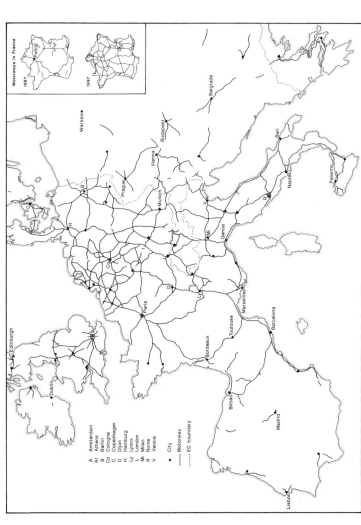

Figure 8.5 The motorways of Europe, 1990. Note that the definition of motorway varies somewhat between countries and that many roads without motorway status are of a high standard. On this map only motorways are shown, but gaps in the system are of course completed by non-motorway roads. The inset map shows plans for further motorway construction in France by 1997

Source: P and O-European Ferries and AA *Europe Road Atlas* (1990), pp. IV–V

Eventually it could be possible to drive on motorway standard roads between any pair of major centres in the EC, with drive-on train passage on some routes across the Alps, as through the Channel Tunnel.

The increasing integration of the road system in the EC in particular and in Europe in general has led to a synthetic, one might even say cosmetic, operation proposed by the United Nations to renumber the main roads of the continent, as shown in Figure 8.6. There is some resemblance to the concept of the earlier US Interstate Highway System, which, however, had a strategic basis as well as a civilian value. In Europe the roads are much too untidy in their layout to form the basis for the imposition of a North American-style grid. Indeed, many of the trunk roads in Europe evolved over centuries, and reflect the location of the capital cities and national boundaries of some 30 different countries. Many busy routes run more NW–SE or NE–SW than in the N–S or E–W routes on which the numbering is based. The system of numbering of the E roads is therefore not compatible with the previous numbering on a national base. To number trunk roads radially from the national capital, as is the practice in most countries, is hardly realistic in the EC as a whole, let alone in the whole of Europe, because a central point, a symbolic capital of the new Europe, such as Brussels, would have to be explicitly recognised.

Attention has been drawn to the E road numbering more for its significance as an attempt at European integration than as an administrative device of importance at present. In some European countries, however (e.g. Spain, Portugal, Belgium), E numbers are widely displayed on road signs alongside national road numbers, whereas in other countries (e.g. UK) E numbering is unknown.

AIR AND WATER TRANSPORT

Air transport

Like road traffic, air traffic in Western Europe has grown greatly since the Second World War right through to the late 1980s. All the major airports of the EC handle three types of traffic – internal, intra-EC, and extra-EC – some of the latter with other European countries, some intercontinental. The data for passenger and goods traffic in Table 8.3 are for all three types. In Figure 8.7 the busiest 20 airports or groups of airports in the EC are shown, together with the busiest routes flown in Western Europe.

Of the 20 busiest cities for passenger air traffic in the EC (see Table 8.3), 16 are in the top 20 also for freight. Nine of the 12 EC capitals are in the top 20 for passenger traffic, while two others, Dublin and Lisbon, are ranked 22nd and 23rd, and Luxembourg figures prominently in freight traffic. Paris and London are outstanding centres of air traffic, each having within their hinterlands about 15 million people, including many of the most affluent. Germany has no such

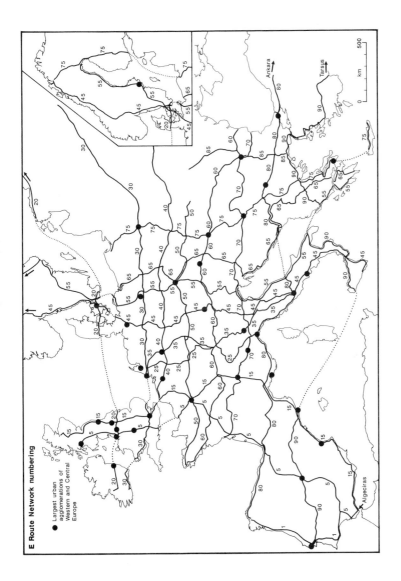

Figure 8.6 The top level of E-numbered routes in Europe. Only north–south roads ending in 0 (zero) and east–west roads ending in 5 are shown on this map (as well as E1 in West Iberia). Only some of the E-roads are motorways. Dotted lines show either ferry links (e.g. E30 Hook of Holland–Harwich) or notional links (e.g. E90 Barcelona–Sicilia).

Table 8.3 Busiest airports of the EC, 1988

| | Special function | Passengers | | | Freight | |
		Rank	Millions	Annual growth 1983–8	Rank	Tonnes (000s)
London[1]	C	1	60	10	2	863
Paris[2]	C	2	41	7	3	814
Frankfurt		3	25	10	1	1,007
Amsterdam	C	4	15	11	4	575
Rome	C	5	15	6	6	202
Madrid	C	6	14	7	7	179
Palma (Spain)	T	7	12	7	small	small
Copenhagen	C	8	12	8	8	155
Athens	C	9	11	4	12	93
Düsseldorf		10	10	9	18	42
Milan[3]		11	10	8	9	142
Manchester		12	10	19	13	77
Munich		13	10	13	16	47
Barcelona		14	8	7	15	56
Brussels	C	15	6	6	5	234
Las Palmas (Spain)	T	16	6	10	19	38
Hamburg		17	6	8	20	35
Tenerife (Spain)	T	18	6	10	small	small
Malaga	T	19	5	6	small	small
Nice	T	20	5	6	small	small
Dublin	C	22	4	15	17	43
Lisbon	C	23	4	6	14	65
Luxembourg	C	59	1	10	10	114
Cologne		n.a.	n.a.	n.a.	11	108

Source: Commission of the EC 1990
Notes: 1 total of Heathrow, Gatwick and Stansted
     2 total of Orly and Charles de Gaulle
     3 total of Linate and Malpensa
     C Capital
     T Tourist
     n.a. not available

single concentration since the former capital, Bonn, was served by Düsseldorf and Cologne, while Frankfurt is the principal airport and focus of trans-continental flights. As its new capital, Berlin should soon figure prominently among European airports. The strong positions of Amsterdam (hub for KLM), Rome, Madrid, and Copenhagen (hub for SAS) may be seen. The other principal airports in the EC are either major regional centres, each serving an area with several million people (e.g. Milan, Manchester, Munich) or centres of resort regions (e.g. Palma in Mallorca, Tenerife in the Canarias, and Nice on the French Riviera).

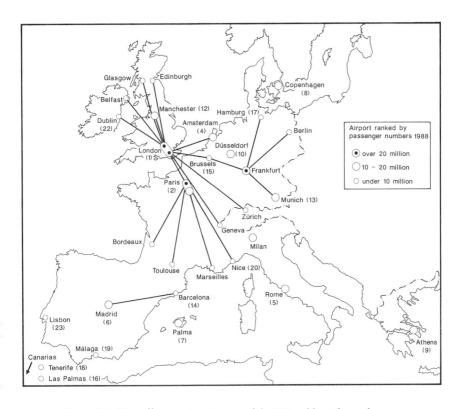

Airport ranked by
passenger numbers 1988

- ● over 20 million
- ◐ 10 – 20 million
- ○ under 10 million

Figure 8.7 Air traffic at major airports of the EC and heavily used routes

The busiest air routes, shown in Figure 8.7, have hitherto usually been served by the national carriers of the countries concerned, with agreements on the sharing of services, usually on a one-to-one basis, and with the pooling of revenues. Less busy and lucrative scheduled routes are usually left to other carriers, which also handle much of the charter business. So long as the national carriers have a monopoly or near monopoly of the main services, fares can be kept high. Only when a major road or rail improvement is introduced do air fares need to be adjusted downwards to compete. For example, the Paris–Lyons TGV rail service makes rail travel between the two cities more attractive than air travel for many people, while the introduction of a fast rail service between Paris or Brussels and London via the Channel Tunnel could have the same effect.

While the above improvements in land links compete with certain air services, the relaxing of constraints on air traffic routes could produce a substantial reduction in air fares throughout Europe, making them more comparable with US internal air fares. While conditions such as availability of air space may be somewhat less favourable in Western Europe than in the USA, the average disparity in pence per mile between four return fares in the EC and four comparable

Table 8.4 Comparison of air fares in the EC and the USA, 1991

	Distance (miles)	Fare (£)	Pence per mile	Ratio (US=100)
Birmingham–Paris	309	142	46.0	368
San Francisco–Los Angeles	337	42	12.5	
London–Athens	1,486	254	17.1	214
Dallas–San Francisco	1,465	117	8.0	
London–Nice	645	201	31.2	166
Dallas–Denver	645	121	18.8	
London–Brussels	206	118	57.3	140
New York–Washington	215	88	40.9	

Source: Birrell and Skipworth 1991

distances in the USA (see Table 8.4) showed the US fares to be less than half those in the EC. There is strong resistance from most Member States to Commission proposals to bring air transport under EC competition rules, but increasing consumer demand and pressure from smaller airlines is likely to push improvements through. The probable effect of greatly reduced EC air fares could be to neutralise much of the gain expected by rail traffic from the costly and laborious construction of a European high-speed system. On the other hand, a proposal to treat all flights between pairs of EC Member States as internal flights, liable to VAT tax, as with domestic flights in most Member States now, would work in the opposite direction. The distribution of passenger travellers among road, rail and air services will be discussed in more detail later (see p. 192).

Sea and inland waterway transport

In Figure 8.8 a distinction should be made between journeys that go all or most of the way by water and those that take the shortest appropriate sea crossing by ferry to link islands to the continent (e.g. Sicilia–Italy), islands to each other (e.g. Ireland to Great Britain) or to cross straits (e.g. Brindisi to Patras, Helsinki to Stockholm). The northern and southern sea routes of the EC each provide useful, reasonably direct access between pairs of ports (e.g. Hamburg–Bilbao, Barcelona–Athens) but in relation to direct distances and land routes, any journey between northern and southern ports is increased by the doubling-back effect. Thus, for example, internal shipping between Bilbao and Barcelona in Spain has to travel about 2,500 km compared with about one-fifth of that distance for land transport by road or rail. The distance from Le Havre to

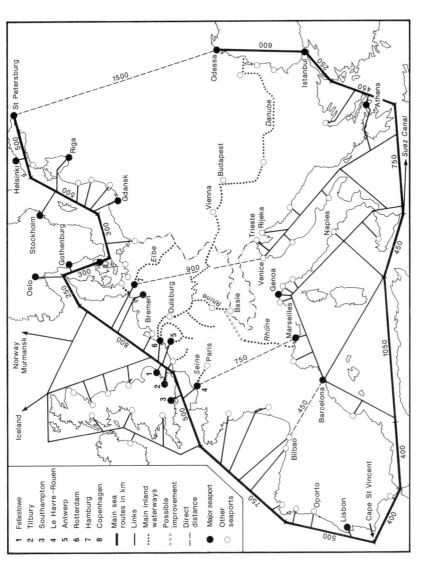

Figure 8.8 Sea and inland waterway routes, and ports of Europe

Note: Distances in kilometres

Plate 18 Reminders of early forms of transport: a canal and a railway viaduct near Llangollen, Wales

Marseilles is 3,350 km against 750, and that from Hamburg to Venice 6,100 km against 900.

Rivers and canals penetrate a long way inland into some parts of Europe. The Rhine and its tributaries provide inland navigation in six countries: the three Benelux countries, Germany, France and Switzerland. Navigation on the Danube reaches into Germany and the river serves places in Austria, Czechoslovakia, Hungary, Yugoslavia, Romania, Bulgaria and the Ukraine. Coastal shipping and inland waterway routes are the sector of the total transport system least likely to change greatly in the next two or three decades apart from the impact of the Rhine–Main–Danube Canal linking the two largest river basins of Europe outside Russia, an engineering feat no less impressive than the Channel Tunnel.

PASSENGER TRAFFIC

As a result of the very dense networks of road, rail and air routes, travellers in the EC often have several possible modes of transport to choose from when planning to make a journey. Since the majority of families in the Community own at least one car, the choice for many people is between private car, coach, rail and air. The choice of mode, therefore, depends to a large extent on the speed of travel and the distance to be covered. Distance can be measured in a straight line; according to the road or rail distance; by time; by cost; or even by convenience. In the study made by the authors that follows, time is used to represent distance, although the relative cost of different modes might outweigh an advantage in time among less affluent travellers.

Most public service journeys (coach, train, plane) can be divided into discrete 'legs'. For example, time on a rail journey would include travel from the place of origin of the journey to a station, waiting for a train to leave, the train journey itself, waiting for transport at the destination station, and journey to destination. To illustrate the data used in this study, the calculations of travel times for two journeys, Paris–Lyons and Paris–Milan, one internal, one international, are shown in Table 8.5. Even though components of each journey have been simplified, it is evident that a large number of influences and variables must be considered. Some time additional to the main journey will be spent in almost all travel. While very short journeys will be made on foot or by bicycle, most comparatively short journeys will be made by car or bus, except those by rail on a metro or suburban train service in larger cities. In contrast, on most journeys over a considerable distance, air will be preferred.

Table 8.6 compares ten selected journeys and shows the information needed to construct the graph in Figure 8.9, giving the relationship between the three modes of travel: road, rail and air. In Figure 8.9 the angles of the three lines reflect the average speed of travel on a journey. The points at which the lines intersect the vertical axis are related to the combined time taken before and after the actual main journey is made. For simplicity, no such delay is counted for road, since it is assumed to be door-to-door. For rail, 60 minutes are allowed, while for air two variants are used, internal flights 150 minutes, international 180 minutes. The average speed of road travel is 60 km/h, of rail travel 100 km/h and of air 600 km/h. In all these modes, time is measured against *direct* distances, whereas in reality there is always some additional distance to be covered through curves, detours and delays (e.g. waiting at ferry crossings, circling above airports) which make the actual journey longer in distance and time than the ideal.

The clear message from the relationship between the lines on the graph in Figure 8.9 is that improvements in the road network of the EC would extend the length of journeys on which road travel would usually be preferred, at the expense of rail travel. A heavy tax on motor fuel and/or an increase in the tax paid for car ownership would have the reverse effect. A heroic effort to increase radically the speed of travel on as many main-line rail routes as possible would improve the position of rail in relation to both road and air. An increase in the speed of aircraft would make little difference to the situation (because time in the air is only a small to moderate part of the total journey on many EC routes), whereas the increased use of airports near the centre of a large city (e.g. the Santos Dumont Airport in Rio de Janeiro, London City Airport in the Docklands) would lower the non-travel threshold for air on the time axis. Flights from London City Airport can reach places 1,600 km distant, thus taking in most of Western and Central Europe. A drastic cut in air fares relative to travel costs or fares by road and rail would threaten rail considerably on longer rail journeys. In general, then, road and air are not in competition, but rail occupies the 'middle distance' between the two, and it is reasonable to infer that unless the costly

Table 8.5 Calculation of travel time on two journeys: Paris–Lyons and Paris–Milan (travel times are in minutes)

	(1) Distance km	(2) Built-up area initial time	(3) Await vehicle	(4) Travel	(5) Leave vehicle	(6) Built-up area	(7) Total time	(8) Speed km/h	(9) Time air=100
Paris to Lyons	400								
Road	461	30	–	310	–	15	355	68	182
Rail (TGV)	427	30	20	120	–	15	185	130	95
Air	(400)	60	30	60	15	30	195	123	100
Paris to Milan	628								
Road	838	30	–	570	–	15	615	61	246
Rail	821	30	20	515	–	15	580	65	232
Air	(628)	60	60	85	15	30	250	151	100

Notes per column:

(1) Road and rail distances exceed direct distance. In reality the distance flown by aircraft also considerably exceeds the direct distance on shorter journeys

(2), (6) Allowance for average time getting through built-up area to fast road 30 minutes for very large city, 15 for smaller one; likewise to reach rail station; 60 and 30 to reach airport

(3) Time allowed between arrival at railway station and departure of train 20 minutes; check in at airport, 30 minutes on internal flight, 60 on international

(4) Road travel with average 100 km/h on motorway (travel on slower roads reduced appropriately) plus time for stops. Train and air times, the fastest service available

(5) Checking out of plane

(6) See (2)

(7) Total time

(8) Speed in relation to *direct* (not route) distance

(9) Speed in relation to air (=100)

Table 8.6 Travel between 10 pairs of places by 3 modes

Journey	Direct distance km	Total time in minutes			Average speed km		
		Road	Rail	Air	Road	Rail	Air
1 London–Birmingham	160	145	155	150	66	62	64
2 Milan–Zürich[1]	216	310	290	190	42	45	68
3 London–Manchester	260	255	215	190	61	73	82
4 London–Paris[*2]	340	430	465	260	47	43	78
5 Paris–Lyons[**]	400	355	185	195	68	130	123
6 Milan–Rome	472	420	295	170	67	96	167
7 London–Edinburgh	518	465	308	210	67	101	148
8 Paris–Milan	628	615	580	250	61	65	151
9 London–Milan	948	985	1,185	280	58	48	203
10 London–Rome	1,420	1,375	1,430	310	62	60	275

Notes: * before opening of Channel Tunnel
** using TGV
1 Journey 2, Milan–Zürich, shows the effect of the Alps on road and rail times.
2 Journey 4, London–Paris, shows the effect of crossing the Channel on road and rail times, also influencing to a smaller degree London–Milan and London–Rome.

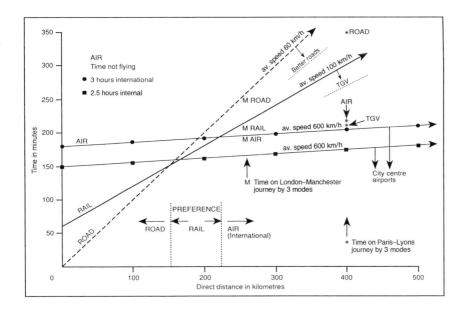

Figure 8.9 The choice of mode of travel for passengers in Western Europe. Calculations by the authors (see text). For simplicity, precise distances and speeds are shown on the diagram but in reality, each line should be a band of considerable width to include a variety of actual journeys

Plate 19 A new road link in the transport network of Europe: the approach to a tunnel to connect south Austria with the newly established country of Slovenia

high-speed rail network is subsidised, the necessary large volume of traffic such a system would have to carry to justify its existence might not materialise.

FREIGHT TRAFFIC

As previously shown, passenger traffic in Western Europe is mainly handled by road, rail and air, with ferry services to support land transport where necessary. Goods, however, are mainly carried by road, rail, inland waterway and sea. Oil, gas and electricity (fuel converted to energy) are taken by special means, while air traffic accounts for an increasing but (in terms of weight) still very small amount of cargo, usually valuable or perishable. Some differences between road and rail should be noted. A good road can accommodate a wider, more bulky load than a railway, which is rigidly restricted by gauge. Road transport also has the advantage of being able to move goods from 'door to door'. On the other hand, rail needs less manpower to move a given quantity of goods on longer journeys, but usually transhipment at one or both ends of a journey.

The movement of goods by rail from the 1950s to the 1980s is shown in Table 8.7 for 10 EC countries, and in Figure 8.10 for the four largest EC countries in population. There has been some increase in traffic during that period in most EC countries, but little change in the UK and Belgium. The data in Table 8.7 show that by the late 1980s road transport handled ten times as much traffic (in terms of weight) as rail transport, but rail journeys on average were considerably longer

196

Table 8.7 Goods handled by rail, road and inland waterway in 10 EC countries, 1986

	(Millions of tonnes transported)			
	Rail	*Road*	*Inland waterway*	*Total*
FRG	321	2,262	222	2,806
France	158	1,233	64	1,455
Italy	48	1,000	2	1,050
Netherlands	20	391	254	665
Belgium/Lux.	90	317	103	510
UK	141	1,412	–	1,550
Ireland	3	91	–	94
Denmark	7	209	–	216
Greece	4	160	–	164
EC (10)	793	7,073	645	8,511

Source: Eurostat 1989b, section 26

than road journeys, and the expression of the flow of traffic in tonne-kilometres shows the rail system to be more important than it appears here. Inland waterways are only used extensively in some EC countries. In France, Germany and Belgium, rail transport is relatively more important than it is in the other EC countries. As the movement of bulky goods such as coal and building materials, associated with rail and waterway, declines in Western Europe, road transport might be expected to increase its share of traffic unless rail can compete in the movement of goods at present largely handled by road. According to Dynes (1991), rail could capture much of the present road freight traffic between Britain and the continent by running fast trains through the Channel Tunnel (35 per day in each direction) between nine terminals in Britain and 20 on the continent. The opening of the Channel Tunnel and the provision of lorry-carrying trains using very long tunnels planned through the Swiss Alps will also reduce journey times by lorry. On the other hand, the introduction (and enforcement) of an 80 km/h (50 mph) speed limit on lorries throughout the EC would reduce the advantages brought to road travel especially since the 1950s through the 'motorway effect'. As the EFTA and Central European countries become more closely linked with the EC countries, the average length of haul of goods is likely to increase to some extent, another trend that could favour rail against road, at least marginally.

As transport links are improved, places gradually come closer together in travel time, while short cuts (e.g. tunnels replacing tortuous Alpine road passes) trim actual distances slightly. It will, however, always be more time-consuming and costly for a producer in Portugal, Greece or Finland to reach the total Western European market than for one in Belgium, eastern France or Switzerland.

This chapter concludes with a study of road distances calculated to give a

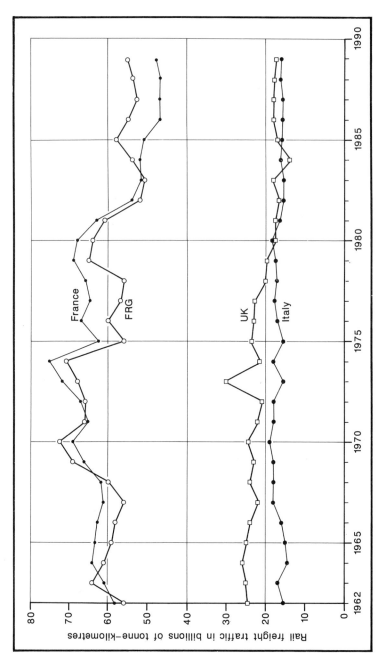

Figure 8.10 The movement of goods by rail in the FRG, France, the UK and Italy, 1962–89

Sources: various years of UNSYB and Eurostat 1991, Table 7.4

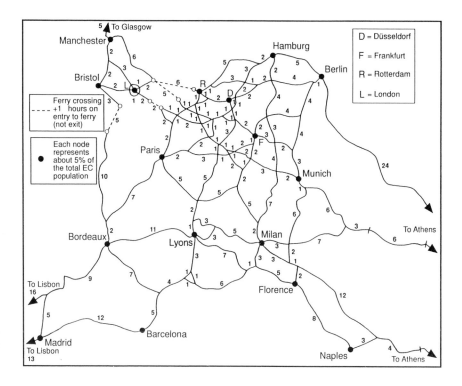

Figure 8.11 Travel times by road for heavy goods vehicles under normal conditions. The time taken on a particular journey would not necessarily take exactly the number of hours indicated on the map as delays are not allowed for. The road system shown on the map includes all the routes calculated to be the shortest in time between all pairs of population nodes. Note: the locations of Glasgow, Athens and Lisbon are outside the frame of the map

broad idea of the favourability of the location of 20 places in the EC, each roughly representing 5 per cent of the total EC population of 345 million (see Figure 8.11). The method of calculation is shown in Table 8.8, in which distances between all of the 20 places (A–T) used are shown to six selected places (in the first six columns). The aggregate travel time from each place to all the other 19, one way, is shown in column (7), the average in time per journey in column (8) and the average in relation to Paris, the place with the lowest aggregate travel, in column (9). The exact values in the table give spurious precision, but an area bounded roughly by a line Paris–Rotterdam–Düsseldorf–Frankfurt–Lyons–Paris contains places not more than 10 per cent above the low Paris and Rotterdam values. Portugal and Greece both have scores more than double the average in the central part of the EC. The matter of centre and periphery will be referred to again in Chapter 10.

Table 8.8 Estimated travel time in hours by heavy goods vehicle between 20 places in the EC, no time being added for obligatory rest times on longer journeys

	(1) K Glasgow	(2) B London	(3) F Paris	(4) M Berlin	(5) R Lisbon	(6) T Athens	(7) Total A–T	(8) Average A–T	(9) Average related to Paris=100
A Manchester	5	5	17	28	51	63	522	26.5	149
B London	10	0	11	24	45	54	428	21.4	122
C Hamburg	28	19	14	5	48	47	447	22.4	128
D Frankfurt	27	15	10	11	44	52	385	19.3	110
E Rotterdam	20	11	6	12	40	48	355	17.8	101
F Paris	22	11	0	21	34	51	350	17.5	100
G Barcelona	44	33	22	39	25	56	547	27.4	156
H Madrid	45	34	23	51	13	68	647	32.4	185
I Milan	36	25	15	22	44	36	414	20.7	118
J Naples	49	38	30	32	55	26	596	29.8	170
K Glasgow	0	10	22	33	56	68	612	30.6	175
L Bristol	9	2	14	27	48	57	472	23.6	135
M Berlin	33	24	21	0	55	42	501	25.1	143
N Münich	35	21	14	12	48	33	423	21.2	121
O Düsseldorf	23	12	8	8	42	45	383	19.3	109
P Lyons	30	19	8	25	36	44	380	19.0	109
Q Bordeaux	31	20	9	30	25	58	435	21.8	124
R Lisbon	56	45	34	55	0	81	837	41.9	239
S Florence	41	30	21	24	47	34	498	24.9	142
T Athens	68	54	51	42	81	0	963	48.2	275
Total	612	428	350	501	837	963			
Average	30.6	21.4	17.5	25.1	41.9	48.2			

In conclusion, some points may be made about the location of places in the EC in relation to the road network. Several main intra-EC routes cross Switzerland or Austria, causing concern in these countries over congestion, pollution and noise. Greece can be reached from other EC countries only by ferry from Italy or across Yugoslavia. The Channel Tunnel is expected to cut two hours off the ferry crossing time. Such a reduction would affect 16 of the journeys in Table 8.8 from UK places, thereby cutting, for example, the aggregate travel time for London by 32 hours from 428 hours to 396. For each of the 16 places on the continent, it would reduce only four journeys (those to the UK and Ireland), saving a total of eight hours. This example shows that the improvement of a particular link in the system does not necessarily benefit all places equally. Finally, the entry of EFTA and the Central European countries into the EC would shift the centre of population to the east and make the UK, Iberia and western France more marginal than they are now, while somewhat improving the relative aggregate travel score of places in Germany in particular.

FURTHER READING

Button, K. (1990) 'The Channel Tunnel – the economic implications for the South East of England', *The Geographical Journal* 156(2): 187–99.
COM (89), 564 final (1990) *Communication on a Community Railway Policy*, Brussels, 25 January.
United Nations (1991) *Transport Information 1991*, Economic Commission for Europe, Geneva, publisher UN, New York.

9

THE ENVIRONMENT

ENVIRONMENTAL ISSUES AND POLICY

Even the most simple human societies have caused changes in the natural environment. In the last 2,000 years Western Europe has experienced increasing pressure on its land, mineral and water resources. For example, in the sixteenth and seventeenth centuries, forests were being heavily depleted in many areas through increasing demand for fuelwood and for timber for construction. According to Nef (1977), a shortage of wood in England in the sixteenth and seventeenth centuries led to the growing use of coal as a fuel. Environmental problems are not new. As early as 1877 a directive was established in Osaka, Japan, to control air pollution from blacksmiths' shops and metal-casting factories. By the turn of the century, travel in parts of London was very unpleasant on account of large quantities of horse dung in the streets and smoke from steam locomotives in the cut-and-cover underground system. In the interwar period, excessive ploughing in the Great Plains of the USA caused extensive soil erosion and 'dust bowl' conditions, producing environmental degradation on a massive scale, a process repeated in the 1950s in the 'new' grain lands of the USSR.

In postwar UK of the 1950s, two separate events, among others, brought home the constant threat of environmental pollution and damage. Dense fog, carrying pollutants, resulted in the widespread presence of 'smog' in some British cities in 1952–3, causing a large number of deaths, especially among older citizens. Subsequent clean air acts introduced 'smoke-free' zones in many urban areas. Early in 1953, many coastal areas of eastern England suffered severe floods, leading eventually to the building of the Thames Barrier to protect London from flooding (see Gilbert and Horner 1984), and to concern over the possible impact of even a small rise in sea level on low-lying coastal areas, a concern felt even more strongly in the Netherlands. Los Angeles can take credit for drawing attention to the influence of motor vehicles as a cause of atmospheric pollution, while Milan and Athens are examples of cities in the EC with such acute problems of pollution from traffic that at times they have been closed to motor vehicles.

In the 1970s and 1980s, thanks particularly to television and instant live viewing through satellites of places anywhere in the world, awareness of a considerable range of environmental problems has grown among politicians and

202

the public alike. A selection of recent environmental disasters is given in Table 9.1. It could correctly be concluded even from the small sample of cases that the accidental release of fuel and toxic chemicals is among the principal causes of environmental disasters.

Not surprisingly, perhaps, polls for the Commission of the EC in 1986 and 1988 showed that the majority of the population in all Member States regarded 'environmental protection as an urgent problem requiring immediate action' (European Parliament 1989, En III/N, p. 1). In 1988, in Italy, Germany, Luxembourg, Greece and Denmark, over 80 per cent of those questioned were 'environmentally aware', but there was less concern in the UK, Portugal, the Netherlands and France (the latter only 59 per cent). In 1990 the EC Council adopted a regulation on the establishment of the European Environment Agency to provide objective and reliable information on the subject. The location had not been decided by the time of writing, but Spain and Denmark were the main contenders. Since concern over the environment has become a widespread issue in the EC and elsewhere only comparatively recently, some facts need to be stated before EC problems are discussed.

Table 9.1 Examples of recent energy-related and environmental disasters

Date	Disaster
1960s	Concern over damage to the natural environment in the USSR first received widespread publicity in connection with discharge from factories into Lake Baykal in Siberia. In 1959 there had been contamination from nuclear discharges over an extensive area in the Urals but this did not receive much publicity.
1967	The tanker *Torrey Canyon* spilt 120,000 tonnes of crude oil off the coast of Cornwall, England.
1974	Flixborough, England, an explosion releasing Cyclohexane killed 28 people and injured 104.
1976	Seveso, North Italy, an air release of TCCP caused over 200 injuries.
1978	The Tanker *Amoco Cadiz* spilt 230,000 tonnes of oil off the coast of Brittany, France.
1979	San Carlos, Spain, propylene transported by road caused 216 deaths and 200 injuries.
1979	Three Mile Island, USA, the failure of a nuclear reactor led to the evacuation of 200,000 people.
1984	San Juan Ixhautepec, Mexico, the explosion of a gas storage tank and subsequent fires caused over 500 deaths and 2,500 injuries.
1984	Bhopal, India, leakage of methyl isocyanate caused approximately 2,800 deaths and 50,000 injuries.
1986	Chernobyl, USSR, nuclear reactor explosion, directly causing (only) about 30 deaths and 300 injuries but contaminating many areas of Europe.
1991	Fires at most of the oil wells in Kuwait following the Iraqi withdrawal caused extensive atmospheric pollution until all were finally extinguished in November of that year. The equivalent of roughly 1 per cent of all world energy consumption in a year was burned up.

Sudden disasters exemplified by those in Table 9.1 attract much attention, but gradual processes can be more serious in the longer term. For example, nitrates from fertilisers have for many decades accumulated in underground water in many EC agricultural areas in sources of water supply. Some sources of pollution have a local impact only, whereas the pollutants from other sources reach further afield before being deposited, often along rivers, or through the atmosphere in the direction of wind at the time of emission. Still others, including carbon dioxide from the burning of fossil fuels, join the global atmospheric 'pool', in which gases are eventually distributed fairly evenly worldwide. The campaign in the EC to convert cars to lead-free petrol is of immediate benefit because the lead is diffused over only a very small area before deposition. On the other hand, the drive to stabilise and even reduce carbon dioxide emissions is largely altruistic if the policy were to be applied only in Western Europe, which accounts for about one-seventh of the world total of carbon dioxide emitted.

The founding Treaties of the EC make no mention of the protection of the environment or of a specific policy in such an area, since environmental issues are a relatively recent concern. The reform of the Treaties under the Single European Act remedied this omission to some extent through the creation of a special Title in the EEC Treaty on environmental protection.

The objectives for EC environmental policy are:

- to preserve, protect and improve the quality of the environment;
- to contribute towards protecting human health;
- to ensure a prudent and rational utilization of natural resources.

(EEC 130r(1))

The principles on which policy is based are the concepts of preventive action, rectification of environmental damage at source, and 'the polluter pays' principle. In addition, the environmental impact of EC economic and social policies and planning must be taken into account, with impact assessment studies now performed on a regular basis, and approval policies for all major public and private projects.

The principle of subsidiarity is also included in the area of environmental policy, with Article 130r (4) stating that 'The Community shall take action ... to the extent to which the objectives ... can be attained better at Community level than at the level of individual Member States', emphasising the usefulness of co-ordinated action, and also the importance of local and regional action being taken at lower environmental levels. With regard to funding, very few measures applied in EC Member States are being financed at Community level, so the Member States are still responsible for funding most environmental initiatives. In 1990, only 42 million ECU were paid out through EC funds for environmental protection, and in the 1991 budget, the first exclusively funded environmental programme, LIFE, was funded with 10 million ECU, both very modest sums.

In terms of decision-making on environmental issues, the Council still acts unanimously in this area, basing its measures on Article 130s of the EEC Treaty, rather than through the co-operation procedure. Article 130t states that the measures adopted in common 'shall not prevent any Member State from maintaining or introducing more stringent, protective measures compatible with the Treaty'. The Treaty of Maastricht has opened up some areas of environmental policy to qualified majority voting and given the European Parliament some powers, although environmental planning and taxes would still require unanimity (TEU Title XII).

It is clear, therefore, that the Member States still retain overall control over environmental policy in the EC, with many proposed measures being introduced very slowly as a result of delays caused by concern over national interests. The lack of a common policy is also illustrated by the fact that some Member States, such as Denmark, continually press for the right to maintain their higher standards.

A major problem, unlikely to disappear quickly, is the difficulty both of detecting pollution of the environment and violations, and of enforcing regulations and recommendations. Ziegler (1987) shows that even in the USSR, where before the 1990s central planners had powerful control over the economy, regulations to protect the environment were very difficult to enforce, particularly so because during the Soviet period the state 'owned' virtually all the means of production, so it was meaningless for it to fine its own enterprises. The same principle holds in market economy countries, even though the offenders are mainly privately owned enterprises or autonomous public sector concerns, rather than entities such as the Post Office or Civil Service directly under state control. The 'polluter pays principle' sounds admirable, but if a company is fined for a particular environmental infringement, the cost will in due course be passed on to the consumer. As in the Soviet case, fines are usually very small compared with the cost of particular environmental damage done, even if such a cost could meaningfully be calculated with any precision. It will at present almost inevitably be much less trouble for the company causing the environmental damage to pay the fine than to pay the cost of removing the source of the pollution.

CAUSES AND TYPES OF ENVIRONMENTAL POLLUTION

For the purposes of a more detailed analysis of environmental issues in the EC, it is necessary to identify and describe various causes and types of pollution and other forms of environmental damage.

Atmospheric pollution

This includes the presence and effects of the following: sulphur dioxide, nitrogen oxides, and suspended particulates mainly from the combustion of fossil fuels, especially in power stations and industrial plants, lead emissions from motor vehicles, and carbon monoxide from the incomplete burning of fuel. All these sources of atmospheric pollution are potentially harmful to human health, while nitrogen oxides in particular are thought to be the cause of acid rain, widely considered to damage Europe's forests. In 1988 the EC adopted a directive to limit the emissions of sulphur dioxide, nitrogen oxides and dust from power stations above a certain capacity, thus requiring considerable expense to provide desulphurization and other equipment. Concessions were made to certain plants burning home-produced coal with an excessively large sulphur content, an example of the EC policy of self-sufficiency in energy overriding environmental policy.

The most rigorous environmental protection targets in the 1990s have been set for the six founding Member States of the EC, together with Denmark. In 1989, standards were set for the limitation of emissions by motor vehicles, including, for example, tax incentives to reduce lead emissions. Although not strictly pollutants, the emission of carbon dioxide from the combustion of fossil fuels, and the use of chlorofluorocarbons (CFCs) in industrial products, give concern on account of their contribution to the 'greenhouse effect', thought to cause global atmospheric warming. Energy conservation policy in the EC is expected to discourage an increase in the consumption of fossil fuels, while the use of CFCs is to be reduced and phased out.

Plate 20 Twentieth-century pollution: coal-fired thermal electric station at Ratcliffe-on-Soar, England. The chimney on the right emits smoke, but the cooling towers emit only steam

Noise

Noise is not only a cause of discomfort but it may also affect health. At EC level, a series of directives establish maximum noise levels from various types of mechanical equipment, thus achieving noise abatement at source. More drastic changes might involve the separation of residential areas from industrial sites and busy traffic routes, but such a scheme would prove extremely costly if applied universally and rigorously.

Water pollution

Water pollution is of two types: that affecting fresh water on the land surface or in groundwater beneath it, and that in sea water. Both water bodies are the destination of a wide variety of discharges from industrial processes, especially from the processing of raw materials, from sewage removed from centres of population, and from oil released from ships. The issues of water quality include standards for bathing water, the suitability of fresh water for fish life, and the quality of water to be used for drinking. Various quality objectives for water were already established in the 1970s. In 1976, a blacklist of 129 particularly dangerous substances was produced, special targets being discharges of cadmium and mercury.

With regard to marine pollution, three seas, the North Sea, the Baltic and the Mediterranean, are of particular concern to the EC, the first area because several heavily polluted rivers flow into it, the other two because they are almost entirely shut off from contact with the oceans. Three meetings were held between 1984 and 1990 to tackle the problem of the dumping of industrial waste and sewage sludge into the North Sea. The Mediterranean is also the subject of EC initiatives, especially against dumping from ships and aircraft. The entry of the former GDR gives the EC extra coastline on the Baltic, which receives pollution, mainly entering via the rivers of Poland and the former USSR. As with atmospheric pollution, monitoring water pollution in addition to identifying offenders and actually fining them, is difficult. In some circumstances, such as the awarding of the European 'Blue Flag' to clean beaches and the publicising of the fact, effective control over pollution can be achieved.

Waste and chemical substances

The volume of waste and chemical substances processed and disposed of in the EC amounts to some 2 billion tonnes every year, about 5 tonnes per inhabitant, 30 million tonnes of which are estimated to be dangerous. Relevant legislation is mostly restricted to individual types of waste disposal considered to cause acute problems, as, for example, waste from the titanium oxide industry, waste oils and the use of sewage sludge in agriculture. In the area of waste management, the Community is working to establish guidelines to adopt clean technologies, to reprocess waste, to improve waste disposal, tighten up the transport of dangerous substances, and reclaim contaminated land. Some very dangerous chemical substances, including polychlorinated biphenyls and terphenyls (components of electricity transformers), pesticides and detergents, have been subjected to special legislation, and there are regulations regarding classification, packaging, labelling and shipment, some in force since 1967.

Some of the sectors of economic activity giving rise to the greatest concern have been identified. Seven industrial sectors have been made eligible for EC support for the introduction of clean technologies: surface treatment (e.g. galvanising, cadmium-plating), leather (e.g. chromium salts), textiles (various chemicals), cellulose and paper (e.g. pulp bleaching), mining and quarrying, the chemical industry (e.g. organo-chlorine compounds), and agri-food (e.g. effluents from sugar refineries and oil mills, fertilisers). While specific causes of serious environmental damage can often be pinpointed and dealt with through legislation, the burning of fossil fuels and wood is a problem of much greater magnitude, less amenable to control through legislation.

Energy efficiency

In Europe, the efficiency with which energy is used varies greatly from country to country. One way of measuring this is to compare energy consumption per inhabitant with GDP per inhabitant. In Figure 9.1 the countries of Europe are plotted according to their scores on these scales. The ratio of the two values can be seen with the help of the diagonal lines. Switzerland, Spain and Portugal are among the most 'efficient' users of energy in the world. The countries of Central Europe, and the former USSR, make much less effective use of their high levels of energy consumption. In the EC, some allowance should be made for the large scale of heavy industry in some countries and the greater need for domestic heating in the more northerly countries. Even then, the extremes within the EC of about 170 dollars (140 ECU) of GDP per 100 kg in the Netherlands and over 420 dollars (340 ECU) in Spain and Portugal, are considerable. The burning of fossil fuels in the EC is heavily concentrated roughly in the triangle from Scotland to the Ruhr, to Paris (see Figure 5.2 and Tables 9.2 and 9.3).

Sulphur oxides are one of the largest groups of air pollutants. About 100 million tonnes are emitted annually in the world from fuel processing and consumption, of which the EC and EFTA account for about 13 million tonnes (see Table 9.2). The UK comes highest in kilograms emitted per unit of GDP produced. Central Europe has a much less favourable record in relation to population size than the EC, the former GDR and Czechoslovakia having particularly bad environmental conditions.

Much background material is available in the OECD (1991) publication, *The State of the Environment*, the publication of which illustrates growing concern with environmental issues. Europe figures prominently among the more highly industrialised regions of the world, which, including the former USSR and

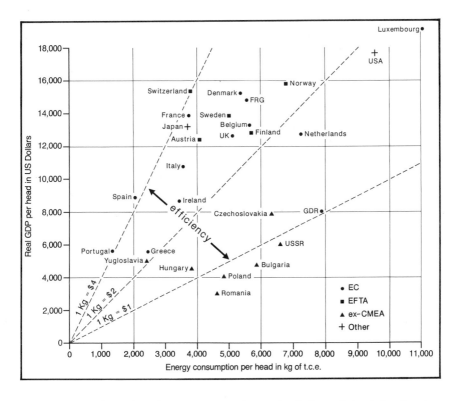

Figure 9.1 Relationship of energy consumption per head of population in kg of coal equivalent to real GDP per head in the countries of Europe and other selected countries, late 1980s

Table 9.2 Emission of sulphur oxides, late 1980s

	Sulphur oxides 1,000 tonnes	Kg per head	Kg/1,000 GDP US$
FRG	1,306	21	1.9
France	1,335	24	2.4
Italy	2,070	36	4.4
Netherlands	256	18	1.9
UK	3,664	65	7.0
Norway	65	15	1.0
Sweden	199	24	1.8
OECD Europe	13,200	37	4.1
Rest of OECD	26,700	65	4.0*
Rest of world	59,100	14	10.0

Source: OECD 1991: 34–5
Note: *estimate

Table 9.3 Carbon released into the atmosphere by selected countries

	Millions of tonnes of carbon		
	1971	*1980*	*1988*
FRG	208	219	190
France	126	139	103
Italy	92	106	108
UK	187	167	163
OECD	2,427	2,756	2,793
Rest of world	2,323	2,772	3,463

Source: based on OECD 1991: 23

Central Europe (neither in the OECD), have less than one-quarter of the world's population, but account for roughly three-quarters of the pollution. As efforts to contain and even reduce environmental pollution in the developed regions of the world take effect, their share of the growing world total may gradually diminish.

THE MOVEMENT AND IMPACT OF POLLUTANTS

Pollutants are not only moved from their sources by natural forces, mainly wind and rivers, but also by man-made conveyances. The exact direction and distance they will be carried in the air before being deposited cannot be predicted precisely, but in some areas prevailing wind directions are experienced. In contrast, along rivers and, unless accidental, when organised by means of waste disposal services such as pipes, lorries and ships, movement is predictable. EC policy is aimed to encourage the disposal of waste at the nearest appropriate location, regardless of whether it is in the country in which the waste originates.

The estimated movement of sulphur dioxide in the atmosphere from three source countries, the UK, Spain and Czechoslovakia is mapped in Figure 9.2 as an example of diffusion through the atmosphere. Sulphur dioxide can be carried hundreds of kilometres, at times even more. Thus, for example, a considerable proportion of the sulphur dioxide originating in Western and Central Europe actually reaches North Africa, itself the occasional source of a reverse flow of harmless particulates from sand storms in the Sahara Desert, reaching far northwards into Europe.

Many rivers in Europe carry large quantities of pollutants, with adverse effects on water quality, fishing and local environments along their courses, and potential harm to marine life and to tourist beaches near their estuaries. The courses of selected rivers of Central and Western Europe are shown in Figure 9.3. Major concentrations of population and industry are also indicated. Some international boundaries follow the watersheds between the main drainage basins.

210

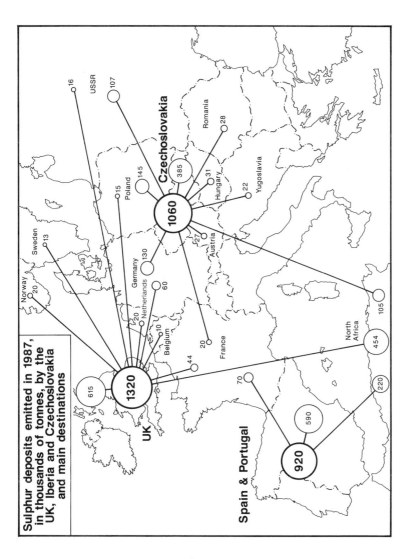

Sulphur deposits emitted in 1987, in thousands of tonnes, by the UK, Iberia and Czechoslovakia and main destinations

Figure 9.2 Destination of sulphur deposits emitted by the UK, Iberia and Czechoslovakia over Europe and North Africa

Source: European Parliament 1990b: 162–3

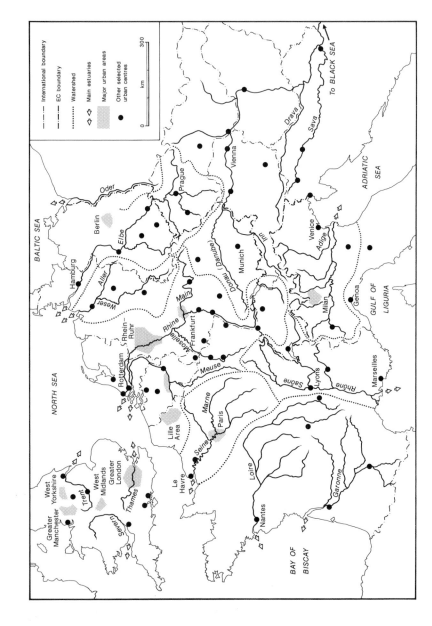

Figure 9.3 Main river basins of parts of Western and Central Europe. No distinction is made between rivers, canalised rivers and canals

Many basins are, however, shared by more than one country (e.g. the Rhine, Elbe, Danube), while in places a river actually forms the boundary between two countries (e.g. the Rhine between France and Germany, the Oder between Germany and Poland). Much transfrontier pollution can therefore be expected, a good reason for dealing with pollution problems internationally or under EC legislation.

The quality of water varies greatly from one river to another, and also along different sections of the same river. The nitrate concentrations in a selection of rivers are shown in Table 9.4 to illustrate the contrasts. The Thames has the highest score of all the rivers included in the table, while the rivers of Belgium and the Netherlands, and the Rhine in Germany, are also seriously affected. The Rhine and its tributaries drain the largest river basin in the EC. These waterways pass through numerous industrial areas, and have many large cities on or near their banks. About one-fifth of the total population of the EC lives in the Rhine basin, while an even larger proportion of the metallurgical and chemicals industries is situated there.

The Elbe, which drains a smaller basin than the Rhine, is also heavily polluted. Although its basin is in both the former GDR and the FRG, it actually starts in Czechoslovakia, where it already receives industrial waste and untreated sewage from Prague and smaller cities. As a result, fish taken from the Elbe are mostly inedible, and among various pollutants the river discharges into the North Sea are mercury, copper, phosphates, nitrogen and ammonia. In North Italy, the River Po and its tributaries drain a comparatively small basin which, however, contains much of Italy's industrial capacity, together with the most intensively farmed agricultural land in the country. An excessively large quantity of phosphates originating in the farms has been blamed for the occurrence in recent years of algae on the Adriatic tourist beaches of the region of Emilia-Romagna, just south of the Po delta, giving rise to one of the worst cases of eutrophication in Europe (Marchetti 1985).

While it is obvious that environmental damage is very unevenly distributed in

Table 9.4 Water quality of selected European rivers: nitrate concentration (mgN/litre)

River	Country	MgN/litre	River	Country	MgN/litre
Thames	UK	7.67	Loire	France	2.53
Escaut-Doel	Belgium	5.06	Danube	Yugoslavia	2.42
Ijssel-Kampen	Netherlands	4.33	Rhine	Switzerland	1.76
Meuse	Netherlands	3.86	Po	Italy	1.68
Rhine	Germany	3.70	Rhône	France	1.38
Guadalquivir	Spain	3.47	Porsuk	Turkey	1.28
Mersey	UK	2.86	Gudenaa	Denmark	1.25

Source: OECD 1991: 61

the territory of the EC and along its coasts and offshore seas, the variety of different ingredients that contribute is so great that it is not possible to quantify the overall occurrence accurately. A hypothetical 'density of pollution' map of the EC would show many small areas with very high scores, including some cities, badly polluted mining areas, and certain stretches of river and coast, as well as extensive areas affected less seriously in some way or other, and a few areas completely free.

Coasts and seas

Compared with most other large regions of the world, the countries of the EC share a very long coastline in relation to their total area, but many of the coasts, together with adjoining seas, have become environmental problem areas, and in some cases, catastrophes have occurred. The sea receives pollutants carried into it by rivers, sewage and industrial waste directly from the many centres of population along the shores, and waste deliberately dumped there by purpose-built ships or spilt there accidentally.

Palmer and Rowland (1990) report on a meeting of EC environment ministers to consider the deteriorating state of the North Sea. Seven of the 12 EC Member States have a coastline on the North Sea or lie in the basin of the Rhine, which drains into it: the eastern side of Britain, northeast France, the Benelux, almost all of Germany, Denmark and Switzerland are involved. Indeed, about 40 per cent of the population of the EC lives in areas draining to the North Sea. Virtually every known source of contamination affects the North Sea: atmospheric pollution, especially from the UK, industrial waste and sewage via rivers or from dumping at sea, radioactive waste. Fishing has been reduced through disease and malformation in the fish, algal growth affects marine life, and many beaches are unsuitable for visitors to use.

In the basins of the rivers entering the Mediterranean, industrial activity is less widespread than around the North Sea, but problems are acute in many localities close to ports and industries, for example Marseilles and the Rhône delta area, Genoa on the Gulf of Liguria, and the northern Adriatic. According to Froment and Lerat (1989: 220) Marseilles, Toulon, Nice, Menton, Antibes, and Ajaccio, all on the Mediterranean coast, made up half of the principal urban agglomerations of France with no *dépollution* (the application of measures against pollution) in 1980 out of over 100 considered. In addition, population is growing fast in the countries of North Africa with coasts on the southern side of the Mediterranean.

Forests

The world's forests have been shrinking over recent decades, in spite of reforestation in many countries. In the 1980s, a great deal of publicity was given to the cutting of the tropical rain forests of the world. At the same time, the effect of acid rain on the coniferous forests of northern and mountain areas of Europe and North America has caused increasing concern. According to the World Watch Institute (*Time*, 9 April 1990) about 70 per cent of the forests of Czechoslovakia are damaged, nearly two-thirds in Britain and around half in Germany, Italy, Norway and Poland. In one influential United Nations report, *The Human Development Report 1990* (UNDP 1990: 7, 62), the following thought is expressed in two places: 'the concept of sustainable development is much broader than the protection of natural resources and the physical environment. After all, it is people, not trees, whose future choices have to be protected.' As shown in Chapter 4, the area of the EC defined as forest has actually increased in recent decades, but the EC has virtually no influence on the conservation of forests in the tropics other than through the banning of trade in such products as tropical hardwoods and some animal products.

Animal life

In addition to the problems of agricultural land, forests and fisheries, already referred to, the protection of wildlife, particularly in the form of hundreds of threatened species of plant and animal, gets frequent if sporadic attention, focused usually only on a local or special feature. For example, the wolf population of the EC is now very small, spatially fragmented and under threat of extinction. The population of foxes is much larger, but no more welcome in view of the propensity of foxes to carry rabies, not forgetting their predatory nature and recent tendency to scavenge in urban environments. Many local and migratory species of bird are finding their nesting areas and temporary stopping places increasingly restricted. The killing of migratory birds for sport, widespread in Italy, bloodsports in the UK, and even cruelty to animals in general, still common for example in parts of Spain and Portugal, are further examples of national practices regarded as undesirable in other Member States of the Community and therefore possible matters for consideration at EC level.

Agriculture

The intensive use of artificial or chemical fertilisers is causing concern in the EC on account of the pollution caused to both surface and underground water. Between the mid-1960s and the mid-1980s the consumption of nitrogenous fertilisers in the world as a whole increased four times. In Europe excluding the USSR, the increase was 2.5 times. Data for selected countries are given in Table 9.5. The increases in yield achieved in Europe were shown in Chapter 4 to correlate closely with the use of fertilisers. Only in the Netherlands, which has a very high level of consumption already, and the more environmentally conscious Sweden, has there been virtually no increase in the last 20 years. The large extent of land in northern France affected by nitrogenous fertilisers shown in Figure 9.4 includes much of the total arable area in the country.

215

Table 9.5 Changes in the level of consumption of nitrogen fertilisers between 1970 and 1988 in selected countries of Europe

	Tonnes per km² 1988	*1970*	*1970–80*	*1970–88*
Netherlands	46.7	100	122	101
UK	20.9	100	143	169
FRG	20.6	100	139	138
France	13.3	100	142	166
Italy	7.6	100	198	182
Sweden	7.6	100	111	103
Spain	5.5	100	161	201
OECD Europe	9.9	100	153	172
World	5.4	100	185	242

Source: OECD 1991: 181

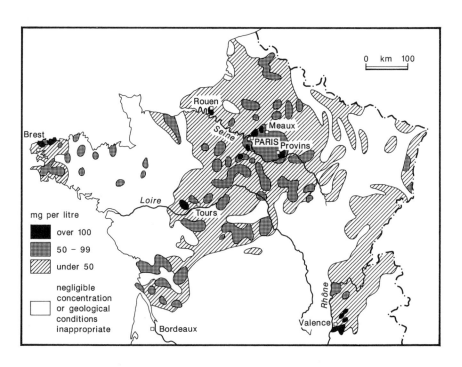

Figure 9.4 Areas of northern France affected by nitrates in subterranean water

Source: Froment and Lerat 1989, Tome 2:208

216

Table 9.6 Sulphur dioxide concentrations in selected cities

Country	City	Base 1975 mg/m³	Index 1975=100			Late 1980s
			1975	1980	1985	
FRG	West Berlin	95	100	95	71	64
France	Paris	115	100	77	47	38
	Rouen	63	100	111	59	56
Italy	Milan	244	100	82	36	23
Netherlands	Amsterdam	34	100	74	47	41
Belgium	Brussels	99	100	63	34	32
UK	London	116	100	60	36	34
	Newcastle	112	100	62	36	32
Denmark	Copenhagen	45	100	69	58	47
Portugal	Lisbon	36	100	122	86	119
Finland	Tampere	103	100	57	40	7
Norway	Oslo	48	100	75	31	27
Sweden	Gothenburg	41	100	59	54	32
	Stockholm	59	100	71	36	24

Source: OECD 1991: 41

Urban Environment

The data in Table 9.6 illustrate the considerable progress made in some cities of the EC and EFTA in reducing sulphur dioxide concentrations. In general, the EFTA countries, particularly those of Scandinavia, have led the way in improving the urban environment. Norway's prime minister, Mrs Brundtland, has been a particularly enthusiastic and influential advocate of the need for greater concern over the environment. Scandinavia has the advantage (in this respect) of a low density of population and no coal industry. Improvements are bound to take longer in the southern EC countries (e.g. Portugal), where the number of motor vehicles in use is still growing fast and population density is higher.

CURE AND PREVENTION OF ENVIRONMENTAL DAMAGE

Only in the 1980s have publicity and awareness of environmental problems become widespread. Politicians have responded in various ways, in particular in the emergence of Green parties and the adoption of green agendas by mainstream parties. Even so, the task of making human activity and environmental stability compatible is only in its infancy. It is therefore difficult to estimate which issues will be foremost in the future, how problems will be tackled, and how much funding will be available.

Davies-Gleizes (1991) notes that with two decades of tough environmental legislation in the USA, US firms are better equipped financially and technologic-

217

ally than EC firms to carry out much of the work on environmental improvement needed in Europe. Nevertheless, a vast industry producing devices to clean the environment has already grown up in the EC, which is ahead of most regions of the world, apart from the USA, in pollution concern and control. It has 2.5 million people engaged in making pollution control equipment, and exports from the Community in the late 1980s were between four and five times the value of its imports of such equipment. The cost of pollution control in the EC has been about 30 billion ECU per year in the late 1980s: a necessary expenditure, but still only accounting for less than 1 per cent of the total GDP of the Community.

One regional example of a Community initiative of environmental concern is ENVIREG, which addresses the environmental problems of the Mediterranean basin and other Objective 1 regions. Its aim is to demonstrate better methods of dealing with waste water in coastal areas, especially where this threatens the future of tourism, of reducing marine pollution arising from the washing of ships' bilges, and of treating industrial and other toxic wastes properly. The Community budget line for the four-year period is 50 million ECU.

The general idea of preventive (as opposed to curative) measures is to reduce if not eliminate the causes of pollution and thereby protect the environment from further damage. One aspect of the preventive approach is to ensure that regulations are enforced. Another is actually to eliminate or cut the consumption of products that cause damage to the environment. These will be discussed in turn.

It often happens that what is regarded as a favourable and beneficial environmental policy has side effects that are not taken into account and which may even be negative. A striking example is the protection of deer from natural predators or adequate culling. The herds may grow to such an extent that their presence damages the natural vegetation, including trees, on which they depend, and which itself is valued (see Gill 1991). The widespread use of battery-powered cars (see Casassus 1991) in urban areas would eliminate emissions from the burning of petrol locally, but the increased electricity needed to power the batteries, unless obtained from solar panels in each home running such a car, would have to be generated somewhere – a case of transferring or exporting pollution, in this instance from the streets to the vicinity of thermal electric stations. Similarly, the replacement of tractors and other machinery driven by hydrocarbons in the agricultural sector by working animals such as horses would require the provision of large quantities of fodder throughout the year, putting extra pressure on the land and conceivably requiring extra inputs of chemical fertilisers, whereas tractors can be laid up when not in use.

Some of the measures that would have to be taken to produce a substantial reduction in the consumption of fuel and materials would not be palatable to many people in the EC. The use of smaller, slower passenger cars might, for example, halve the consumption of motor fuel. Organic farming is practised on about 1 per cent of the farms in Western Europe. Such a practice, if widespread, would reduce the consumption of chemical fertilisers, but would also result in generally lower yields and, without the extension of cultivation into new areas, a smaller total of agricultural production, eventually making the EC more dependent than at present on agricultural imports. Indeed Hornsby (1991) reports a proposal by a group of English farmers to introduce compulsory nitrogen rationing in the EC with a target of a 20 per cent cut. Although such a measure would reduce overproduction and help to preserve the landscape, it is unlikely to be received enthusiastically by the majority of EC farmers. The generation of electricity from 'clean', renewable sources of energy derived from solar, wind and tidal power is also attractive environmentally (if not always aesthetically) but even with the successful development of the technology, and large-scale investment, could in two decades only supply about 10 per cent of the quantity of electricity expected to be needed by then in the EC, according to the informed view of Lord Marshall, chairman of the CEGB in the late 1980s.

CONTINENTAL AND GLOBAL ENVIRONMENTAL ISSUES

As already stressed several times in this chapter, many sources of actual and potential damage to and pollution of the environment affect large areas and even the whole globe. To appreciate adequately the future prospects for the EC it is necessary, therefore, to consider environmental issues and prospects beyond Western Europe. In this section EFTA, Central and Eastern Europe will first be discussed, followed by the world as a whole.

The EFTA countries suffer more environmental damage from EC countries than they cause to them. It is claimed in Scandinavia that acid rain from the burning of fossil fuels in the EC and Central Europe damages the trees there. Switzerland and Austria are crossed by roads (mainly motorways) heavily used by intra-EC traffic, causing pollution, noise, and congestion. As noted in Chapter 8, the ultimate solution for Switzerland is to 'ferry' vehicles in transit on trains, a procedure already used for cars in the Simplon and Lotschberg Tunnels. Such a procedure would require the costly construction of long tunnels, not a new experience for the Swiss. Figure 9.5 shows the places of origin/destination of EC traffic crossing the Brenner Pass between Austria and Italy. Austria is mainly located in the basin of the River Danube, Switzerland in those of the Rhine and the Rhône, and each country in its turn contributes to the pollution of these waterways.

The former GDR deserves special mention because it has been estimated that some 80 billion ECU would be needed to ensure that EC environmental standards are respected in its territory. Among environmental issues that require to be confronted in the GDR are the use of lignite as the main source of energy, unsafe nuclear power plants, excessive motor vehicle emissions, the pollution of waterways and the problem of concentrations of livestock in some small areas. In Leipzig in the former GDR, surrounded by lignite quarries and lignite-burning power stations, industries and homes, life expectancy is six years below the average for the remainder of the former GDR. In the industrial centre of

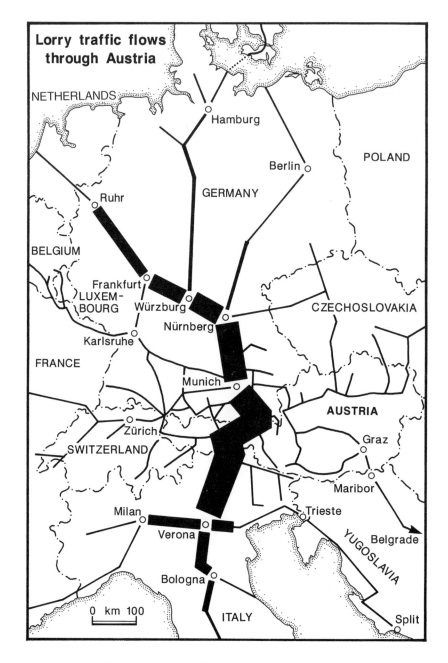

Figure 9.5 Main flows by lorry of traffic using the Brenner Pass between Austria and
Italy

Source: OECD 1991:209

220

Espenhain, near Leipzig, four out of five children suffer from chronic bronchitis. The cost of rendering safe a district in the extreme south of the GDR, where uranium has been extracted for export to the USSR since the Second World War, is expected to be very high.

Poland, Czechoslovakia and, to a lesser extent, Hungary have environmental problems similar to those of the former GDR. Czechoslovakia is of particular concern to the EC because much of its mining and heavy industry is concentrated in the extreme northwest (Bohemia), close to Germany. An EP Report (see European Parliament 1991: 1) refers to catastrophic devastation, with a third of the country affected by sulphur pollution: 'The children of Tiplice are forbidden to play outdoors in winter and for six weeks a year schoolchildren are sent to less polluted areas.' Both lignite-fired and nuclear power stations give concern and bring problems, the former causing atmospheric pollution by burning the fuel without filtering, the latter admitted to have safety problems arising from leaks of contaminated material. Dangerous metals, untreated sewage and damage to agricultural land are other problems in Czechoslovakia. The neighbouring Land of Bayern in Germany is adversely affected by pollution from power stations in nearby Bohemia, and there is a plan to reduce the generation of electricity, cutting sulphur emissions, and to top up Czechoslovak supplies from Germany itself.

Other countries of Central Europe also have serious environmental problems. Bulgaria's one nuclear power station at Kozloduy is crucial for the supply of electricity to the country but its safety record is poor and its future prospects bleak. Some of the industrial areas of Romania have very bad environmental records. The plan to dam and divert the Danube in its middle course is a project of international scope, but one that has been the subject of much controversy. One among various reasons why the EC is likely to be reluctant to admit the former CMEA countries of Central Europe to full membership very soon is the great cost that would fall on the richer EC Member States to improve the environment there.

If the environmental problems of Central Europe and the former USSR have suddenly come to the attention of the EC and EFTA, in the longer term there are likely to be even greater environmental problems elsewhere in the world, especially in many parts of the developing world. Western Europe (or even Europe as a whole) will not be able to isolate itself from global environmental issues. It is therefore appropriate to step back and to look briefly at the EC in a global context.

In the last 200 years, from the time when the Industrial Revolution was already beginning to spread from Britain to other parts of Europe, the population of the world has increased about five times. The use of fuel and raw materials has increased roughly a hundred-fold during that time. The use of materials is highly concentrated, with 25 per cent of the world's population using about 75 per cent, and accounting for roughly a similar proportion of all pollution and waste. If the developing countries, almost all with fast-growing populations, are to reach or even approach the levels of consumption of energy and materials currently found in the developed countries, then the pressure on natural resources, including water and agricultural land, would become much greater than now. China, for example, has doubled its production and consumption of coal in the 1980s and India is also increasing coal output. Droughts have been affecting parts of Africa and the interior of Asia, with implications for food production. In Brazil and in many other tropical countries, the cutting of the tropical rain forest continues.

Global environmental issues are, however, still of greater concern in the developed than in the developing world, where governments seem less inclined to put environmental protection high on the agenda. The impact of higher environmental standards and measures such as a "green" tax on industry will be a burden on the competitive position of EC industry in the world economy unless comparable measures are applied universally.

One of several global issues illustrates the interdependence of the countries of the world, the expected accumulation in the atmosphere of 'greenhouse' gases, which could cause a considerable increase in global atmospheric and ocean temperatures. The effects a warmer atmosphere might have on future climate and weather cannot be predicted with certainty. In the opinion of Jones and Wigley (1990: 73) 'Although this is obviously an unsatisfactory situation as far as policy

Table 9.7 Origins of 'greenhouse' gases (a) by sector and (b) by country (percentage of world total), late 1980s

(a) By sector

	CO_2	CFC	CH_4	O_3	N_2O	Total
Energy	35	–	4	6	4	49
Deforestation	10	–	4	–	–	14
Agriculture	3	–	8	–	2	13
Industry	2	20	–	2	–	24
% warming by gas	50	20	16	8	6	100

(b) By country

Developed*		Developing	
USA	18	Brazil	10
EC and EFTA	12	China	7
Japan	4	India	4
Other OECD	3	Rest of world	30
Former USSR	12		

Source of both tables: OECD 1991: 21
Note: *excludes Central Europe

implications are concerned, these uncertainties must not be used as excuses to delay formulating and implementing policies to reduce temperature increases caused by greenhouse gases.' In the 1980s a debate began on how to deal with such sources of greenhouse gases as fossil fuels, thus affecting EC policies on various issues (see Table 9.7). With about 7 per cent of the total population of the world, the EC and EFTA account for about 12 per cent of emissions of greenhouse gases, mainly through the burning of fossil fuels. Deforestation and agricultural practices in the developing world also make a substantial contribution. Flooding of low-lying areas by the sea and changes in rainfall and temperature (see Parry 1990) over large areas of the earth's land surface are possible future problems. There is no doubt that the environment, both in the European and global context, will continue to be a very controversial and widely debated issue in the decades ahead.

FURTHER READING

Commission of the EC (1987) *The State of the Environment in the European Community 1986*, Luxembourg (EUR 10633).

—— (n.d.), *European Year of the Environment*, 21 March 1987–20 March 1988 (EUR 10960), Brussels.

—— (1991), *Environment Statistics 1989*, Luxembourg: Office for Official Publications of the European Communities.

OECD (1991) *The State of the Environment*, Paris: Publications Service, Organisation for Economic Co-operation and Development.

Warrick, R. A., Barrow, E. M. and Wigley, T. M. L. (1990) *The Greenhouse Effect and its Implications for the European Community*, Luxembourg: Office for Official Publications of the European Communities (EUR 12707 EN).

White, R. M. (1990) 'The great climate debate', *Scientific American*, July, 263(1): 18–25.

10

REGIONAL ISSUES

REGIONAL POLICY

At the beginning of this book it was emphasised that one of the policy aims of the EC is to encourage convergence of economic performance and production of GDP between poorer and richer regions. Disparities have been shown to exist between EC Member States and also between regions at levels below State in every aspect of Community life examined so far. As implied in Chapter 2, to some extent the actual networks or systems of regions in use influence the perception and interpretation of disparities. In this chapter, various aspects of the regions are brought together. Two indicators of economic development, GDP per capita and level of unemployment, are examined at regional level. The causes of regional disparities in the EC and ways of reducing them are then considered. Economic disparities have dominated EC thinking on regional differences, but reference is made in Chapter 11 to subnational cultures and their relevance to convergence.

Following the signing of the Single European Act, the Treaty of Rome was amended to include a 'title' or section devoted to 'Economic and Social Cohesion' (EEC Title V). The objectives of the EC in regional policy terms are made clear:

> In order to promote its overall harmonious development, the Community shall develop and pursue its actions leading to the strengthening of its economic and social cohesion.
>
> In particular, the Community shall aim at reducing disparities between the various regions and the backwardness of the least-favoured regions.
>
> (Art. 130a EEC)

Economic growth is considered to be beneficial for two reasons. First, it raises living standards in general, and, second, it has been associated with economic and social convergence between Member States and between regions, an equalising process that is reduced or ceases during economic recessions. With or without concurrent economic growth, a deliberate policy to reduce regional disparities can be achieved in various ways. People can move or be moved from more backward to more advanced regions, a process that has generally been slow in the EC apart from special occasions such as the exodus of East Germans to the West in 1989–90. Alternatively, financial assistance can be provided by more advanced to more backward regions through the EC budget. Such a transfer can be made either sectorally, as, for example, under the Common Agricultural Policy, or spatially as, for example, the transfer of resources through the Cassa per il Mezzogiorno from North to South in Italy, especially in the 1950s and 1960s, in this case a national rather than an EC initiative. The EC Structural Funds are both regionally and sectorally based. They include the European Regional Development Fund (ERDF), the European Social Fund (ESF) and the European Agricultural Guidance and Guarantee Fund (EAGGF). As was shown in Chapter 2, the EC budget is modest in proportion to the total GDP of the 12 Member States, and interregional transfers of resources are correspondingly small.

Two different ways can be used to raise consumption and living standards in disadvantaged regions through the transfer of resources: first, to assist in public housing, unemployment benefits and similar ways of improving living standards or, second, to improve infrastructures. The second approach is considered preferable to subsidies because it enables lagging regions to increase their productivity and output of goods and services, and therefore the per capita GDP. This important concept is discussed as follows in COM 90-609 (1991), 8–4 to 8–5.

What then will be the real effects of Community resources on recipients' production, income and employment levels? If these resources are used for consumption instead of investment in human and physical capital, barely any lasting effects on production potential, output growth and income levels can be anticipated. If instead these resources are used for additional investment in raising labour force qualifications, infrastructures and the real capital stock of firms (actions which are 'eligible' in Community terms), substantial lasting effects should materialize. It is of course for this reason that the maintenance of additionality is of crucial importance. While the direct and indirect dynamic effects of using transfers to enhance economic capacity cannot be quantified at regional level at present for data reasons, it can be taken for granted that the increase in regional GDP will exceed substantially the value of the transfer itself over the medium and longer term and help to set the weaker regions on a path to faster growth, consistent with the aim of converging economically on the stronger regions. Of course, in the light of the size of disparities described earlier, and of the time required to reduce these disparities ... a marked relative improvement in the situation of the weaker regions remains a long term challenge, even after the doubling of the Structural Funds.

Various theories have been developed and policies adopted to ensure that the best use is made of resources transferred from richer to poorer regions, whether internally in Member States, or at EC level. One of the criteria taken into

225

consideration in the allocation of resources is based on the assumption that each region should be encouraged and if necessary assisted to specialise in what it is best suited to perform (COM 90-609, 1991: 79–82), known as the concept of comparative advantage. Unfortunately some regions are better endowed overall than others in their attributes and their locations. In some cases, the best that poorly endowed regions can hope for is to be encouraged to concentrate on what they do least badly.

One notable characteristic of the EC has been its readiness to accept new members on several occasions since the EEC came into existence in 1958. The list and distribution of advanced and backward or problem regions in the EC has therefore changed. Before 1973, the South and Islands of Italy were the main problem regions of the EC, although there were other smaller regions with difficulties, such as Corse in France and parts of southern Belgium. More emphasis was given then to poor agricultural regions than to industrial regions in decline. The entry of the UK, Ireland and Denmark in 1973 brought into the EC industrial regions already in decline in the UK, together with the comparatively backward, still very agricultural, Irish Republic. The entry of Greece (1981) and then of Spain and Portugal (1986) greatly increased the number of people in backward agricultural regions and added some stagnating industrial regions in Spain. Finally, the inclusion of the former GDR has added a substantial new industrial problem region. With the exception of Denmark, all the additions to the original six of the EEC have been countries with GDP levels per capita below the EC average at the time of their entry. In anticipation of Chapter 11, in which further possible new members are considered, it should be appreciated that the six EFTA countries are all at or above the present EC average, whereas Poland, Hungary and Czechoslovakia, like the GDR, are a long way below it.

In the late 1980s the EC was already having to devise new regional polices to take into account the three new, comparatively backward, members, the entry of which, to complicate matters, introduced three additional languages. The entry since then of the GDR has had repercussions on the Community and serious negative effects, initially at least, on the FRG. Given the state of uncertainty and rapid change in the EC in the early 1990s, various aspects of regional features and problems may be drastically modified at short notice. Nevertheless, basic distributions and regional characteristics will change only slowly. Stuttgart, Birmingham and Milan will long remain far more highly industrialised than the Canarias, Crete or Calabria.

CAUSES OF REGIONAL DISPARITIES

The fortunes of some regions have fluctuated over the centuries but other regions, such as North and Central Italy, and the Low Countries have generally prospered while still others, such as the Massif Central in France, and South Italy, have always been poor. In order to provide a framework for studying the causes of regional disparities in the EC, two of many possible aspects will now be

226

discussed. First, the attributes of regions will be assessed and, second, the summary will be given of the findings of a survey by the Commission of the EC covering some 900 companies.

The geographical literature of some decades ago contained much evidence intended to support the view that the natural environment affects human activities profoundly. A more controversial explanation of differences between societies, now discredited, was related to the actual mental capabilities and cultural attitudes of various groups of people. Much has also been said about the importance of location on the success (or otherwise) of economic activities. For various conceptual and methodological reasons, the influence of regional environmental and locational differences on development has been played down in recent decades, if not ignored altogether. Instead, overwhelming importance is attached to economic organisation (e.g. the movement of capital, the cost of labour) and the effect of political and economic decisions. The present authors are of the view that even within the comparatively small EC, regions differ so profoundly in their attributes and locations that the study of their past performance and future prospects must take into account these differences, notwithstanding the great influence of organisational decisions. For simplicity, two influences have been distinguished: first, the various elements that make up the region and, second, its location in a given context relative to other regions. The two influences are together comprehensive enough to cover most aspects of regional disparities and to answer most questions about them.

Each region contains a particular combination of natural resources, people (often referred to as human resources), and means of production (capital resources). Natural resources include water, bioclimatic resources (the quality of the land and soil), fossil fuel and non-fuel mineral reserves. Attributes of people, especially educational levels and skills in new and growing activities, are important, as is also financial organisation. Means of production, as for example the quantity, quality and efficiency of factories, farms and hospitals, and the level of mechanisation, are guides to the state of the means of production of goods and services in sectors that are expanding, stagnating or declining. Location in the EC, however it is defined, is broadly related to the supposed advantage of being central rather than peripheral in a spatial sense (see Chapter 3).

In order to exemplify the possible effects of the *attributes* and the *locations* on regional disparities in the EC, four NUTS 2 level regions are compared in Table 10.1, two from the UK, two from Italy. At present levels of performance, Lombardia in Italy and South Central England are roughly similar, and each is well ahead of arguably the most backward region in each of the two countries, Calabria and Northern Ireland. On the scale used, using points subjectively awarded by the authors in order to illustrate the way the situation can be viewed, no EC region could score 75 out of 75 or 0 out of 75. Some regions of southern Germany might exceed Lombardia by a few points but few if any in the EC would be lower than Calabria. An examination of the scores of the four regions in Table 10.1 shows that there is little room for quick, profound changes.

Table 10.1 A comparison of the attributes of four NUTS 2 level EC regions. Notional scores: maximum 5 favourable, 0 unfavourable

	Lombardia	Calabria	Berks Bucks Oxon	Northern Ireland
Water	4	2	3	3
Agricultural land quality	4	1	3	3
Forests	3	1	1	1
Hydro-electricity	3	1	0	0
Fossil fuels	0	0	0	0
Non-fuel minerals	0	0	0	0
Higher education	4	0	4	2
Financial	4	0	4	1
Agricultural sector	4	1	3	3
Industrial sector	4	1	4	2
Service sector	4	1	4	2
Research	4	0	5	1
Tradition and skills	4	0	4	3
EC location	3	1	3	1
National location	3	1	5	1
Local variations	great	great	small	small
Total score	48/75	10/75	43/75	23/75

Source: The scores for each attribute range between 5 (for a position among the top few in the whole EC) to 0 (either absence of the attribute or a position among the bottom few in the EC). The judgements are subjective, and although made with considerable thought, are presented primarily to draw attention to reasons why regional differences exist in the EC.

Calabria and Lombardia have been vastly different for centuries, as have South Central England and Northern Ireland. Indeed, the creation of the EC may actually have slightly enhanced the locational advantages of Lombardia and South Central England over their national positions in a pre-EC context.

Location cannot be changed, although places can be brought closer together in time distance by the improvement of communications. On the other hand, a firm looking for the optimum location in the EC for a given function has locational freedom, and the decision about location would presumably take into account the various relevant advantages and disadvantages of a number of possible regions. The accessibility scores for representative places in the EC in Figure 8.8 could be a guide. Some of the ingredients, such as improved educational levels, and the introduction of new industries, can produce changes gradually.

An extensive survey of the views of 900 EC Companies (see COM 90-609 (1991)) on regional issues was directed at firms in three types of region: backward agricultural regions; declining industrial ones; and a control group. A feature of the findings is a lack of concern about location in the EC. If a location is unsatisfactory for a particular industrial or service activity, then that activity can be moved to a place regarded as more favourable, but the locational features of its initial position can only be changed slightly by an improvement in transport and communications links with other regions. Since improvements in the transport sector are numerous, ongoing, and widely distributed in all kinds of region, the relative improvement of a particular link may be matched and in effect cancelled out by improvements in others.

Many problems connected with non-locational features were universally regarded as serious in the survey. Many of the companies questioned hoped that income and corporate taxes could be lowered, although this was somewhat unrealistic. Another concern was the quality and suitability of the skills of the labour force. Economic growth was regarded as essential for progress. In the lagging regions, the cost of credit caused concern, together with the attitude of bureaucracy. In Italy, for example, interest rates tend to be higher in the South than in the North. Business services were lacking and inadequate. In Portugal and Ireland the provision of the energy supply was regarded as a serious issue, while in Ireland, southern Spain, Sicilia and Sardegna, transport (including presumably a peripheral location) was referred to as a problem, and suitable industrial sites were not available in southern Italy. Educational provision is inadequate at all levels in Spain. In declining industrial regions, a need to retrain unemployed people and to improve the qualifications of the workforce was referred to, while at the same time labour costs have to be reduced. The former GDR, not included in the survey, has immediately become the most critical declining industrial region in the EC.

According to the survey, even the most successful regions had problems, with labour shortages a common feature. Indeed, vocational training and professional expertise are perhaps the greatest single need for the 1990s. According to COM 90-609 (1991: 39): 'in an increasingly competitive world in all regions both process and product innovations are constantly needed'. In the EC a related problem is the great concentration of research and development in a few regions, as in Madrid for the whole of Spain and in Northwest Italy for that country. Due to a long-standing policy of decentralisation in France, Paris is less dominant than it was some decades ago.

In spite of the dramatic recent reduction in fertility rates, the population of many regions of the EC continues to grow and immigrants add significantly to the number of young adults in some regions, so there will be more young people seeking jobs, as the extremely high unemployment levels among under-25s show. How many young people in EC countries will be able and willing to continue in full-time education into their twenties is likely to be a prominent issue in the 1990s.

Although it is convenient to consider each region as homogeneous, taking average values for variables, in reality there are great disparities, both environmental and human, within regions, however the regions are delimited. To be sure, the more finely a part of the world is subdivided, the smaller should be the differences within each region. In the EC, only at NUTS 3 level are regions small

229

enough in some cases to have a considerable degree of homogeneity. Two examples will serve to illustrate the diversity found in the EC regions at NUTS 2 level.

1   *Lombardia* (Italy), which is an entity at both NUTS 1 and 2 levels, consists of nine provinces. Three of these are entirely or partly in the Alps, where a particular set of problems is to be found. A zone of highly industrialised centres of various sizes, including Milan, extends over all or part of several more provinces. Finally, the southern part of Lombardia, in the North Italian Lowland, contains some of the most productive farmland in the EC.

2   *Derbyshire and Nottinghamshire* (NUTS 2 level) include the Peak National Park, with upland farming, many coalfield settlements, some now with their collieries closed, two large manufacturing centres specialising in engineering and textiles, and a zone of mainly agricultural land of reasonably good quality.

In both the regions described above, it is unrealistic to generalise about conditions and to pretend that development assistance, if forthcoming, should be distributed evenly over the region. A comparable degree of diversity can be found in many other NUTS 2 level regions of the EC, and even greater diversity usually at NUTS 1 level.

Another consideration in the planning of the best allocation of resources to regions regarded as backward is to ensure that resources actually help the more needy. In the UNDP, this issue is given prominence:

A major conclusion from all the evidence is that not all government spending works in the interest of the poor and that great care must be taken in structuring social spending to ensure that benefits also flow to them. The very rationale for government intervention crumbles if social expenditures, far from improving the existing income distribution, aggravate it further.

(UNDP 1990: 33)

For example, a road improvement programme in a relatively backward agricultural region of southern Spain or Italy might improve the conditions for public passenger and goods traffic but would also benefit car owners, by definition already the more affluent members of the community. Ideally, every family, household or even individual should be considered if the most appropriate benefactors are to be targeted. In practice however, with 345 million individuals, or about 100 million households, in the EC, generalisations have to be made and decisions based on these.

GDP PER CAPITA IN THE REGIONS OF THE EC

Gross Domestic Product (GDP) measures the income generated in the Member States and regions by the resident producer units. GDP is the most comprehensive single index of the economic success or lack of success (by EC standards) of a region and a guide to the eligibility of the region for some kind of assistance because it measures the total production of goods and services in a given period. When GDP is used to compare regions that differ in population size, as indeed all the EC regions do, it should be expressed in terms of the notional GDP per inhabitant, whether of the whole population or of some subset of it, such as per person employed. The participation rate (percentage of population actually economically active) varies greatly between regions in the EC, so measurement of GDP against total population and against economically active population does not bear a constant relationship. Another problem in the interpretation of GDP data, especially for some lower-level regions in the hierarchy, is that people may work in one region but reside in an adjoining one (e.g. there is a net flow of commuters from Kent to Greater London and back). They will contribute to the GDP of the region in which they work but will be counted against the GDP of the region in which they reside. Figure 10.1 shows the GDP per capita of the NUTS 1 level regions of the EC.

The effects of the aggregation of population and production into regions must now be noted. First, there is a general tendency for the extremes in GDP per capita between regions to increase in accordance with the number of regions into which the EC (or any other major region) is subdivided. This effect is enhanced by the lack of consistency in the size of the regions at each level in the hierarchy. Second, in each region there will be disparities between the subregions of which it is composed. This effect is illustrated in Table 10.2, in which GDP per inhabitant is given for four NUTS 1 level regions, Bayern (Germany), Southeast (UK), Noord-Nederland, and the Sud (Italy), and for regions within them at NUTS 2 level. The averages for the subregions of each NUTS 1 level region vary enormously, and further disparities appear within the NUTS 2 level regions when they, in turn, are broken down.

Since, in practice, the regions of the EC at NUTS 1 and 2 levels with high GDP per inhabitant are ordinarily net providers of assistance through the EC budget, their features and problems are of less immediate concern than those with low GDP levels per inhabitant. Their very 'success' should however be appreciated and accounted for, since they are at levels to which more backward regions should in theory be aspiring, although some of them also have serious problems such as the great size and congestion of London and Paris, and the heavy dependence on natural gas in Groningen (the Netherlands). The 'top' 12 regions of the EC in GDP per inhabitant at NUTS 2 level are listed in Table 10.3 and brief comments about them are included. One group comprises large cities with sophisticated services, a considerable concentration of industry, and a comparatively small surrounding area: Hamburg, Ile-de-France, Greater London, Bremen, Hovedstadsregionen (Greater Copenhagen). Another group consists of sophisticated, highly industrialised regions with industries developed mainly in the twentieth century: Darmstadt, Lombardia, Stuttgart, Emilia-Romagna. Groningen has a natural resource of exceptional importance and a small population (Grampian in the UK is similar). The Valle d'Aosta is so small

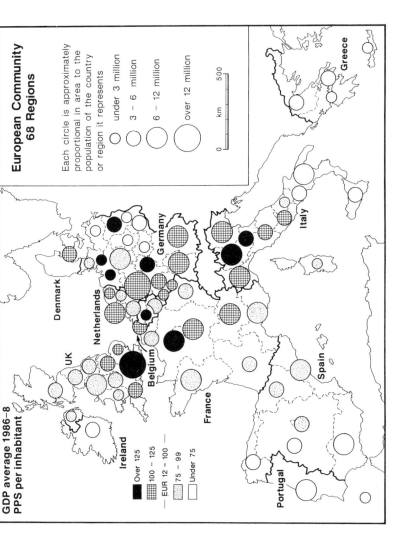

Figure 10.1 GDP per inhabitant at NUTS 1 level of the European Community, average 1986–87–88

Source: COM 90-609 (1991), Table A of Statistical Annex

Note: See Figure 2.3 for the names of the regions

Table 10.2 Gross Domestic Product per inhabitant in four selected regions of the EC at NUTS 1 and 2 levels (EC average = 100), average 1986–8

Region	GDP per inhab.	Region	GDP per inhab.
Bayern (Germany)	113.6	**Southeast (UK)**	128.3
Oberbayern	135.1	Greater London	164.0
Mittelfranken	122.3	Berks, Bucks, Oxon	118.3
Schwaben	107.8	Beds, Herts	111.3
Oberfranken	97.8	Hants, I. of Wight	109.0
Unterfranken	94.7	Surrey, E. and W. Sussex	107.0
Niederbayern	90.9	Kent	97.1
Oberpfalz	90.7	Essex	96.8
Noord-Nederland	123.6	**Sud (Italy)**	67.4
Groningen	183.1	Puglia	72.5
Drenthe	100.7	Basilicata	64.0
Friesland	84.6	Calabria	58.7

Source: COM 90-609 (1991), Annex Table A

Table 10.3 Top 12 NUTS 2 level regions for GDP per inhabitant in PPS, average 1986–8 (EC average = 100)

	GDP per inhabitant	NUTS 2 region	Country	Attributes
1	183.1	Groningen	Netherlands	Gas fields and processing
2	182.7	Hamburg	Germany	World league sea port, city only
3	165.6	Ile-de-France	France	Contains Paris and suburbs
4	164.0	Greater London	UK	Contains London and suburbs
5	148.9	Darmstadt	Germany	Contains Frankfurt and various industries
6	146.8	Bremen	Germany	Major sea port, city only
7	137.3	Lombardia	Italy	Italy's industrial and financial heartland
8	135.1	Oberbayern	Germany	Contains Munich and various industries
9	133.8	Stuttgart	Germany	EC's most highly industrialised region
10	133.8	Valle d'Aosta	Italy	Small 'freak' region in Italian Alps
11	132.6	Hovedstadsregionen	Denmark	Contains Copenhagen and suburbs
12	127.6	Emilia-Romagna	Italy	Industrial expansion, good agriculture

Source: COM 90-609 (1991), Annex Table A

(115,000 inhabitants) that it would not merit its NUTS 1 level status but for a degree of autonomy granted to it on account of its cultural uniqueness in Italy.

Thus the group of regions at the top of the GDP 'league table' is rather mixed. Together the 12 regions contain 12.8 per cent of the population of the EC. When broken down into smaller areas and then into families and individuals, it can be seen that they contain some extremely poor people such as the homeless who sleep 'on the streets' in London and Paris. Indeed, unemployment levels are high in some regions at the 'top', such as Hamburg (8 per cent) and Groningen (11.3 per cent), and by definition the unemployed have no earned income. Concentrations of immigrants from developing and Central European countries are growing in and around several EC capital cities and ports including London, Paris, Marseilles, Naples and Berlin.

The lower end of the GDP spectrum looks very different. At NUTS 2 level, 35 regions have a GDP per inhabitant of less than 75 per cent of the EC average. Thirty-three of these are distributed by countries as follows:

Greece	13 (all)	Italy	5 (out of 20)
Portugal	5 (all)	Ireland	
Spain	8 (out of 16)	Netherlands	1 (out of 12)

(*Note:* the Départements d'outre-mer (DOM) of France, and Ceuta and Melilla of Spain, are not counted here.)

The above 33 regions have approximately 18 per cent of the total population of the EC. Most of the regions are in Greece, Portugal, southern Spain and southern Italy. They are more dependent on agriculture than most other regions of the EC and are generally more rural.

Just as the regions of the EC with the highest GDP per capita contain relatively poor people, although by class rather than by areal concentration, so the regions of the EC with the lowest GDP per capita contain affluent people. What is also noticeable is the low level of unemployment in most of the Greek and Portuguese regions, a result presumably (at least partly) of the recording and definition of the unemployed, which differs from that elsewhere in the EC and is less rigorous in the registration of people out of work.

UNEMPLOYMENT

The European Commission has yet to produce an entirely consistent definition of unemployment throughout the EC. Since levels fluctuate substantially over quite short periods, it is also difficult to keep up to date with changes. The problems of interpreting EC unemployment data are shown in Table 10.4. Some of the variations between the four sets are due to actual changes in levels during 1987–90, but differences in definition may be partly responsible. Even if the low level in Luxembourg is disregarded, given the very small size of the country, yet the contrast between the extremes, Denmark and Spain, is very marked. Variations in unemployment level in the EC are shown at NUTS 1 level in Figure 10.2.

Table 10.4 Unemployment levels (percentage of workforce unemployed) in the EC according to four sources, the countries ranked according to position in 1987

	(1) *COM 87-230* *1986*	*(2)* *Eurostat* *1987*	*(3)* *CSO* *1988*	*(4)* *COM 90-609* *1990*
Luxembourg	2.5	2.7	2.3	1.5
Denmark	6.5	6.1	6.4	7.9
FRG	7.1	6.3	6.3	5.2
Portugal	8.7	7.1	6.1	5.1
Greece	7.5	7.4	7.7	7.5
Netherlands	9.8	9.7	10.0	8.0
France	10.1	10.4	9.8	8.7
Italy	10.0	10.6	11.0	10.2
EC	**10.8**	**10.6**	**10.1**	**8.3**
UK	12.0	11.1	9.3	6.3
Belgium	10.2	11.3	10.1	7.6
Ireland	18.7	18.1	17.8	16.4
Spain	21.5	20.8	20.2	16.1

Sources: (1) COM 87-230, 1987
 (2) Eurostat, 1989a
 (3) CSO, 1990
 (4) COM 90-609, 1991

In Table 10.5 and in Figure 10.3 it can be seen that within the five largest EC countries there are very big differences in unemployment at NUTS 2 level. What is more, quite sharp contrasts occur between many pairs or groups of adjoining regions. Thus, for example, West-Vlaanderen (Belgium) with 3.8 per cent adjoins Hainaut (also Belgium) with 13.1 per cent and Nord-Pas-de-Calais (France) with 11.8 per cent. In Italy, Lazio (with Rome) has 10.9 per cent unemployment but adjoining Campania (with Naples) has 19.8 per cent.

Many NUTS 2 level regions are well below half the average unemployment level of 8.3 per cent for the whole of the EC in 1990. The regions with the lowest levels are found in a variety of places in the Community, in some cases these are unexpected: some counties in the Southeast region of the UK, several regions in southern Germany, and the northernmost regions of Italy, as well as in Greece and Portugal. They form a far from homogeneous group in other respects. Some have very high GDP per capita levels, while others have very low levels.

While it is interesting to consider the characteristics of those EC regions with the lowest unemployment, it is of more relevance for the allocation of assistance to identify the features and problems of the regions with the highest unemployment. All NUTS 2 level regions with unemployment of more than twice the EC average of 8.3 per cent are listed in Table 10.6 (DOM and Ceuta and Melilla are excluded). All of these 11 regions are either in Spain or Italy. Those between 50 and 100 per cent above the EC average include Ireland and Northern Ireland

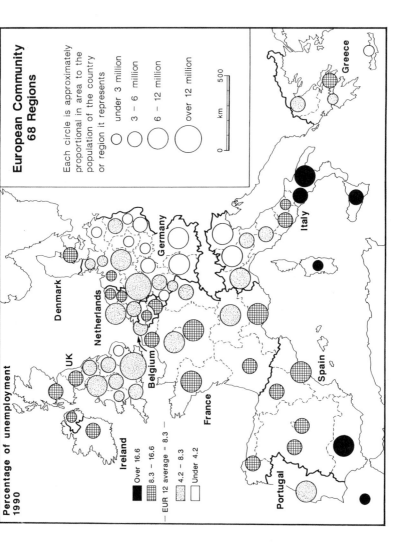

Figure 10.2 Percentage of unemployment at NUTS 1 regional level of the European Community

Source: COM 90-609 (1991), Table A for Statistical Annex
Note: See Figure 2.3 for names of the regions

Table 10.5 Extremes of unemployment level in selected EC countries in 1990, at
NUTS 2 level, percentages of total workforce

National unemployment levels		Regions of highest unemployment		Regions of lowest unemployment	
FRG	5.2	Bremen	10.4	Stuttgart	2.7
France	8.7	Languedoc-Rousillon	12.9	Alsace	4.5
Italy	10.2	Calabria	22.6	Valle d'Aosta	2.4
UK	6.3	N. Ireland	15.7	Berks, Bucks, Oxon	2.2
Spain	16.1	Andalucía	25.4	Rioja	7.3
Netherlands	8.0	Groningen	11.3	Zeeland	5.6
Belgium	7.6	Hainaut	13.1	West-Vlaanderen	3.8
Greece	7.5	Attiki	9.7	Ionia Nisia	3.3
Portugal	5.1	Alentejo	12.4	Centro	3.1
EC*	8.3	Andalucía	25.4	Luxembourg GD	1.5

Source: COM 90-609 (1991), Annex Table A
Note: * excluding the GDR

(UK), and five more in Spain. Most of the regions with high unemployment are heavily dependent on agriculture, but the País Vasco and Cataluña, Spain's most industrialised regions, together with Hainaut (Belgium) and Merseyside, are highly urbanised and have traditional industries. The largest areas of high unemployment in the EC are in Italy roughly south of Rome and, across the western Mediterranean, in most of Spain.

A particularly disturbing feature of unemployment in the EC is brought out by data for levels among persons under the age of 25. Table 10.7 shows which EC regions at NUTS 2 level have unemployment among the under-25s at more than half. The overall EC unemployment level (see Eurostat 1989a: 127–34) in 1987 of 10.6 per cent breaks down into an average of 21.6 per cent for the under-25s and only 7.9 per cent for the over-25s. The unemployment situation for the under-25s is a rough indication of future economic prospects for the countries and regions. The FRG had a good record because there is virtually no difference between the levels of unemployment in either age group. In contrast, Spain and Italy have very bad records. The addition to the FRG of the GDR, reported in mid-1991 to have as much as 20 per cent unemployment, has raised considerably the overall level in the new Germany.

While it is desirable on the grounds of equity and justice to guide employment to the most deprived regions, the EC does not have the powers or the financial resources to create many new jobs. Since the late 1980s, there has actually been a net loss of jobs in many parts of the EC, so the problem is, in practice, how to stem the growth of unemployment and soften its effects.

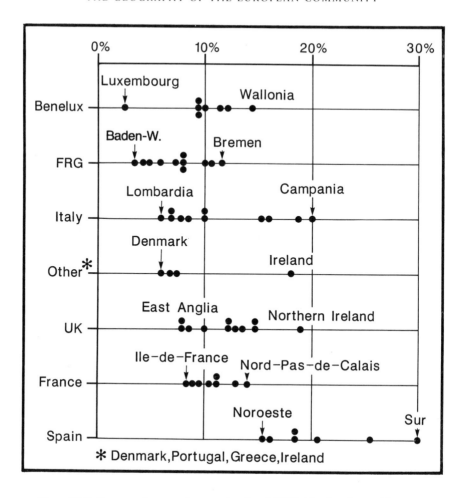

Figure 10.3 Contrasts in unemployment levels at NUTS 1 level within and between
countries of the European Community

Source: COM 90-609 (1991), Table A for Statistical Annex

A MULTI-VARIATE VIEW OF THE REGIONS OF THE EC

A number of variables related to regional contrasts in the EC have already been
discussed in different chapters of this book. Two of them, regarded as highly
significant, GDP per capita and unemployment, were referred to in the two
previous sections of this chapter. In this section, 13 variables are brought
together for 69 regions of the EC at NUTS 1 level, including the new Länder of
the former GDR. All EFTA countries except Iceland have been added, to give a
total of 74 regions. The 74 by 13 data matrix is shown in Table 10.8. It is of

Table 10.6 Regions at NUTS 2 level with levels of unemployment more than twice the EC average in 1990 (percentage of total workforce)

Region	Country	% of workforce unemployed
1 Andalucía	Spain	25.4
2 Extremadura	Spain	24.8
3 Canarias	Spain	22.7
4 Calabria	Italy	22.6
5 Sicilia	Italy	21.7
6 Basilicata	Italy	21.5
7 Campania	Italy	19.8
8 País Vasco	Spain	19.0
9 Sardegna	Italy	18.9
10 Asturias	Spain	17.0
11 Cantabria	Spain	16.6

Source: COM 90-609 (1991), Annex Table A

Table 10.7 Highest under-25 employment rates (in percentages) in 160 regions of the EC

Italy		Spain	
Campania	63.2	País Vasco (Nordeste)	58.9
Calabria (Sud)	54.8	Andalucía (Sur)	53.8
Sardegna	53.7	Asturias (Noroeste)	50.0
Molise (Abruzzi e Molise)	50.8		

Source: Eurostat 1989a: 127–34

general interest, and also of relevance to the study of regional characteristics and trends, to know how closely the variables correlate, and also which regions are similar in their various attributes. Principal components analysis has been applied to the data set to achieve these aims. The results of the application of a similar technique (factor analysis) were reported in Commission of the EC (1984: 211–51). Greece, Spain and Portugal were not included in that study. The procedure and results of the present study will be set out for clarity step by step.

1   *The data matrix.* All but four of the variables ((1), (2), (7) and (13)) have been taken from the definitive data set in COM 90-609 (1991) and are therefore considered to be information of relevance to regional policy. The first two variables show locational attributes, one based on the calculation made for the EC (see Chapter 2), the other by the authors, referred to in Chapter 3. Additional variables are unemployment levels among under-25s and infant mortality rates. Some of the data for the GDR are estimates. West and East Berlin have been kept separate for technical reasons. It is appreci-

239

Table 10.8 Data set for 69 NUTS 1 level EC regions and five EFTA countries

	(1)	(2)	(3)	(4)	(5)	(6)	(7)	(8)	(9)	(10)	(11)	(12)	(13)
		Centrality	Population				<25				GDP	Per	Inf.
	EC	Coles	Change	15–64	Part.	Unem.	Unem.	Agric.	Ind.	Serv.	PPS	empl.	mort.
1 Schleswig-Holstein	3	3	-0.1	70	48	6	10	5	30	65	95	101	8
2 Hamburg	5	3	-0.6	70	49	8	15	1	26	73	183	134	10
3 Niedersachsen	3	3	-0.1	69	47	7	9	6	37	57	98	99	9
4 Bremen	4	3	-0.7	70	46	10	15	0	33	67	147	116	10
5 Nordrhein-W.	5	4	-0.2	71	45	7	9	3	44	54	109	108	10
6 Hessen	5	5	-0.1	70	49	4	5	3	37	60	128	116	9
7 Rheinland-P.	5	5	0.0	70	47	5	7	5	41	54	101	101	10
8 Baden-W.	4	5	0.2	70	49	3	4	5	47	48	120	103	7
9 Bayern	3	4	0.1	70	51	3	4	8	41	51	114	100	8
10 Saarland	4	5	-0.3	71	42	7	12	2	42	56	105	101	10
11 Berlin West	3	3	0.4	68	52	7	10	1	31	68	125	105	11
12 Berlin East	3	3	0.3	67	60	2	3	1	35	64	75	75	9
13 Mecklenburg-V.	3	2	0.3	67	60	2	3	20	33	47	65	65	8
14 Brandenburg	3	3	0.1	67	60	2	3	15	43	42	65	65	9
15 Sachsen-A.	3	3	-0.1	67	60	2	3	12	48	40	70	70	9
16 Thuringen	3	4	-0.1	67	60	2	3	10	52	38	70	70	10
17 Sachsen	3	3	-0.2	67	60	2	3	7	54	39	75	75	10
18 Ile-de-France	5	5	0.3	69	50	7	16	1	26	73	166	140	8
19 Bassin Parisien	3	5	0.5	65	44	9	24	9	34	57	100	104	8
20 Nord-P.d.C.	5	5	0.0	65	40	12	29	4	36	60	88	105	9

21 Est	9	107	99	59	37	4	19	7	44	67	0.2	5	3
22 Ouest	8	96	91	57	29	13	24	9	44	64	0.6	4	3
23 Sud-Ouest	9	97	93	60	26	14	25	10	44	65	0.5	4	2
24 Centre-Est	8	101	105	59	34	7	21	8	45	66	0.5	5	3
25 Méditerranée	8	109	96	70	22	8	27	12	41	65	1.0	4	3
26 Nord-Ouest	8	101	104	58	32	10	33	10	42	68	0.3	5	3
27 Lombardia	8	122	137	53	43	4	20	3	46	71	0.1	4	3
28 Nord-Est	7	101	117	55	37	8	21	4	44	69	0.1	4	3
29 Emilia-R.	9	109	128	52	37	11	22	4	46	69	0.0	4	3
30 Centro	9	98	111	55	37	8	27	7	43	68	0.1	3	3
31 Lazio	9	110	117	76	19	5	44	11	41	70	0.4	3	3
32 Campania	12	81	67	63	24	13	63	20	40	66	0.7	2	2
33 Abruzzi-M.	11	88	87	54	28	18	37	11	42	67	0.4	2	2
34 Sud	12	79	67	59	22	19	47	18	38	66	0.6	1	1
35 Sicilia	12	88	70	62	21	16	50	22	37	66	0.6	1	1
36 Sardegna	10	89	75	63	24	13	54	19	39	67	0.6	2	1
37 Noord-Nederland	7	176	124	64	30	6	18	9	42	67	0.4	4	3
38 Oost-N.	8	113	87	64	30	6	15	9	44	68	1.0	4	4
39 West-N.	8	126	112	74	22	4	13	8	47	69	0.4	5	5
40 Zuid-N.	8	119	95	62	33	5	14	8	45	71	0.6	4	5
41 Vlaams-G.	10	115	101	62	35	3	17	6	41	68	0.2	4	5
42 Région Wallonne	9	104	83	69	28	4	31	11	39	67	0.0	5	4
43 Région Bruxelles	9	93	154	80	20	0	25	10	38	65	-0.6	5	5
44 Luxembourg GD	9	104	122	67	29	4	6	2	43	70	0.3	5	3
45 North	8	91	92	62	36	2	21	9	49	66	-0.2	3	3
46 Yorks and H.	10	90	97	62	36	2	19	7	49	66	0.0	3	3
47 E. Midlands	8	89	100	57	41	2	14	5	51	66	0.4	3	3
48 East Anglia	9	90	104	63	32	5	12	4	52	65	1.0	3	3
49 Southeast	9	101	128	71	28	1	11	4	52	66	0.2	4	4

Table 10.8 continued

	(1)	(2)	(3)	(4)	(5)	(6)	(7)	(8)	(9)	(10)	(11)	(12)	(13)
		Centrality Population											
	EC	Coles	Change	15–64	Part.	Unem.	<25 Unem.	Agric.	Ind.	Serv.	GDP PPS	Per empl.	Inf. mort.
50 Southwest	2	3	0.7	64	50	4	12	4	29	67	101	94	9
51 W. Midlands	3	3	0.0	66	50	6	18	3	40	57	96	86	11
52 Northwest	4	2	-0.3	65	50	8	20	1	35	64	99	95	9
53 Wales	3	3	0.1	65	45	7	20	3	34	63	88	93	10
54 Scotland	2	1	-0.2	66	49	9	23	4	32	64	100	92	9
55 N. Ireland	2	1	0.2	63	43	16	27	5	28	66	81	85	10
56 Ireland	1	1	0.8	60	38	16	26	16	29	56	65	83	9
57 Denmark	2	2	0.1	67	56	8	8	6	27	67	113	87	5
58 Voreia Ellada	1	0	0.5	66	42	7	25	36	26	38	53	53	14
59 Kentriki E.	1	0	0.2	66	44	6	25	46	19	35	55	56	14
60 Attiki	1	0	0.9	66	38	10	25	2	31	67	59	64	14
61 Nisia	1	0	0.4	66	42	4	25	35	18	47	49	50	14
62 Noroeste	1	1	0.3	65	40	14	40	33	26	41	68	78	9
63 Nordeste	1	3	0.4	67	38	15	47	9	40	51	87	105	9
64 Madrid	2	2	0.9	66	37	12	39	1	31	68	85	111	9
65 Centro	1	2	0.4	65	37	17	39	24	29	47	63	86	7
66 Este	2	3	0.6	66	40	13	41	7	41	52	83	104	8
67 Sur	1	1	1.0	64	35	24	52	18	26	56	59	92	9
68 Canarias	1	0	0.7	65	38	23	49	10	23	67	72	107	8
69 Portugal	1	1	0.8	64	46	5	17	21	35	44	54	56	18
70 Switzerland	3	5	0.3	68	50	1	2	2	35	67	205	205	7

		(1)	(2)	(3)	(4)	(5)	(6)	(7)	(8)	(9)	(10)	(11)	(12)	(13)
71	Austria	2	3	0.1	68	50	2	3	4	39	57	117	110	8
72	Norway	1	1	0.3	65	55	2	3	4	38	58	150	150	8
73	Sweden	1	1	0.2	64	55	2	4	4	36	61	144	140	6
74	Finland	1	0	0.3	68	50	8	12	8	34	58	140	130	7

Notes on the variables in Table 10.8

(1), (2) Indices of centrality

(1) *Source*: COM 87-230, 1987, p. 120 of Annex, five types, 'scoring' as follows: 5 points Inner Central, 4 Outer Central, 3 Intermediate, 2 Inner Peripheral, 1 Outer Peripheral

(2) Distance from the centre of gravity of population of the EC, see Chapter 2 and Figure 3.3

(3), (4) Population. *Source*: COM 90-609 (1991), Annex Table A

(3) Annual percentage change of population, 1978–88

(4) Percentage of total population within age range 15–64 years inclusive, 1987

(5) Participation rate, percentage of total population economically active 1988. *Source*: as for (3)

(6) Unemployment as a percentage of the total workforce 1990. *Source*: as for (3)

(7) Percentage unemployed among persons of under 25 years of age, 1987. *Source*: Eurostat 1989a

(8)–(10) Percentage of total economically active population in three sectors, 1987

(8) Agriculture

(9) Industry   *Source*: as for (3)

(10) Services

(11), (12) Gross Domestic Product in PPS, (11) per total population, (12) per person employed. *Source*: as for (3)

(13) Infant deaths per 1,000 live births, 1985. *Source*: CSO 1990

ated that by their nature some variables are bound to correlate quite highly with each other negatively or positively: in particular, the two measures of centrality ((1) and (2)) and the two types of unemployment ((6) and (7)) positively, and the three sectors of the economy ((8), (9), (10)) negatively.

2   Table 10.9 shows the *coefficients of correlation* between all possible pairs of variables in the data set. The general impression of the correlations is that there is not a high degree of 'agreement' between variables except where, as noted above, they are describing roughly the same attributes or are mutually exclusive. In other words, the EC is very complex, and changes in one variable would not necessarily lead to corresponding changes in others. The variables used are predominantly demographic and economic, and further depth could have been added by the inclusion, for example, of environmental, cultural or social variables. The results of the exercise described here are, however, quite close to two other exercises carried out earlier by the authors with a smaller number of variables, in one case with 60 NUTS 1 level regions, excluding the GDR and EFTA, and in the second case only without EFTA.

3   *Eigenvalues* are indices that serve as a guide to the degree of intercorrelation of the variables. From the correlation matrix, 13 uncorrelated principal components were calculated. In this study, only the first two, the strongest, are considered. The first component picks out a set of intercorrelated variables that accounts for 40 per cent of all the variation (5.2 units out of 13), while the second adds another 21.6 per cent (2.8 units out of 13). Thus, more than three-fifths of all the variation in the 13 variables can be expressed on two scales or dimensions.

4   *The loadings of the variables on the two components* are shown in Table 10.10. The percentage of each of the 13 variables loading on each of the first two (strongest) components is also shown in Table 10.10.

5   *The scores of the 74 regions on each component.* The first component is a broad consensus of a considerable proportion of most variables, placing the regions that are more central and more stable demographically, with low employment in agriculture and high GDP per capita at one end, and those with the opposite characteristics at the other. The positions of the 74 regions on this component can be read on the horizontal axis in Figure 10.4. Although the second component has little more than half of the weight of the first one, it has been stretched by standardisation to equal the first component. It is hardly influenced by locational or demographic features, but reflects strongly the service sector of employment (variable 10). The 74 regions are positioned on the vertical axis according to their scores on this second component. Each region is therefore located on the graph according to its position in two-dimensional socio-economic 'space', which reflects demographic and economic aspects of the EC, but which also has a spatial ingredient in the two centrality variables. The 74 regions would be repositioned into another dimension if the third component were also used,

Table 10.9 Matrix of Pearson product-moment correlation coefficients (from +1.0 perfect positive to −1.0 perfect negative, and no significant correlation around 0.0)

	(1) Cen. EC	(2) Coles	(3) Pop. Ch.	(4) 15–64	(5) Part. rate	(6) Unem.	(7) Unem. <25	(8) Agri.	(9) Serv.	(10) Ind.	(11) GDP	(12) GDP Empl.	(13) Inf. Mort.
1 Centrality EC	1.0	0.8	−0.5	0.6	0.2	−0.4	−0.4	−0.6	0.3	0.3	0.5	0.3	−0.3
2 Centrality Coles	0.8	1.0	−0.3	0.5	0.1	−0.4	−0.3	−0.5	0.3	0.2	0.5	0.4	−0.4
3 Population change	−0.5	−0.3	1.0	−0.4	−0.4	0.4	0.4	0.3	−0.4	0.0	−0.4	−0.1	0.1
4 % 15–64	0.6	0.5	−0.4	1.0	0.2	−0.4	−0.3	−0.3	0.3	0.1	0.4	0.3	−0.2
5 Participation rate	0.2	0.1	−0.4	0.2	1.0	−0.7	−0.8	−0.2	0.5	−0.2	0.2	−0.0	−0.2
6 Unemployment	−0.4	−0.4	0.4	−0.4	−0.7	1.0	0.9	0.2	−0.5	0.2	−0.4	−0.1	−0.1
7 Unempl. under 25	−0.4	−0.3	0.4	−0.3	−0.8	0.9	1.0	0.3	−0.5	0.1	−0.4	−0.2	0.2
8 % Agriculture	−0.6	−0.5	0.3	−0.3	−0.2	0.2	0.3	1.0	−0.3	−0.7	−0.6	−0.5	0.5
9 % Industry	0.3	0.3	−0.4	0.3	0.5	−0.5	−0.5	−0.3	1.0	−0.5	0.1	0.0	−0.2
10 % Services	0.3	0.2	0.0	0.1	−0.2	0.2	0.1	−0.7	−0.5	1.0	0.5	0.5	−0.3
11 GDP per capita	0.5	0.5	−0.4	0.4	0.2	−0.4	−0.4	−0.6	0.1	0.5	1.0	0.8	−0.5
12 GDP per employed	0.3	0.4	−0.1	0.3	−0.0	−0.1	−0.2	−0.5	0.0	0.5	0.8	1.0	−0.6
13 Infant mortality	−0.3	−0.4	0.1	−0.2	−0.2	0.1	0.2	0.5	−0.2	−0.3	−0.5	−0.6	1.0

Table 10.10 Component loadings

Variable	Component loadings		Percentage explained on Component	
	I	II	I	II
1 Centrality EC	+0.76	+0.14	58	2
2 Centrality Coles	+0.72	+0.19	52	3
3 Population change	−0.58	+0.23	33	5
4 % 15–64	+0.61	−0.01	37	0
5 Participation rate	+0.55	−0.62	30	38
6 Unemployment	−0.67	+0.58	45	34
7 Unemployment under 25	−0.74	+0.51	54	26
8 % Agriculture	−0.73	−0.38	54	15
9 % Industry	+0.52	−0.58	27	33
10 % Services	+0.28	+0.82	8	68
11 GDP per capita	+0.77	+0.38	59	15
12 GDP per employed	+0.59	+0.57	35	32
13 Infant mortality	−0.53	−0.31	28	10

and into more dimensions, in reality each of less weight, if even more components were considered. The position of each region on the graph in Figure 10.4 is determined therefore by only three-fifths of the information in Table 10.8. The distance apart of the various regions measures the extent of their similarity or dissimilarity. Thus, for example, Switzerland and Portugal are 'poles apart' in many respects, as are Sicilia and Sachsen.

Some further implications of the results for the future of the EC may be noted. In the graph in Figure 10.4 the 'outer' regions (in a non-spatial sense) of some of the countries have been joined. The great diversity of Italy (even after several decades of efforts to bring the North and South together) shows very clearly. Post-unification Germany also shows great diversity. The UK is comparatively homogeneous, as is most of France. It is worth noting that these latter countries have been organised as single states much longer than has Italy or Germany.

Wales emerges as the most 'average' of all the 74 regions, a position it still retains even if the third component is added. Indeed, Great Britain in total is remarkably near average and therefore not likely to be a notable net donor or recipient of assistance to or from the rest of the EC. The most affluent and service-based regions of the EC are found in the upper-right area of the graph. The heavily industrialised regions of the former GDR, with a weak service sector, are situated to the lower right. The regions in which the agricultural sector is comparatively prominent are on the left side of the graph, with unemployment higher towards the upper part. Denmark, and all of the EFTA countries except Switzerland, fit comfortably into the space occupied by the FRG and Great Britain.

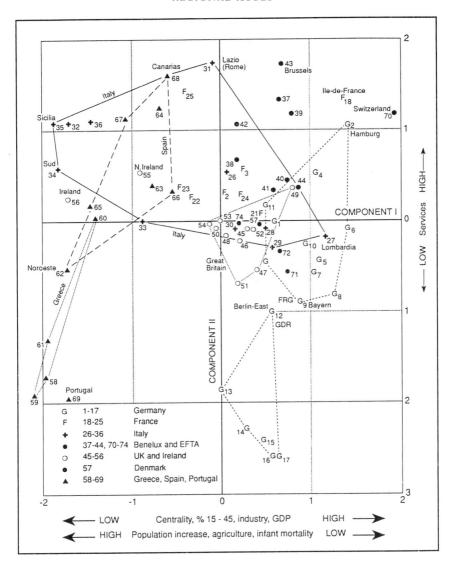

Figure 10.4 The positions of EC regions and the countries of EFTA in socio-economic space determined by principal components analysis. See text for explanation. The numbering of the regions in the diagram corresponds to the numbering in Table 10.8

What developments in the EC might change the positions of the regions on the graph? If, for example, unemployment increases in the GDR from the estimated pre-unification levels used here, the Länder would move towards the upper left of the graph, actually distancing themselves further from the FRG than they were at unification. Most of the less affluent, lagging or backward regions of the EC apart from the GDR are in the left-hand half of the graph. A notable change in the conditions of some of these regions (or of any others) would however result in a change in the position of the centre (or 'average') of the space. The addition of a dozen new regions from Poland, Czechoslovakia and Hungary, all placed somewhere between the GDR and Portugal, would shift the average on component I to the left and the average on component II downwards. In contrast, a dozen new regions from Turkey would fall far out to the left of Greece and southern Italy and would pull the average a good way in that direction along the horizontal axis of component I. Without the addition of new members, however, the present relative positions of the regions of the 12 in socio-economic space seems likely to change only very slowly.

THE REDUCTION OF REGIONAL DISPARITIES IN THE EC

Given the irregular nature of economic growth in the EC since the late 1970s, the accession of new members, and the great diversity within the Community in spite of its inclusion under the umbrella of the 'developed world', it is a daunting task for the Commission to decide where regional assistance should be directed. According to COM 90-609 (1991): 'the ten least developed regions, located mainly in Greece and Portugal, presently have average incomes per head which are one third of the average of the ten most advanced regions.' Similarly, disparities in unemployment are noted: 'the regional differences remain substantial, and in 1990, in the 10 regions with the lowest unemployment, the rate averaged just over 2.5 per cent while in the ten regions with the highest rate it averaged 22 per cent.' The Community may therefore be commended for taking a positive view of the problem of disparities by doubling the funds allocated to tackle it and by clearly identifying places to be assisted. Regions eligible for aid through the Structural Funds are shown in Figure 10.5. Table 10.11 contains basic data for five priority objectives for 1989–93. Only three are mapped in Figure 10.5, namely Objectives 1, 2 and 5b; Objectives 3, 4 and 5a affect the whole Community.

Much of the assistance goes to Objective 1 regions. These mostly have a GDP per capita level of less than 75 per cent of the EC average. They include Greece, Portugal, southern Italy, much of Spain, Ireland, and Corse in France. In all these regions, agriculture is a comparatively large employer of labour, and in most, industry is less developed. Even so, much of the population in these regions actually lives in large cities. The population of some areas of Objective 1 regions is growing by almost 1 per cent per year. In the late 1980s, the GDP per capita and employment have been growing in Spain and Portugal but have been declining in Greece and southern Italy.

Three criteria have to be satisfied for a NUTS level 3 region to be eligible under Objective 2:

(a) the average rate of unemployment recorded over the last three years must have been above the Community average;

248

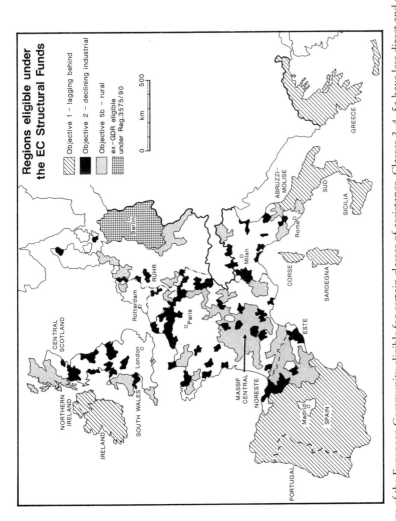

Regions eligible under the EC Structural Funds

⬚ Objective 1 – lagging behind

■ Objective 2 – declining industrial

⬚ Objective 5b – rural

⊞ ex-GDR eligible under Reg.3575/90

0   km   500

Figure 10.5 Regions of the European Community eligible for certain classes of assistance. Classes 3, 4, 5a have less direct and obvious regional significance and are not shown

Source: Commission of the EC (1991a: 3, Map 4)

Table 10.11 Assistance allocated from the EC Structural Funds 1989–93 (1989 prices)

	Member States (MS) or Regions	Proportion of		
		Community territory involved %	Population involved %	Billion ECU
Objective 1	7 MS	40.7	21.5	38.3
Objective 2	60 regions	–	16.5	7.2
Objectives 3 and 4	9 MS	100	100	7.45
Objective 5a	9 MS	100	100	3.4
Objective 5b	50 regions	17	5	2.8

Source: COM 90-84, 1992: 18
Notes:
Objective 1 – regions where development is lagging behind
Objective 2 – conversion of areas affected by industrial decline
Objectives 3 and 4 – combatting long-term unemployment and occupational integration of young people
Objective 5a – adjustment of agricultural structures
Objective 5b – development of rural areas

(b) the percentage share of industrial employment in total employment must have equalled or exceeded the Community average in any reference year from 1975 onwards;

(c) there must have been an observable fall in industrial employment compared with the reference year chosen in accordance with point (b).

(COM 90-609, 1991: 5-5)

In the event, NUTS 3 level regions eligible for assistance under the above criteria were to be found in 9 of the 12 Member States, and had a combined population of about 25 per cent of the whole EC. As 15 per cent had been the limit of the Community population to be included in such areas, subdivisions within NUTS 3 regions were used to distinguish areas in most need.

Objective 5b regions, selected for consideration for assistance, are a more mixed set, mostly small in population, rural, and peripheral or marginal. Some are mountain areas with a low density of population, poor communications and problems with regard to the high cost of maintenance of services.

While the precise destinations of EC assistance to the regions of the Community has not been worked out for the mid-to late 1990s, Figure 10.5 shows where assistance will be broadly targeted. The situation of East Germany remains to be made more precise, while the accession of new Member States would also lead to modifications. It is of interest, also, to refer to the distribution of assistance in recent years. Figure 10.6 shows the amount per inhabitant placed during 1975–87 (inclusive) in NUTS 2 level regions (NUTS 1 level for the UK). Greece, Spain and Portugal joined after 1975. Altogether, 96 regions received

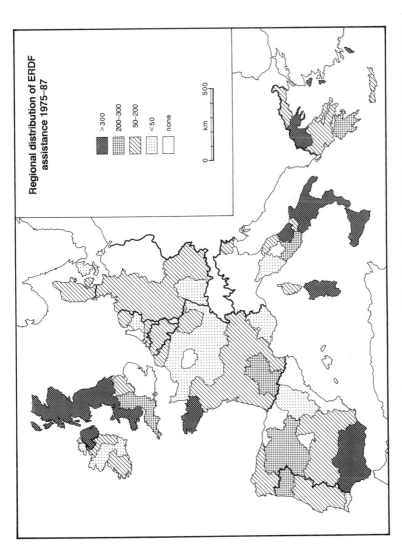

Figure 10.6 Regional distribution of ERDF assistance 1975–87 in millions of ECU at NUTS 2 level (UK at NUTS 1 level)

Source: Commission of the EC (1989: 65, Table 20)

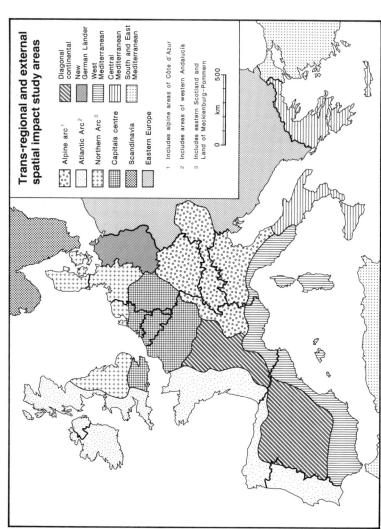

Trans-regional and external spatial impact study areas

- Alpine arc [1]
- Atlantic Arc [2]
- Northern Arc [3]
- Capitals centre
- Scandinavia
- Eastern Europe
- Diagonal continental
- New German Länder
- West Mediterranean
- Central Mediterranean
- South and East Mediterranean

1 Includes alpine areas of Côte d'Azur
2 Includes areas of western Andalucía
3 Includes eastern Scotland and Land of Mecklenburg–Pommern

0 — 500 km

Figure 10.7 Trans-regional and external spatial impact study areas (see text for explanation). Note that Atlantic Andalucía is not shown and Pommern is Vorpommern

Source: Commission of the EC 1991a: 23

some degree of assistance, including the four DOM regions of France. Amounts per inhabitant varied greatly, especially when the fact that only part of the population of some regions was eligible is taken into account. Details can be found in the annual *European Regional Development Report* (see Commission of the EC 1989).

Several features of the distribution of assistance shown in Figure 10.6 may be noted. All the Länder of West Germany received some assistance whereas North Italy received none, in contrast to the South and Islands, which were among the most lavishly assisted. In the UK (Southeast), Denmark (Copenhagen), the Netherlands (West Nederland), France (Ile-de-France) and Spain (Madrid), the regions in which the capital city is located were not assisted. In the mid- and late 1990s, more of the same may be expected, since the gap between the richer and poorer regions of the EC (counting all Member States, even when some had not joined) has not shown much reduction relatively since the early 1970s, even though the total GDP of the Community has increased considerably.

The reduction of regional disparities in GDP per inhabitant and in material conditions in the EC will no doubt be a matter of concern for the next two decades at least. The further integration of the Community may, paradoxically, encourage smaller national groups within some of the Member States to assert themselves, a matter to be discussed in Chapter 11. In the longer term, as a result of increasing contacts within what is gradually becoming effectively a new sovereign state, cultural and economic similarities between sets of regions located in two or more present Member States may form areas of common interest. Figure 10.7 is based on a map in Commission of the EC (1991a). Each of the five largest Member States of the EC together with the Netherlands breaks up into two to four parts, which join similar parts of other Member States. Thus, for example, almost the whole 'Atlantic arc' of the EC, from southern Portugal through Spain, France, England, Wales and Ireland to Scotland, is identified as one region: an entity hardly likely to be recognised yet by most of its inhabitants. Non-EC countries of Europe are included in the scheme; some, like Switzerland and Austria, associated with EC countries, others waiting for a clearer view of their future prospects to emerge. Such 'transregional and external spatial impact study areas' are unlikely to form useful regions for detailed policy and planning decisions since, as well as overriding existing sovereign state boundaries in a refreshing way, they are implicitly credited with homogeneity, in reality based in most cases on only a broad unifying physical feature, whether a complex of mountains (e.g. the Alps) or a coast on a particular sea (e.g. the North Sea).

FURTHER READING

Clout, H. (1986) *Regional Variations in the European Community*, Cambridge: Cambridge University Press.

Cole, J. P. and Cole, F. J. (1990) 'The East Midlands and the European Community: a geographical appraisal', *The East Midlands Geographer*, vol. 13, part 1: 19–32.

Com (87), 230 (1987) *Third Periodic Report from the Commission on the Social and Economic Situation and Development of the Regions of the Community*, Brussels, 21 May.

Commission of the EC (1991) *The Regions in the 1990s*, Brussels: Office for Official Publications of the European Communities.

—— (1991) *Europe 2000 Outlook for the Development of the Community's Territory*, Brussels: Office for Official Publications of the European Communities.

Economic and Social Consultative Assembly (1988) *Disadvantaged Island Regions*, European Communities, Economic and Social Committee, Brussels.

11

DISINTEGRATION, INTEGRATION AND UNION IN EUROPE

HISTORICAL PERSPECTIVES

Up to its traditional limits of the Ural Mountains and the Ural River, Trans-caucasia, and the Black and Mediterranean Seas (see Figure 1.1) Europe covers 10,400,000 sq km, only 7 per cent of the world's land area. Although it is roughly comparable in area to Canada, China, the USA or Brazil, each of which is a single political unit, it has been politically fragmented throughout its history. The great diversity of Europe's geographical features may have contributed to its political fragmentation, with mountain ranges and seas forming obstacles to movement, and major rivers sometimes offering convenient markers at the limit of political units. Linguistic, ethnic and religious differences also contributed to the separation of peoples. For 2,000 years, large parts of Europe have formed states or 'empires', only to disintegrate and later gather again into new combinations. During that period the whole of Europe has never been organised as a single political unit, and recent events in Central and Eastern Europe point to continuing regional and local interest predominating over more centralised structures.

A review of the periods in the history of Europe when substantial parts of the continent were for one reason or another organised into single entities, while not expected to be more than a rough guideline to possible future situations, can serve as a basis for speculation. With the help of the six political maps in Figures 11.1a to 11.1f, six configurations of Europe will be briefly considered, and each compared with the area of the EC, with its 12 Member States as in 1991.

11.1a The Roman Empire around AD 200 included territory in Asia and North Africa while also extending in places eastwards and southwards in Europe beyond the limit of the EC, but it did not contain Scotland, most of Germany, the northern Netherlands and Denmark. The area of modern Germany proved difficult for the Romans to conquer. Most of the area in the Roman Empire in Figure 11.1a around AD 200 was successfully held and governed from Rome for several centuries.

11.1b The medieval German Empire of around 1190 was a loosely organised entity emerging as a major force in Western Europe, bounded in the west

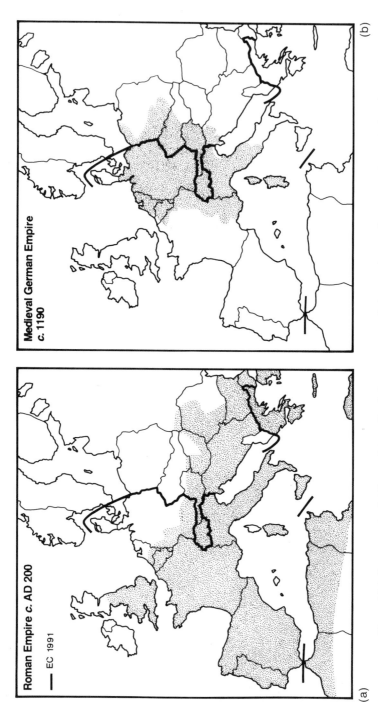

Roman Empire c. AD 200

EC 1991

(a)

Medieval German Empire
c. 1190

(b)

Figure 11.1 Europe under (a) Rome, (b) medieval Germany, (c) Habsburgs, (d) Napoleon, (e) Hitler, and (f) Stalin

Source: based on maps in *The Times Atlas of World History,* pp. 90–1, 118–19, 170–1, 204, 273, 275

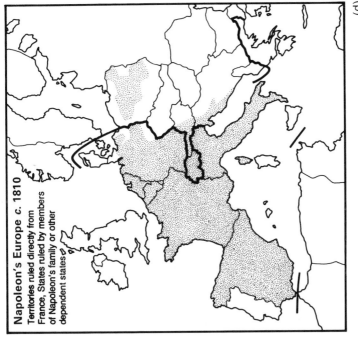

Napoleon's Europe *c.* 1810

Territories ruled directly from France, States ruled by members of Napoleon's family or other dependent states

(d)

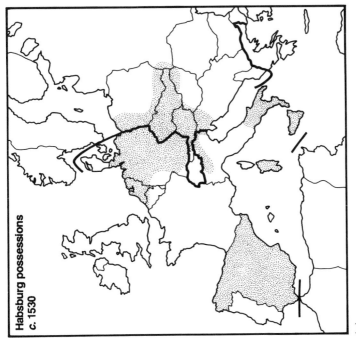

Habsburg possessions *c.* 1530

(c)

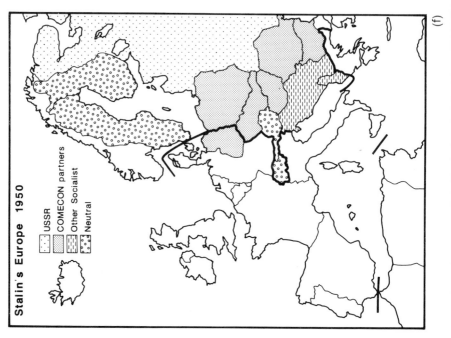

Stalin's Europe 1950

USSR
COMECON partners
Other Socialist
Neutral

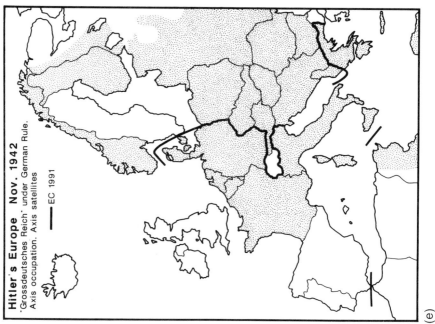

Hitler's Europe Nov. 1942

'Grossdeutsches Reich' under German Rule.
Axis occupation. Axis satellites

—— EC 1991

(f)

(e)

by France and in the east by Hungary and Poland. It bore some resemblance to the original EEC of the Six in 1957.

11.1c Following its final integration in 1492 with the conquest of Granada and the expulsion of the Moors, Spain became a leading power in Europe in the sixteenth century. Although separated by France from its central European territories, it controlled an appreciable part of Western Europe through the Habsburg Empire.

11.1d Around 1810 Napoleon's France, which included territories ruled directly from Paris, states ruled by members of Napoleon's family, and other dependent states, resembled the present EC with 12 Member States, except for Portugal, Great Britain and Ireland, and Denmark, but it included the Grand Duchy of Warsaw.

11.1e Hitler's hold over Europe at its greatest extent in 1942 consisted of the Grossdeutsches Reich plus a much larger territory occupied by German forces. Of the present EC it did not include the UK, Ireland, Spain, Portugal or, notionally at least, Vichy France.

11.1f The USSR superseded Germany as the dominant power in Europe after 1945; in around 1950 Stalin's Europe including the satellites of Central Europe extended well into Western Europe in the Soviet zone of occupied Germany. The neutrality of several non-Communist countries could be regarded indirectly as a consequence of Soviet pressure. Of the original EC Six, West Germany formed the front line against perceived Soviet pressure, with NATO forces from other countries stationed there.

Geo-political changes rather than physical ones have led to the formation of new structures in Europe. A new shakeup, largely unexpected, started in 1989 and is likely to lead to a substantially different Europe by the year 2000. The apparent cause this time was not the rise of a major power in Europe, as in the past, but the abandonment of an ideology, Marxism-Leninism, assumed to override feelings of nationalism and cultural heritage. It is argued by many that the impressive economic strength of the European Community has contributed to the disintegration of CMEA. On the other hand it would be foolish to pretend that, on the basis of recent or long-term history, the future shape of Europe could be predicted with any confidence. It may be noted that all or part of Germany was in all six entities (Figures 1.1a–f), albeit only minimally under Rome, while England was in none of them except the Roman Empire; Scotland and Ireland even escaped Roman rule. If a nation, or rather its population, does have a memory going back centuries that influences its present attitudes and decisions, then England has never been occupied by or politically merged with anywhere on the continent since the Middle Ages, whereas most of the rest of Western Europe has been invaded on various occasions.

In NATO since 1949 and in the EC since 1973, the UK and Germany have finally joined the same 'camp' along with three other major European nations, France, Italy and Spain, removing the prospect of any further military conflicts between two or more of them, so frequent in European history. While the sovereignty of the main powers of Western Europe, regarded in the 1930s as sacrosanct, has been greatly reduced since the 1950s, new independent countries are emerging from Yugoslavia and the former USSR. In Western Europe, economic considerations have become as significant as political and military ones since the ending of the Cold War. It is appropriate, therefore, to refer briefly next to the changes in the economic scene in European history.

Impressive advances were made in the Roman Empire in construction work (e.g. aqueducts, roads, stadia), but energy was provided by animate sources (humans, animals), by the power of wind and falling water, and from the use of wood for fuel. Further advances were made with the same sources of energy in medieval Europe with, in particular, the construction at enormous cost to local communities of lavish ecclesiastical buildings, and the development of complex and sophisticated machines driven by water power. Several hundred years ago northern and central Italy, Germany and Flanders, were centres of scientific discoveries and technical inventions. After the Reformation the Protestant north tended to be more supportive of the scientific research and technological developments than the Catholic South.

The extensive use of coal in Britain towards the end of the seventeenth century and in the eighteenth century, used to smelt iron ore and then to produce steam power to drive machinery, gave rise to the Industrial Revolution. Many of the innovations were first developed and applied in Britain, subsequently spreading in the nineteenth century to France, Belgium and Germany in particular. Coal-field areas were initially favourable and preferred for the location of new industries. The growth of railways in the second half of the nineteenth century reduced the relative cost of transporting fuel and raw materials by land, and the development of hydro-electric power late in the century allowed a further dispersal of modern industrial activity.

The economist R. Soltau (1935) recognised two Europes, referred to unassumingly as Europe A and Europe B (see Figure 11.2). By the 1930s it was quite meaningful to draw a line joining the places chosen by Soltau to enclose Europe A, in which almost all of the modern industry was concentrated, apart from that in the USSR. The central position of what became West Germany after 1945 is striking. The 1930s was perhaps the time when the differences between Europe A and Europe B were most marked.

Since the 1930s there have been considerable changes. Crash programmes in the countries of CMEA led to rapid, although unbalanced, industrial growth beyond the Soltau line to the east and southeast. Since the 1950s there has been a deliberate policy to industrialise southern Italy and to a lesser extent some parts of Spain. North Sea oil has made an impact on the economies of Scotland and Norway on the northern fringes of Europe A. Events in the late 1980s (see also Chapter 6) point, however, to the continuing industrial dominance of Europe A in the continent as a whole. From north to south, the most successful regions extend from southern Sweden and southern Britain through eastern France, the

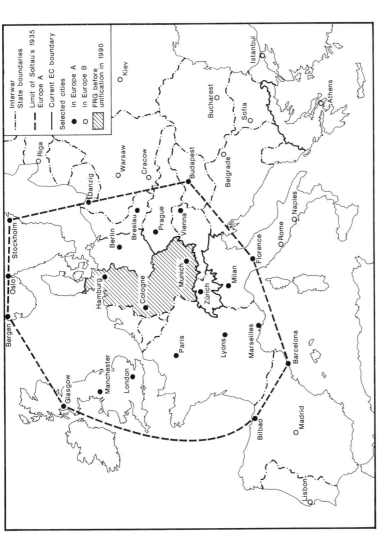

Figure 11.2 Europe A and B of R. Soltau, 1935

Source: Soltau 1935

Table 11.1 Human Development Indicators in Europe and the Maghreb
(EF = EFTA, CM = former CMEA except SU = former USSR)

		(1) Life expectancy	(2) Adult literacy	(3) Real GDP	(4) Log GDP	(5) HDI (1990)	(6) HDI (1992)
EF	Sweden	77	99	13.8	4.14	987	976
EF	Switzerland	77	99	15.4	4.19	986	977
EC	Netherlands	77	99	12.7	4.10	984	968
EF	Norway	77	99	15.9	4.20	983	978
EC	France	76	99	14.0	4.14	974	969
EC	Denmark	76	99	15.1	4.18	971	953
EC	UK	76	99	12.3	4.09	970	962
EF	Finland	75	99	12.8	4.11	967	953
EC	FR Germany	75	99	14.7	4.17	967	955*
EC	Italy	76	97	10.7	4.03	966	922
EC	Belgium	75	99	13.1	4.12	966	950
EC	Spain	77	95	9.0	3.95	965	916
EC	Ireland	74	99	8.6	3.93	961	921
EF	Austria	74	99	12.4	4.09	961	950
CM	German DR	74	99	8.0	3.90	953	–
EC	Greece	76	93	5.5	3.74	949	901
SU	Lithuania	72	99	7.6	3.88	943	896†
SU	Belarus	72	99	6.7	3.82	943	896†
SU	Georgia	72	99	5.5	3.74	943	896†
CM	Czechoslovakia	72	98	7.8	3.89	931	897
SU	Estonia	71	99	9.2	3.97	927	880†
SU	Latvia	71	99	8.7	3.94	927	880†
SU	Ukraine	71	99	5.7	3.76	927	880†
SU	USSR	70	99	6.0	3.78	920	873
CM	Bulgaria	72	93	4.8	3.68	918	865
CM	Hungary	71	98	4.5	3.65	915	893
	Yugoslavia	72	92	5.0	3.70	913	857
SU	Armenia	69	99	4.9	3.69	913	866†
CM	Poland	72	98	4.0	3.60	910	874
EC	Portugal	74	85	5.6	3.75	899	850
SU	Moldova	68	99	5.3	3.73	897	850†
SU	Azerbaijan	70	98	3.6	3.56	887	840†
CM	Romania	71	96	3.0	3.48	863	733
	Albania	72	85	2.0	3.30	790	791
	Turkey	65	74	3.8	3.58	751	671
	Tunisia	66	55	2.7	3.44	657	582
	Algeria	63	50	2.6	3.42	609	533
	Morocco	62	34	1.8	3.25	4.89	429

Sources: UNDP, *Human Development Report 1990*, Table 1 and UNDP, *Human Development Report 1992*, Table 1

Key: * All Germany

   † Former Soviet Republics, all reduced from 1990 by 47 points, as for all the USSR

Notes per column:

(1) Life expectancy in years at birth 1987

(2) Adult literacy rate (%) 1985
(3) In thousands of US dollars
(4) Logarithm of (3)
(5) HDI – Human Development Index calculated by a method of 'lost points' based on the positions of (1), (2) and (3) on a scale between 0 and 1
(6) A more recent calculation of the Human Development Index, modifying the 1990 version, the major difference being a more complex calculation of educational attainment, taking into account mean years of schooling as well as adult literacy rate. The highest scores out of 1,000 are Canada with 982 and Japan with 981; the lowest score Guinea (Africa) with 52

Benelux, the former FRG, and Switzerland, to northern and central Italy. The southern regions of the EC, together with the countries of Central Europe, have serious problems with many of their industries. In contrast, the more advanced region of Scandinavia contains very few inhabitants. Most of all, the ex-Soviet economies face problems of enormous proportions.

It is hoped that the reviews of the political and economic histories of Europe in this section will throw some light on the changes that might be expected in the EC in the next decade and beyond. Which other countries, if any, are likely to become full members of the EC in the near or not too distant future? How widely can the EC extend? Can it afford the financial burden of persisting with the concept of convergence when, apart from EFTA, countries applying for membership are much poorer than the present EC average? In the next sections the aspirations and attributes of various countries will be considered.

COMPARING THE COUNTRIES OF EUROPE

An introductory data set for the countries of Europe was given in Chapter 1, Table 1.3. In this section, use is made of a new Human Development Index, calculated as the basis for United Nations policy in its drive to improve conditions among the poorest regions of the world, to focus on the eligibility of non-EC countries for future membership. All the present Member States of the EC and most of those that have shown an interest in joining in the future come high on the scale used. The Index is based on the assumption that a long and healthy life (the body), reasonable educational levels (the mind), and basic material needs, should be enjoyed by everyone in the world (see Table 11.1). The measures used are life expectancy at birth (1987), percentage of adult literacy (1985), and 'North minimum purchasing power' (position in relation to the average poverty line of about 4,800 US dollars per head in nine industrial countries). Countries lose 'points' according to how far they fall below a maximum of 1.00. For the three criteria described, life expectancy of 78 years in Japan is the highest, 100 per cent adult literacy rate is the maximum, and the logarithmic value of real GDP at the minimum purchasing power value referred to above is the ceiling. Equal weight is given to each of the three indices, which are then combined to produce a possible maximum score of 1.00 and a possible minimum score of 0.00. In Table 11.1 the final score is multiplied by 1,000 and is given in column (5). In addition to all the countries of Europe except the smallest, nine of the 15

THE GEOGRAPHY OF THE EUROPEAN COMMUNITY

former Soviet Socialist Republics are included for comparative purposes. By comparison, the extremes are Japan, with 996 points out of 1,000 and Niger with only 116.

From the Human Development Index in Table 11.1, it can be seen that the five EFTA countries compare economically with the more developed and affluent members of the EC (Iceland falls between Norway and Sweden). The former GDR (953 points) and Greece (949 points) are followed by the remaining Central European countries and the former Soviet Socialist Republics (SSRs) of the USSR. Portugal lags well behind the rest of the EC, pulled down particularly by its relatively low adult literacy score, and it comes below several Central European countries and seven former SSRs. Any country below Portugal has a long way to move up the scale to reach the weighted average EC score of about 965 out of 1,000.

In considering future membership of the EC it is also helpful to view the GDP situation of the EC through data provided by Eurostat (1989a). The extent of the GDP 'gap' is very large. In Figure 11.3, each column is proportional in area to the total GDP of the country or countries it represents, being a rectangle formed by total number of inhabitants on the horizontal axis 'multiplied' by the average number of US dollars per inhabitant in that region on the vertical axis. The diagram shows the adjustments that would be needed to bring particular groups of countries to the same level. Several averages are shown, a new one as each new country or group of countries is brought in, adding successively and cumulatively EFTA, the six East European countries (excluding the GDR), the nine Soviet Socialist Republics in Europe (excluding the RSFSR), and then finally Turkey and the Maghreb countries.

The EFTA countries are all above the EC average whereas the East European countries and the nine European SSRs are well below. Turkey and the Maghreb countries are still lower. The total of about 700 million people in all the countries of Europe and the Maghreb combined has an average of 8,360 dollars per capita, about double the world average. To equalise GDP per inhabitant throughout, hypothetical transfers would be needed on a massive scale into Central Europe, the nine former Soviet Republics, Turkey, and the Maghreb. Germany, EFTA and France would each have to 'lose' about half of their GDP. The expected fast rate of population growth in Turkey and in the Maghreb countries in the future means that their columns in the diagram will extend to the right along the horizontal axis and, if they do not increase GDP correspondingly, their columns will flatten.

It is not seriously suggested that any substantial transfers will be made in the near future to Central Europe apart from those committed to the former GDR. There are many relatively poor regions in the present EC, while beyond the countries of Europe is the whole developing world. Belton (1990) quotes the Italian finance minister Guido Carli as saying, 'We have to reconcile our domestic needs with help for Eastern Europe and the developing countries'.

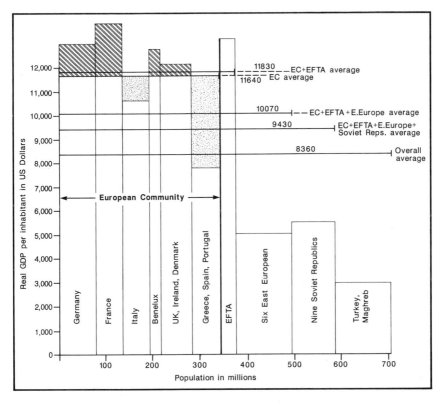

Figure 11.3 The extent of hypothetical transfers of GDP needed to produce uniform GDP per capita in various groupings of European countries and the Maghreb

THE ENLARGEMENT OF THE EC

Since Spain and Portugal entered the EC in 1986, many other European countries have expressed an interest in joining, and some have submitted applications. McMillan-Scott (1990), in his provocative pamphlet 'Greater Europe: 12 plus 6 plus 6', explicitly accepts the possibility that the EC could admit the six EFTA countries plus six Central European countries into the Community. The sudden enthusiasm on the part of the British government to enlarge the EC shortly before the Maastricht Summit in 1991 was seen by some as a devious attempt to distract the Member States most dedicated to closer political and economic union on the assumption that enlargement and intensification are mutually exclusive. In this section various features of these and other countries that could affect their prospects of entry will be assessed.

In *A Strategy for Enlargement* it is stated:

Enlargement is firmly on the Community's agenda. But whilst politicians and commentators talk of a Community of 20 or 24 there has been little serious thought or analysis of the implications of enlargement. The deeper one examines the subject, the more complex seem the problems. But despite the difficulties surrounding enlargement the Community cannot shirk the historic challenge it now faces.

(Commission of the EC 1991b)

In the above publication, four characteristics of 15 possible candidates for admission to the EC are examined: motives for joining, popular support, a democratic tradition, and participation in international organisations. Verbal descriptions are given for each characteristic. On the four criteria, Sweden, for example, is credited with economic/political motives, a broad consensus in favour of joining, a good democratic tradition, and strong participation in international organisations. In contrast, Cyprus, for example, has political motives and a description of weak for the remaining three considerations. Apart from Iceland, the EFTA countries emerge as generally favourable; six Central European countries as currently far from suitable; Cyprus, Malta and Turkey unsatisfactory.

Cole (1990: 26) published a checklist with numerical scores for each possible candidate for EC membership. The authors have updated and modified the checklist, the new one being given in Table 11.2. Although the use of numerical scores gives a spurious impression of precision, it makes comparison between candidates more easy than when only words are used. A 'points lost' basis is used, so the higher the score the less attractive the applicant. Ten separate criteria have been used to produce a consensus, all given equal weight. The candidates are seen through the eyes of the Member States of the EC, rather than having their own aspirations taken into account.

A number of criteria virtually exclude most countries of the world from entry. Location within Europe would exclude for example New Zealand or Uruguay, however attractive their profiles. Failure to reach required minimum standards of respect for democratic principles and/or human rights would at the time of writing exclude some of the countries in Table 11.2. Absolute size of population, area and/or the Gross National Product could be a major consideration, since the larger the country, the greater its impact on the existing Community. A generous endowment of natural resources (in relation to population) and a high GDP per capita would be positive attributes, since in general the EC is poorly endowed with non-renewable natural resources, particularly in relation to its population size and the rate at which primary products are consumed, while the more prosperous the country the larger its per capita contribution to the Community budget. Many other considerations would no doubt also enter. Even on the basis of the scores awarded in Table 11.2 it is evident that some countries have much better credentials than others. Each of the countries in the Table will now be examined, singly or in groups.

In all respects *Austria* could join with a minimum of difficulty, although it lacks natural resources and has few industries of special importance to the EC.

One of the two major obstacles has now disappeared, the commitment to neutrality required for the USSR to withdraw its forces from the Soviet occupation zone after the Second World War, but failure to renounce wholeheartedly its past Nazi associations is still a matter of concern in some quarters.

Switzerland, like the UK, claims a tradition of democracy going back centuries (to 1291). Since 1815 it has maintained a position of neutrality in Europe and the world, and entry into the EC may compromise its position in this respect. Geographically it is virtually embedded within EC territory and numerous land and air routes cross it. Linguistically it presents no problems, although financially it is a world apart, and the erosion of its independence in this area could deter entry, as could the prospect of loss of control over immigration. The most likely solution is a compromise, with Switzerland becoming in effect a large 'onshore island', analogous to the Isle of Man and the Channel Islands.

Norway has a strong card to play in the form of its large reserves of oil and natural gas, a strategic asset to the Community, which imports almost half of its energy needs. The peripheral position of Norway and the consequent need to support economic activities in the thinly populated northern areas should not prove a great problem to the EC, although there is opposition to membership from fishermen and farmers in these very areas.

Sweden's prosperity this century, and especially since the Second World War, and its well-developed social services, have been recognised in Europe. Even with Norway and Finland as substantial markets for its various industrial products, its strong economic position is now threatened as competition increases in shipbuilding, the manufacture of motor vehicles, and other industries in which it has excelled. Its primary products, timber and iron ore, are useful to the EC, but not vital. The changing political situation in Sweden may hasten entry into the EC.

Finland has traditionally had strong links with both Sweden and the USSR and, like Sweden, useful forest and mineral resources. As Soviet pressure has diminished if not entirely disappeared, the neutral position of Finland previously demanded by the former USSR no longer precludes its entry into the EC. The sudden reduction in trade with its neighbour has forced it to rethink its position.

Iceland depends very heavily on its fisheries. Entry into the EC could result in the sacrifice of fishing grounds and rights. On the other hand any strategic and military advantage Iceland enjoyed after the Second World War, attracting financial support from the USA, has diminished since the USSR ceased to be perceived as a military threat to NATO.

All the EFTA countries mentioned above have strengthened their commercial links with the EC through the signing of the European Economic Area (EEA) Agreement, due to enter into force on 1 January 1993. This agreement may in effect only have a limited relevance since several of the EFTA countries are expected to join the EC by the end of 1995.

Poland, *Hungary* and *Czechoslovakia* might all see entry into the EC as a possible answer to their acute economic problems. Unfortunately for them, there is no affluent paymaster to support their rehabilitation in the way that the FRG

SOVIET SOCIALIST REPUBLICS

	(1)	(2)	(3)	(4)	(5)	(6)	(7)	(8)	(9)	(10)	Total
Estonia	1	3	4	5	5	1	4	1	3	1	28
Latvia	1	2	4	5	5	1	4	1	3	1	27
Lithuania	1	2	4	5	5	3	4	2	3	2	28
Moldova	1	3	4	5	5	3	5	3	2	3	33
Belarus	2	3	3	5	5	1	4	2	3	3	29
Ukraine	5	2	3	5	5	1	5	3	3	3	33
Georgia	1	5	4	5	5	3	5	3	3	3	35
Armenia	1	5	4	5	5	3	4	3	3	3	35
Azerbaijan	1	5	3	5	5	3	5	4	3	3	36

EXTRA EUROPEAN

	(1)	(2)	(3)	(4)	(5)	(6)	(7)	(8)	(9)	(10)	Total
Cyprus	0	5	4	5	0	1	4	3	2	3	25
Turkey	5	4	3	0	3	5	5	4	3	4	35
Algeria	3	3	1	5	3	5	5	4	3	4	37
Morocco	3	4	2	5	3	5	5	5	3	5	39
Tunisia	1	3	4	5	3	5	5	4	3	4	37

Notes per column of Table 11.2

Impact-producing, negative effect and/or nuisance value of 10 attributes of each non-EC European country, Soviet Republics and countries in Asia and Africa closely associated with the EC.

(1) Population: 0 for under 1 million, 1 for 1–10 million, 2 for 10–20 million, 3 for under 20–30 million, 4 for 30–40 million, 5 for over 40 million

(2) Total fertility rate: 0 for under 2.0, 1 for 2.0–2.4, 2 for 2.5–2.9, 3 for 3.0–3.9, 4 for 4.0–4.9, 5 for over 4.9

(3) Distance from the centre of population of the EC

(4) Natural resources per inhabitant

(5), (6) Democratic elections, more than one political party, human rights respected

(7) Healthcare and educational levels

(8) General assessment of state of economic development

(9) Dollars per inhabitant: 0 for over 10,000, 1 for 8,000–10,000, 2 for 6,000–8,000, 3 for 4,000–6,000, 4 for 2,000–4,000, 5 for under 2,000

(10) Language(s) compatible with those already used in EC or different to varying degrees

set about salvaging the GDR. The funds from the EC budget allocated to the GDR for 1991 are very modest, and if any of the three former CMEA countries entered, they would be in competition with the poorer existing Member States of the EC and with the former GDR. According to various estimates, the cost of raising the GDR to the level of the FRG is some 700 billion US dollars over ten years. To reach even the average per capita GDP level of the EC, the sum would be 400 billion. On the same basis, to raise Poland, Hungary and Czechoslovakia from their present GDP per capita levels to the EC average would cost about 400 billion dollars each for Czechoslovakia and Hungary, and about 1,800 billion dollars for Poland. Such astronomical amounts could not be obtained from the richer EC countries, concerned already with pushing Spain, Portugal, Greece, southern Italy and Ireland up towards the present EC average. Poland, Hungary and Czechoslovakia each has problems similar to those in the GDR (see next section, pp. 273–5). High-cost coal, exported at subsidised prices, and lignite, are sources of fuel threatened with decline or even extinction in the EC. Subsidised oil and natural gas from the former USSR are no longer forthcoming. Rail networks are extensive, but tracks and rolling stock are poor. Road networks and motor vehicles are also poor in quality. Agricultural yields have increased impressively in the last 20 years, but agricultural surpluses rather than shortages are the problem in the EC. Many branches of industry would have difficulty competing in the EC.

Bulgaria, Romania, Yugoslavia and *Albania* all have a long way to go before their political and economic circumstances make them likely contenders for EC entry. On the other hand, *Slovenia* and *Croatia* could be joined to the EC to rescue them from Serbian domination, although probably not until Austria joined.

Of the nine former *Soviet Socialist Republics* listed in Table 11.2, only the three Baltic Republics can seriously be considered for entry this century, possibly after an initial association with the Scandinavian members of EFTA. In spite of many glowing statements about the resources and productivity of Ukrainian agriculture, mines and industry, the republic actually has a vast complex of high-cost coal mines and steel mills, gas deposits nearing exhaustion, and a belt of good soil that has lacked moisture resources during some growing seasons and is likely to suffer in the future if the effects of global warming on rainfall prove correct. Shloma (1992) gives a very depressing picture of the Ukraine, stressing its dependence on imported fuel and raw materials, almost all from Russia (90 per cent of its oil, 77 per cent of gas, 93 per cent of timber). In 1991 it produced only 60 per cent of its grain needs. Industrial production has dropped by 25 per cent. A massive budget deficit and a depression similar to the world depression of the 1920s and 1930s are forecast, hardly conditions likely to put the republic near the head of the queue for membership.

Turkey and the *Maghreb* countries are too poor, too large and demographically too explosive to be considered for entry as full members of the EC. Turkey and Morocco have both applied for membership but both applications have received a cool response from EC institutions. Culturally they are fundamentally different from Europe, and have questionable records on human rights. Some formula might be worked out whereby the migration of workers to the EC is based on less arbitrary rules, while local job creation schemes are assisted and tariffs are reduced to encourage the countries to benefit more from trade with the EC.

The prospect of enlarging the EC in the 1990s is closely related to trends in trade. One of the main reasons often given to justify the creation, expansion and integration of the EC countries has been the increasing and now large proportion of the foreign trade of each member with the other 11 members. Similarly, one reason for the applications of new members is their present and future expected trade with the EC. Here only the trade between the more hopeful and/or persistent candidates for EC membership is referred to: the six EFTA countries, Poland, Czechoslovakia and Hungary, Turkey, Morocco, and the two small aspirants Malta and Cyprus.

In Table 11.3, the trading pattern before the great rises in oil prices is shown by data for 1972. For some years after the oil price rises in 1973–4 and 1979, the relative price of oil against almost all other products increased in total world trade. Since oil imports are a large item of trade for almost all the countries in Table 11.3, and the oil comes to them and to their EC trading partners mainly from outside Europe, the effect was to reduce apparently the importance of intra-European trade between many pairs of trading partners, whether intra-EC, between EC and third countries, or between other countries themselves. This special influence of oil prices on trading patterns must be appreciated in the discussion that follows.

Two features may be noted in Table 11.3: first, the percentages of trade between each country and the EC as a whole; second, the changes in these percentages. The most noticeable trend during the 1970s and 1980s has been little change, and indeed for many of the countries, there has even been a decline in the trade with the EC, although for 1972 the trade figures are only for 10 EC countries, excluding Spain and Portugal. In other words, the attraction of joining the EC on purely commercial grounds is not markedly different now from what it was 20 years ago. On the other hand, the percentage of trade with EC countries varies greatly, with Switzerland and Austria very heavily dependent on the EC, as well as being key transit countries. In 1987, 72 per cent of the imports of Switzerland came from the EC, and another 7 per cent from other EFTA partners, while Austria took 68 per cent of its imports from the EC and another 8 per cent from EFTA partners. In comparison, the other four EFTA countries are less oriented towards the EC in their trade, but are more closely associated with each other. Sweden is a large market for Norwegian oil, Norway for Swedish manufactured goods. Finland had a considerable volume of trade with the USSR. Nevertheless, all six EFTA countries are closely associated in terms of trade with the EC, which is one good reason for them to join. Cyprus and Malta are also similarly tied to the EC.

Turkey and Morocco both trade extensively with the EC. However, the

Table 11.3 Trade of selected non-EC countries with EC and with EFTA in 1972, 1980 and 1987

	Trade with EC[1]						Trade with (other) EFTA					
	% imports from			% exports to			% imports from			% exports to		
	1972	1980	1987	1972	1980	1987	1972	1980	1987	1972	1980	1987
Austria	65.5	63.1	68.1	49.7	56.1	63.4	11.4	7.6	7.8	19.1	12.1	11.1
Switzerland	68.9	68.5	72.2	47.1	53.3	55.6	10.0	6.5	7.4	12.9	8.4	7.1
Finland	42.3	34.7	44.2	44.9	40.4	41.6	25.3	17.1	22.6	25.0	23.2	18.3
Norway	45.1	49.3	49.6	55.3	72.2	64.4	25.7	23.4	26.1	21.3	12.4	15.2
Sweden	54.9	50.9	57.3	50.6	51.3	51.0	18.2	15.4	16.4	21.4	19.9	20.7
Iceland	52.6	47.4	52.1	33.2	46.9	57.3	19.2	18.8	20.7	17.5	10.4	8.2
Czechoslovakia	14.2	13.8	9.5	12.8	14.0	8.3	6.4	6.8	4.8	4.9	6.4	3.0
Hungary	19.0	23.2	24.6	16.8	20.9	20.0	5.7	10.5	10.8	5.5	7.9	9.2
Poland	–	19.7	19.3	–	22.8	21.3	–	7.0	8.3	–	7.8	7.4
Turkey	53.0	29.9	40.0	47.0	44.7	47.8	8.5	7.8	5.7	12.2	7.1	6.2
Morocco	55.1	53.3	53.0	64.6	62.7	58.2	6.5	3.1	4.2	2.9	3.2	2.3
Cyprus	61.1	52.4	56.4	61.2	31.0	41.1	5.7	4.3	5.6	4.1	1.7	3.4
Malta	71.3	75.4	68.0	74.5	73.6	67.8	3.4	3.8	3.5	3.5	4.1	2.0

Source: various years of UN Yearbook of International Trade Statistics
Notes: – not available
1 1972 EC 10, 1980 and 1987 EC 12

Community's share of Turkish trade has tended to decline in the last two decades. Many other countries in the developing world have equally strong trading ties with the EC, but no expectation of joining the Community. Of the three most eligible Central European countries, Hungary and Poland have developed stronger trading ties with the EC than Czechoslovakia has, but all three have depended primarily on CMEA links. The former GDR was similarly orientated away from the EC so its experience in becoming integrated with the EC could have useful lessons for other countries, although its instant absorption into the new Germany, and its loss of sovereignty, are more drastic even than full membership of the EC would be for the other countries. The GDR is the subject of the next section.

The structure and efficiency of the institutions of the EC in the light of future enlargements is under close scrutiny at present. One example of the increasing complexity of an expanded European Community is the question of the size of the membership of the European Parliament. It was noted in Chapter 2 that 518 members were elected in 1989. As a result of the principle of degressive proportionality, the smaller the Member State, the smaller the number of people per seat. Thus with 400,000 inhabitants, Luxembourg has 6 seats while Germany has only 81 seats for over 79 million inhabitants. De Gucht (1992) projects seat allocation for an extended European Parliament. The cumulative increase in seats might be as follows (with degressive proportionality still applied): adjustments to the seats of the current 12 Member States would raise the total from 518 to 570 (e.g. Germany gains 18, Ireland loses 3). The addition of all the EFTA countries plus Malta and Cyprus would increase it to 667. The three most eligible Central European countries, Czechoslovakia, Hungary and Poland, together with the three Baltic Republics, bring it to 823, while Turkey takes it to 906. Once Iceland, Albania, Bulgaria, Romania, Croatia, Slovenia and the Ukraine are added, the astronomical number of 1,099 is reached. Even then, most of Yugoslavia is excluded, as are Belorus, Moldova, and the Transcaucasian republics of the former USSR, as well of course, as Russia itself.

After a drastic reduction in the thresholds for seat allocations based on the size of countries, De Gucht reduces the number of seats for the present EC 12 Member States to 374 (no doubt there would be dismay as, for example, Italy, France and the UK each drops from 81 to 58 seats), giving a new grand total of 733 instead of 1,099, coincidentally almost exactly the number of seats in the European Parliament building under construction in Brussels in 1992.

GERMAN UNIFICATION

The enlargement of the EC through German unification, the merging of an existing Member State with another state, is a one-off event in EC history. The creation of a new sovereign state has resulted in some developments and problems of the merger that are special, others that any new member of the EC would experience on joining. For further aspects of German unification, see J.P. Cole and F.J. Cole (1990).

The need for compatibility of political and administrative functions and organisation between the two Germanies required, among other changes, the unification of the two currencies, the creation of a single national parliament, a standard electoral procedure, and federal divisions (the Länder) identical in status and comparable in size. In due course Berlin is to be the national capital, although Bonn retains the day-to-day function for the present. The freedom of movement of people, goods, services and capital between the two Germanies has been implemented. The ownership of means of production in agriculture, industry and services was almost exclusively public in the GDR and the new Germany has had to address this basic difference. Public sector areas such as healthcare, education and unemployment benefit have also had to be standardised.

The GDR was the most developed and 'richest' of all the countries in the CMEA. Nevertheless its GDP per capita was only about half that of the FRG, so it is vital for the FRG to reduce the GDP gap, if not remove it, and to ensure that unemployment levels between the two Germanies do not differ greatly. Unless that is done, migration is expected to continue from the less attractive GDR to the FRG. A number of problems will now be referred to.

1   *Unemployment* has been relatively low in the FRG compared with that in the rest of the EC since the foundation of the Community. In the GDR it has, in theory, been non-existent but, in practice, disguised by overmanning. Since German unification in 1990, the unemployment level has risen enormously in the GDR. The payment of unemployment benefit could cost several billion dollars annually per million people out of work. According to Murray (1991) the number of jobless in the GDR rose from 370,000 in July 1990 to 787,000 in February 1991, while in the West it was 1,860,000 at both those times, but for nearly four times the population.

2   *Transport.* The GDR depends heavily on rail transport for the movement of goods and passengers. The quality of track and rolling stock and the maximum speed for trains severely limit the efficiency of the system. It is estimated that 40 billion dollars would be needed to bring the system up to the level of that in the FRG and in other more advanced parts of the EC. Road transport suffers from poorly surfaced roads, including existing motorways, passenger cars that produce emissions exceeding EC standards of freedom from pollutants, and a fleet of commercial vehicles far too modest and antiquated to function efficiently in the road-dominated EC transport system. Several hundred kilometres of new motorways need to be provided.

3   *Energy.* About 70 per cent of GDR energy was provided by lignite, which is the worst of all the fossil fuels in terms of impurities to weight and to energy equivalents. Most of the rest of the energy was obtained from oil and natural gas imported from the USSR, which is a net exporter of both. After January 1991 Soviet oil was no longer sold to former CMEA partners at prices below those in the world market. The nuclear power generating capacity in the

GDR has been closed down because it is unsafe. The system of electricity transmission would not be compatible with that in the FRG without major conversion works.

4 *Agriculture.* In this sector the level of productivity per worker and yield per unit of cultivated area does not differ greatly between the two Germanies. The greatest difference is in the size of unit of land tenure. Farms in the FRG are small even by standards of the northern countries of the EC, and many are actually family farms. Agriculture in the GDR is organised in enormous state farms for arable farming and in large livestock farms with animals concentrated in comparatively small areas.

5 *Industry* in the GDR has produced a wide range of manufactures not only for the home market but also for export to the 'captive' CMEA market. Both capital and consumer manufactured goods were exported to the USSR and CMEA partners, in exchange for primary products and capital goods, mainly for heavy industries. One estimate of the situation before unification was that one-third of the industries of the GDR should be written off, one-third could be updated at a cost, and one-third could survive more or less as they were. As in the rest of the EC, industries such as shipbuilding, iron and steel, and textiles, are expected to decline, but even industries such as optical goods and electronics products, for which the GDR excelled in CMEA, have to be rehabilitated, cut or even closed down.

6 *Environmental problems* in the GDR have assumed huge proportions. The widespread use of lignite in industry, in the generation of electricity, and in domestic heating, has resulted in high levels of atmospheric pollution and poor conditions of health locally. Motor vehicles add to pollution levels, especially in urban areas. The legacy of uranium mining has left one area devastated environmentally (see Chapter 9).

ENLARGEMENT OF THE EC AND THE RISE OF THE REGIONS

Two future scenarios for the EC are now considered in geographical terms. First, all the countries and Soviet Republics discussed in pp. 265–73, except Iceland, are located to the east of the present centre of gravity of population of the EC; any addition of territory will draw the centre of population eastwards. Second, as the EC exercises more powers formerly vested in national parliaments or governments, a similar trend will lead to the emergence of new regional bodies in the EC representing identities submerged by the centralising influence of the main powers. These two prospects will be discussed in turn.

Figure 11.4 shows the location of the demographic and the economic centres of the EC under changing circumstances. There is a brief commentary on the various locations in the caption of Figure 11.4. In Europe the overall distribution of population has not changed markedly in recent decades, but the changing

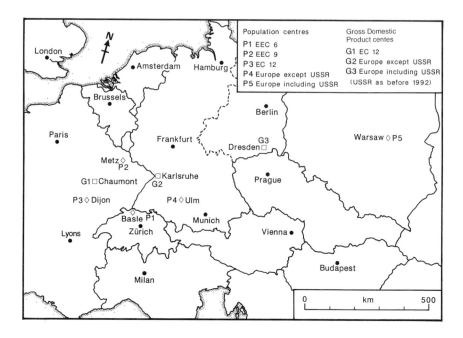

Figure 11.4 The locations of the centres of population and of GDP in different groupings of countries in Europe

membership of the EC has resulted in the movement of the notional centre of the Community.

P1 Near Basle (outside the EC), this was the centre for the founding members in the late 1950s.

P2 The entry of the UK, Ireland and Denmark moved the centre some distance to the northwest to a point near Metz in France.

P3 The entry of Greece, Spain and Portugal moved it to the southwest to a point near Dijon in France, Iberia having more 'weight' on the relocation than Greece. When the GDR entered, the centre moved northeast, about one-twentieth of the way from Dijon towards the centre of the GDR.

P4 If the countries of EFTA and Central Europe join the EC, then the centre will move roughly to Ulm in southern Germany, with almost all the pull coming from the east rather than the west.

P5 The centre of population of the whole of Europe plus European USSR is roughly in Warsaw.

As a result of the shift eastwards, the UK and Spain would become increasingly peripheral, Germany more central. The 'economic' centre of Europe, that of GDP, would not shift eastwards as far as that of population because of the greater 'weight' of GDP per inhabitant in the EC and EFTA than in Central

Europe and the former USSR. Whilst the eastward shift of the centres of population and of production may only influence economic life in Europe to a modest degree, it does point to southern Germany as the future central area of a much enlarged EC (see Figure 11.5).

A second issue that could become more significant in the future is that of the cultural differences and nationalist movements within the EC. Developments in Central Europe and the former USSR have shown that one of the most centralised and strictly controlled large regions of the world, CMEA, could suddenly disintegrate. Czechoslovakia, Yugoslavia (not in CMEA) and, above all, the USSR were countries in which two or more national groups were merged into single sovereign states (see Figure 11.6). There are at least two reasons why new strength may be given to movements within the EC towards more autonomy for suppressed or subnations: first, the example of the Republics of the former USSR, and second, the growing strength of the supranational nature of the European Community. The second influence impinges on the role of the national parliaments of the 12 Member States. As shown in Chapters 2 and 10, within the NUTS 1 level regional framework, areas such as Wales, the País Vasco, Sicilia, and the two halves of Belgium, Vlaanderen and Wallonie, are kept intact. Economically, for example, it might have been more realistic to join North Wales to Northwest England and South Wales to Southwest England, while industrially, Wallonie in Belgium and Nord-Pas-de-Calais in France have very close links.

Over 100 different languages are spoken in Europe. In Figure 11.6 the main language divides are shown, those between the Germanic, Romanic and Slavic groups, which are all subdivided. Finnish, Hungarian and Greek do not belong to these groups. In addition, three Christian groups (Orthodox, Catholic and Protestant) divide Europe into subregions on a religious basis and still influence allegiances, while in the Balkans significant groups of Moslems complicate the situation. Even when there is no marked difference between languages or religions, national feeling can be strong, as in Scotland, distinguished by the nature of its peripheral location.

Along with further moves towards European Union at the summit in Maastricht, it is likely that the principle of subsidiarity, now included in the new Treaty, will govern the future of the EC to a greater extent:

> This Treaty marks a new stage in the process creating an ever closer Union among the peoples of Europe, where decisions are taken as closely as possible to the citizens.
>
> (Art. 1 TEU)

and

> The Community shall take action ... only if ... the objectives of the proposed action cannot be sufficiently achieved by the Member States
>
> (Art. 3b TEU)

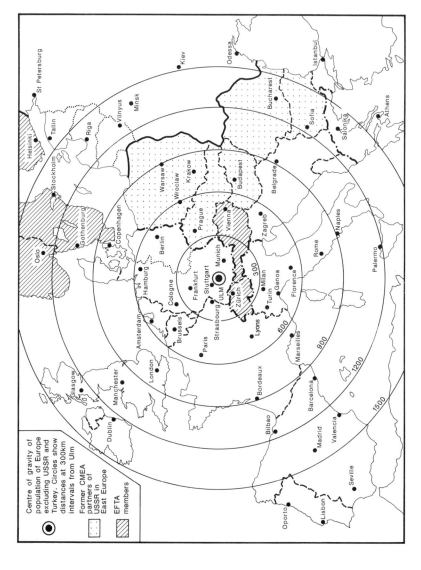

Figure 11.5 Ulm in southern Germany as the centre of population of Europe excluding the former USSR

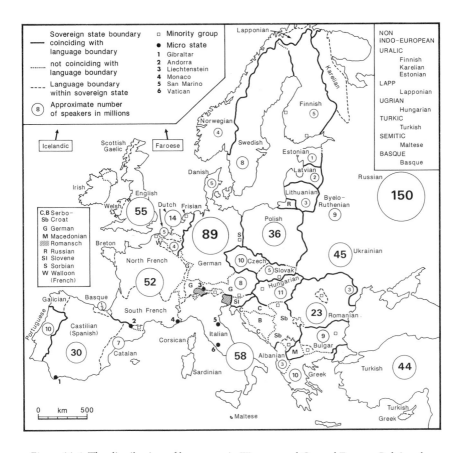

Figure 11.6 The distribution of languages in Western and Central Europe. Belgium has no language of its own. Dutch (Flemish) is spoken in the north, French in the south. The language of administration in Luxembourg is French. German is also used. In the former Yugoslavia, the subdivisions and newly separate States are shown, but Serbo-Croat is spoken by about 17 million people in Croatia, Serbia and Bosnia-Hercegovina

Sources: based on Rand McNally 1987: 152–3 for language areas and on Gunnemark and Kenrick 1985 for numbers speaking main languages

The significance of regional and local interests is recognised by the setting-up of the 'Committee of the Regions', a consultative organ consisting of representatives of regional and local bodies from the 12 Member States. The 1990s will therefore see a further shift in influence and powers from the national level within the EC upwards towards the EC institutions and in influence downwards towards the regions. In the latter, individual cultural and geographical characteristics will be reasserted, in particular in Belgium, the UK, France, Spain and Italy.

FURTHER READING

Centre for Economic Research Policy (1990) *Monitoring European Integration*, The Impact of Eastern Europe, CEPR Annual Report, London, October.

Cole, J. P. (1990) 'Europe: looking towards the 21st Century' in Cipolato, M. J. (ed.), *The Community and Europe*, Brussels: AD Consult S.P.R.L.

European Parliament (1990) *The Impact of German Unification on the European Community*, Directorate-General for Research, Working Document No. 1, 6-1990.

Le Bras, H. and Todd, E. (1981) *L'Invention de la France*, Paris: Collection Pluriel.

Merritt, G. (1991), *Eastern Europe and the USSR: the Challenge of Freedom*, EC/Kogan Page.

Sword, K. (ed.) (1990) *The Times Guide to Eastern Europe*, London: Times Books.

Todd, E. (1990) *L'Invention de l'Europe*, Paris: Editions du Seuil.

Williams, C. H. (1986) 'The question of national congruence', in R. J. Johnston and P. J. Taylor (eds) *A World in Crisis*, Oxford: Blackwell, pp. 196–230.

—— (ed.) (1988) *Language in Geographic Context*, Clevedon-Philadelphia: Multilingual Matters Ltd.

12

THE EC AND THE WORLD
BEYOND EUROPE

THE EC AND THE REST OF THE DEVELOPED WORLD

North America

On 1 January 1989 a free trade agreement between Canada and the USA came into force. According to Charles (1989), although not primarily attributable to increasing integration in Western Europe, the agreement is of interest to the EC in the sense that the resulting trade bloc resembles the Community in some respects. In the late 1980s, 80 per cent of Canada's trade was with the USA, and 19 per cent of US trade was with Canada. Although most of the goods traded actually pass between the two countries duty free, protectionist measures against and surcharges on Canada's exports to the USA have at times been imposed. The prospect that the Single Market in the EC would strengthen the protectionist walls of that group also influenced the Canadian government in its decision to link up more closely with its neighbour.

Foreign trade is only equivalent to a small proportion of the total GDP of the USA. Less than a quarter of US foreign trade is with the EC, compared with over a fifth with Canada. The latter, however, has only 27 million inhabitants whereas the EC has 345 million (see Table 12.1). In 1988 the USA had a very unfavourable balance of trade with the rest of the world (imports worth 441 billion dollars against exports 308 billion), because its imports from Canada, the EC and Japan greatly exceeded its exports to each of those regions.

About one-tenth of the value of US imports is of crude oil and refined products, much of which comes from the Middle East. Some 74 billion dollars worth of imports consisted of automobiles and parts, with Japan the largest single supplier. If the USA is to improve its balance of trade, the EC is one of the regions of the world in which it might hope to improve its position. One way in which the USA can penetrate the EC market is by investing in the Community. Between 1980 and 1987 the value of US investments in the EC increased from 80 billion dollars to 122 billion, slightly more quickly than its total investments worldwide (see Table 12.2). In terms of dollars invested per inhabitant, the UK and Ireland, together with the Benelux three, were the preferred destinations.

Table 12.1 Selected US foreign trading partners, 1988

	Imports		Exports	
	billion dollars	%	billion dollars	%
Total	440.9	100.0	308.0	100.0
Canada	80.9	18.3	69.2	22.5
Latin America	48.9	11.1	40.1	13.0
Western Europe	100.5	22.8	88.0	28.6
EC	85.0	19.3	75.9	24.6
FRG	26.5	6.0	14.3	4.6
France	12.2	2.8	10.1	3.3
Italy	11.6	2.6	6.8	2.2
Netherlands	4.6	1.0	10.1	3.3
Belgium + Lux.	4.5	1.0	7.4	2.4
UK + Ireland	19.4	4.4	20.6	6.7
Denmark	1.7	0.4	1.0	0.3
Greece + Portugal	1.2	0.3	1.4	0.5
Spain	3.2	0.7	4.2	1.4
EFTA	13.0	2.9	9.0	2.9
Japan	89.9	20.4	37.7	12.2
USSR	0.6	0.1	2.8	0.9

Source: Statistical Abstract of the United States 1989

During the same period, however, foreign direct investments in the USA increased more than three times, the contribution of Europe rising from 55 billion dollars to 178 billion dollars. As can be seen in Table 12.3, the contribution of the UK grew more than five times, and accounted for over 40 per cent of Europe's investment in the USA. The USA is likely to attempt to reverse the trend of the 1980s, either by discouraging the continued rapid expansion of foreign investment at home or by stepping up investment globally, with the EC and Japan as prime targets. To what extent the new, more open nature of the economies of the former CMEA countries will attract US investment cannot yet be judged.

Japan

The relationship between the EC and Japan was an uneasy one in the 1980s. The French and Italians have been particularly outspoken about the unfavourable balance of trade, the obstacles to their export initiatives in Japan, and the threat to industries and employment in their countries. It is less widely publicised in Europe that many Japanese businessmen feel that they, in turn, are unfairly treated in the EC and that they see the consolidation of the European market in 1993 as a threat (see McVeigh 1991). Whoever is justified in their views, the facts show that the balance of trade is greatly in Japan's favour.

Table 12.2 US investment position abroad, 1980 and 1987

	Billions of dollars		1987 (1980 = 100)	Dollars per capita
	1980	1987		
Total	215.4	308.8	143	62
Developed	158.2	233.3	147	196
Developing	53.2	71.2	134	19
Canada	45.1	58.9	131	2,265
FRG	15.4	24.5	159	402
France	9.3	11.5	124	207
Italy	5.4	8.4	156	146
Netherlands	8.0	14.2	178	973
Belgium + Lux.	6.9	7.8	113	757
UK + Ireland	30.8	50.2	163	833
Denmark	1.3	1.1	85	218
Greece + Portugal	0.6	0.6	100	30
Spain	2.7	4.0	148	104
EC	80.4	122.3	152	377
4 EFTA	15.0	25.7	171	959
Japan	6.2	14.3	231	117

Source: *Statistical Abstract of the United States 1989*, p. 779

Table 12.3 Foreign direct investment position in the USA, 1980 and 1987

	Billions of dollars		1987 (1980 = 100)	Dollars per capita
	1980	1987		
Total	83.0	261.9	316	52
Canada	12.2	21.7	178	837
Europe*	54.7	178.0	325	499
FRG	7.6	19.6	258	321
Netherlands	19.1	47.0	246	3,219
UK	14.1	74.9	531	1,319
Switzerland	5.1	14.3	280	2,167
Other Europe	8.8	22.0	250	101
Japan	4.7	33.4	712	273
Other areas	11.5	28.9	251	6

Source: *Statistical Abstract of the United States 1989*, p. 777
Note: * excludes CMEA and other socialist areas

It can be seen in Table 12.4 that in 1980 the value of Japanese exports to the EC was more than twice the value of Japanese imports from the EC, the deficit being almost 9 billion US dollars. By 1990 the imbalance had been reduced considerably, EC exports to Japan being almost two-thirds the value of Japanese exports to the EC. The absolute difference had, however, doubled to 18.5 billion

Table 12.4 Japanese trade with and investment in the EC

	(1) (2) Japanese imports from EC (millions of dollars)		(3) (4) Japanese exports to EC (millions of dollars)		(5) EC imports from Japan per capita 1990 (dollars)	(6) Japanese investments in EC 1951–89	
	1980	1990	1980	1990		Per capita 1990 (dollars)	Total (millions of dollars)
FRG	2,501	11,487	5,756	17,782	282	56	3,448
France	1,296	7,590	2,021	6,128	108	51	2,899
Italy	938	5,008	955	3,409	59	12	684
Netherlands	380	1,170	2,061	6,165	411	671	10,072
Belgium	372	1,557	1,419	3,807	385	137	1,353
Luxembourg	3	59	6	53	133	13,458	5,383
UK	1,954	5,239	3,782	10,786	188	275	15,793
Ireland	78	636	221	944	270	161	565
Denmark	321	1,126	428	969	190	10	50
Greece	36*	149	545*	828	82	10	96
Spain	389*	793	410*	2,092	54	40	1,546
Portugal	54*	215	264*	560	54	11	114
EC	7,842	35,028	16,650	53,518	163	128	42,003

Source: JETRO 1990: 9, 13
Note: * not in EC in 1980

US dollars, due to the great overall increase in trade. It may be of some consolation to the EC to know that for the USA the difference in imports from and exports to Japan was 50 billion US dollars a year in the late 1980s.

The data in column (5) of Table 12.4 show that some EC countries trade much more heavily with Japan than others; the Netherlands and Belgium, for example, each receiving imports valued at some 400 dollars per capita, while Spain and Portugal each import only one-eighth of that amount. A comparison of the values in columns (2) and (4) shows also that the balance varies greatly, with France and Italy actually exporting more to Japan than they import from it, but the FRG and the UK being much less favourably placed, and the Netherlands with a very large deficit.

In the 1990s, both the USA and the EC are likely to try to reduce the unfavourable balance of trade with Japan. If they succeed, Japan will be in a precarious position because it has to import about 90 per cent of the fuel and raw materials it uses as well as a considerable proportion of its food. Oil comes both from rich countries (such as the United Arab Emirates and Saudi Arabia) and from Indonesia and other developing countries (most with small populations and without the capacity to absorb large quantities of manufactured goods from Japan). Canada and Australia export coal, non-fuel minerals and food to Japan. They also are comparatively small in population. Japan therefore depends heavily on maintaining a large excess of exports over imports in its trade with the USA and Western Europe, whether through the efficiency of its industries (e.g. it has a much lower rate of consumption of energy per capita for the GDP it produces than does the USA) or through subsidising exports covertly by keeping living standards down at home.

One way in which Japan has been preparing for the Single Market has been to invest in industry and services within the Community. In column (6) of Table 12.4, the Japanese investment per capita in EC Member States shows great disparities, with Italy, Denmark, Greece and Portugal attracting very little, but Luxembourg excelling. The UK has received more than twice the EC average per capita, the Netherlands about five times. By January 1990 there were about 530 Japanese companies in the EC, varying considerably in size, and covering a wide range of manufactured products. Over half of all Japanese foreign investment is however in the USA compared with 20 per cent in the EC.

THE EC AND THE DEVELOPING WORLD

Transactions between the EC, the USA, Japan, and smaller developed market economy countries are conducted broadly as among equals in both a political and an economic sense. These transactions have not been marked by great surprises, or experienced sudden changes in postwar trends, once the economies of Japan and Germany were restored after the Second World War. More of the same is what is generally expected. The rapid changes in Central Europe and the USSR, on the other hand, have produced reforms and realignments in the relationships of those regions with the EC, making the prospects for the 1990s very difficult to anticipate. Some aspects of this relationship were discussed in the previous chapter. Even more uncertain are the overall prospects for the remaining 75 per cent of the population of the world. Figure 12.1 shows how the population of the developed and the developing worlds can be expected to change between 1990 and 2020. Most of this population is in the less-developed market economy countries. China and a few smaller, still solidly Communist, centrally planned, economies, form the other group. The developing world as a whole will be discussed in this section, but in view of its great size and potential future importance to the EC, China will be discussed in greater detail at the end of the section.

As one of the richest regions of the world, the EC has contributed with development assistance to poorer regions since the end of the Second World War. The global amount of assistance has been small and sometimes misplaced. The disparity between rich and poor regions of the world has actually grown in absolute terms in the last few decades, one of the reasons why there is widespread concern and dissatisfaction about the great development gap. At present, development assistance provided from the EC budget, as opposed to that provided by individual Member States, is concentrated in three directions: to the poorer regions within the EC itself, in increasing amounts to parts of Central Europe and to the former USSR, through the PHARE and TACIS programmes; and traditionally to the developing world, especially to former colonies of some members of the EC; also to many small, mostly poor countries of Africa, the Caribbean and the Pacific area. EC development assistance is part of a larger amount contributed by all the developed countries of the world.

Official development assistance has mostly been provided by governments, commercial enterprises or private charities, or by pooled resources from such international bodies as the World Bank. It is transferred in the form of grants, loans or investments. Some assistance has been in the form of arms, while some has been used to stimulate industrial development or to boost agricultural production. It has often been given on condition that it is spent in the donor country. In general, assistance that leads to an improvement in infrastructure and the capacity and quality of means of production is regarded as more beneficial to the world as a whole than transfers of food and other consumer goods, except, of course, in cases of emergency.

Some of the countries providing assistance have been more forthcoming than others. In Table 12.6 it can be seen that Norway is the only European country contributing more than 1 per cent of its GNP while the Netherlands, Denmark and France are the only EC countries to exceed a UN target of over 0.7 per cent which was set two decades ago. With continuing economic stagnation in some EC countries, the urgent need to raise the backward regions of the EC itself to enable further integration in the Community, and the perceived obligation to help to overcome acute economic and environmental problems in Central Europe and the USSR, it seems unlikely that either the EC as a whole or its Member

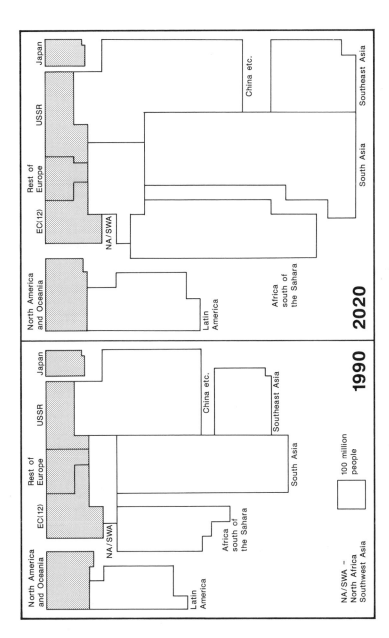

Figure 12.1 The population of the world in 1990 and the estimated population in 2020. China, etc. includes for convenience Taiwan, Hong Kong and Korea

Source: PRB, *WPDS* (1990)

Table 12.5 Population of the world, 1990 and 1992

	1990		1992	
	Millions	%	*Millions*	%
World	5,320	100	5,420	100
Developed regions[1]	1,215	23	1,224	23
China	1,120	21	1,166	21
South Asia[2]	1,120	21	1,156	21
Rest[3]	1,865	35	1,874	35

Sources: PRB, *WPDS* 1990 and 1992

Notes: 1 Europe, USSR, USA, Canada, Australia, New Zealand, Japan

2 India, Pakistan, Bangladesh, Sri Lanka, Nepal

3 Latin America, Africa, rest of Asia, rest of Oceania

Table 12.6 Official development assistance given as a percentage of GNP, 1987

Top donor countries	Aid as % of GNP	Top donor countries	Aid as % of GNP
1 Saudi Arabia	3.40	9 Belgium	0.49
2 Kuwait	1.23	10 Canada	0.47
3 Norway	1.09	11 FRG	0.39
4 Netherlands	0.98	12 Italy	0.35
5 Sweden	0.88	Japan	0.31
6 Denmark	0.88	UK	0.28
7 France	0.74	USSR	0.25
8 Finland	0.50	USA	0.20

Source: UNDP 1990: 164–5

Table 12.7 Official development assistance received as a percentage of GNP, 1987

Top eight		Other selected	
1 Somalia	57.0	Bangladesh	9.3
2 Mozambique	40.9	Pakistan	2.4
3 Lesotho	29.4	Indonesia	1.8
4 Tanzania	25.2	India	0.7
5 Malawi	22.8	China	0.5
6 Zambia	21.1	Nigeria	0.3
7 Chad	20.3	Brazil	0.1
8 Mauritania	19.0	Mexico	0.1

Source: UNDP 1990: 164–5

States individually will increase their assistance to the developing world in absolute terms in the 1990s.

In order to classify the developing countries of the world into the more and the less needy, with regard to the distribution of the modest resources available from development assistance, the Index of Human Development, explained in Chapter 11, has been used. In Table 12.8 column (5) the final scores are the combination

Table 12.8 Human Development Indicators in selected countries

	(1) Life expectancy in years	(2) Adult literacy %	(3) Real GDP	(4) Log GDP	(5) HDI (1990)	(6) HDI (1992)
Japan	78	99	13.1	4.12	996	981
Netherlands	77	99	12.7	4.10	984	968
Canada	77	99	16.4	4.21	983	982
Australia	76	99	11.8	4.07	978	971
UK	76	99	12.3	4.09	970	962
New Zealand	75	99	10.5	4.02	966	947
Belgium	75	99	13.1	4.12	966	950
USA	76	96	17.6	4.25	961	976
Israel	76	95	9.2	3.96	957	939
Greece	76	93	5.5	3.74	949	901
Hong Kong	76	88	13.9	4.14	936	913
Chile	72	98	4.9	3.69	931	863
Korea Rep.	70	95	4.8	3.68	903	871
Portugal	74	85	5.6	3.75	899	850
Mexico	69	90	4.6	3.67	876	804
Malaysia	70	74	3.8	3.59	800	789
Brazil	65	78	4.3	3.63	784	739
South Africa	61	70	5.0	3.70	731	674
China	70	69	2.1	3.33	716	612
Indonesia	57	74	1.7	3.22	591	491
Egypt	62	45	1.4	3.13	501	385
India	59	43	1.1	3.02	439	297
Haiti	55	38	0.8	2.89	356	276
Nigeria	51	43	0.7	2.82	322	241
Bangladesh	52	33	0.9	2.95	318	185
Zaïre	53	62	0.2	2.34	294	262
Ethiopia	42	66	0.5	2.66	282	173
Afghanistan	42	24	1.0	3.00	212	65
Niger	45	14	0.5	2.66	116	78

Source: UNDP 1990: 128–9

Notes: (3) Real GDP per capita (PPP $) 1987
  (4) Logarithmic value of (3)
  (5) Human Development Index, maximum 1,000
  (6) Human Development Index, maximum 1,000, 1992 (see note 6 in Table 11.1 for further details)

of the scores of each country on the three variables in columns (1)–(3). Japan has the highest score, 996 out of a possible maximum of 1,000. Niger is not the lowest country on all three scales but it is the lowest on the combination of the three. The table includes five representative members of the EC, five other developed countries, and 19 developing countries. The lowest are mostly in Africa or South Asia. It can be seen in Figure 12.2 that some developing countries

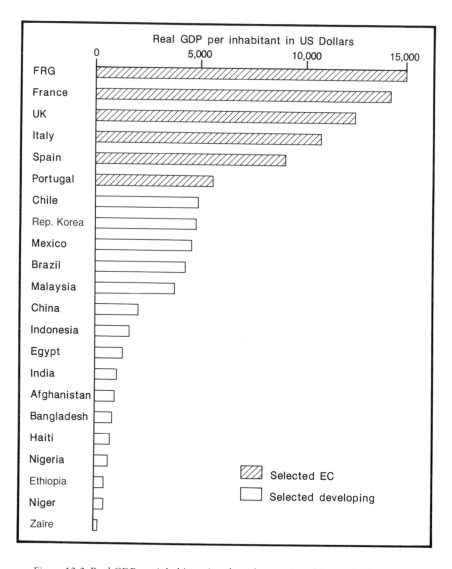

Figure 12.2 Real GDP per inhabitant in selected countries of the world, late 1980s

of Latin America and East Asia came close to the two poorest in the EC, Greece and Portugal.

Increasingly it seems that small, poor countries in the developing world with virtual states of emergency are becoming the main targets for assistance (see Table 12.7). Some, it could be inferred, have been favoured because they were former colonies of the EC countries. It is evident also that although India and China each receives a substantial absolute amount of assistance, as a consequence of their large size it is in practice a negligible quantity per head. In both countries there are very marked regional disparities, and if their respective states and provinces were individual sovereign countries, some would be very low on the Human Development scale (e.g. Bihar in India, Guizhou in China), thereby qualifying at least in theory for more assistance from developed countries.

The 1990 UN Human Development Programme is very explicit with regard to what the goals for development assistance should be and which countries should receive it. A number of qualified global targets already exist for the year 2000. These include the following (see UNDP 1990: 67):

- complete immunisation of all children;
- reduction of the under-5 child mortality rate by half or to 70 per 1,000 live births, whichever is lower;
- elimination of severe malnutrition, and a 50 per cent reduction in moderate malnutrition;
- universal primary enrolment of all children of primary school age;
- reduction of the adult illiteracy rate in 1990 by half, with the female illiteracy rate to be no higher than the male illiteracy rate;
- universal access to safe water.

Such goals seem modest when compared with conditions currently enjoyed by virtually all the citizens of the EC but, with a fast-growing population in the developing world, the resources needed to provide these are large.

The Newly Industrialising Countries

Some countries conventionally included in the developing world are actually donors of development assistance, some, mainly oil-exporting countries with small populations, have very high levels of GNP per capita, while several others have industrialised rapidly since the Second World War, especially since the 1960s (for example, the Republic of Korea and Taiwan). The EC is not only a voracious importer and user of primary products, especially fuels and raw materials but, contrary to its traditional trading practices, increasingly also an importer of manufactured goods, many supplied by Newly Industrialising Countries (NICs). Although the principal non-European suppliers of manufactures to most EC countries are Japan and the USA, Western European countries are increasingly targeted by various developing countries, some of which are the NICs. While some of the NICs and other countries included in Table 12.9 are

Table 12.9 Exports of selected developing countries (percentages)

	Agric.	Mining	Mfg	Of which		
				Textiles	Metals[1]	Other
Korean Republic			96	33	41	
Hong Kong			96	38	33	
Singapore			93		48	23 chemicals
Philippines	13	6	81			45 food, other
Pakistan			80	58		11 food
Turkey	18	3	80	34	13	10 chemicals
Bangladesh	24		76	71		
Brazil	18	8	76		17	20 food
China	22	8	70	26[2]	10	
Thailand	28	5	68	17	13	25 food
Argentina	37		63			31 food
Malaysia	20	22	58		27	13 food
India	21	25	54	23	11	10 food
Mexico	7	57	36		18	9 chemicals
Indonesia	17	52	31			10 wood

Source: *United Nations Yearbook of International Trade Statistics*
Notes: 1 includes engineering products
2 textiles and clothing

quite small in population (e.g. Singapore, Taiwan) or large but with very low GDP per capita (e.g. Bangladesh, Pakistan), in a growing number of them manufactured goods account for over half of the value of their exports. The countries listed in Table 12.9 actually have over half of the population of the world, although less than 10 per cent of total world GDP. In four, the Republic of Korea, Hong Kong, Singapore, and Taiwan, manufactured goods make up over 90 per cent of the value of exports. In all the others apart from Mexico and Indonesia, whose main export is oil, products of manufacturing make up over half of the value. The four most sophisticated all have an important contribution from metallurgical and engineering branches, but textiles, clothing and food products largely account for the processed and manufactured goods exported from most NICs. In addition to the many developing countries for which the EC is increasingly seen as a market for the exports of manufactured goods, the former CMEA partners of the USSR will be seeking outlets in the EC and EFTA, as intra-CMEA trade declines. Disregard for actual production costs in CMEA countries enabled them to export manufactured goods (e.g. Czech and Soviet cars) to Western Europe at unrealistically low prices. If such practices continue, then conditions may become more competitive for EC manufacturers in the 1990s from that quarter, as well as from the NICs.

The EC and China

Since the Second World War many of the Pacific countries of Asia have experienced fast economic growth for considerable periods, and have in turn made their presence felt in Western Europe. Japan's trade with the EC has grown rapidly since the early 1960s, that of the Korean Republic, Taiwan, Hong Kong and Singapore since the early 1970s, and currently the economy of some ASEAN countries have been expanding fast. Given its vast population size, the impact of China on the EC has been comparatively modest so far, although its foreign trade has increased greatly in the 1980s.

A number of issues and problems have been widely aired in the media and have been confronted if not solved by the government of China in the 1980s. The need to reduce the rate of population growth has been accepted, urbanisation and further industrialisation are to be encouraged, and central planning and Communism are to be modified, but not abandoned, in the hope that with appropriate incentives to individuals and the operation of some market forces, production and efficiency may increase and improve without increasing existing inequalities.

In relation to the size of its population, China is poorly endowed with most natural resources. It has 21 per cent of the population of the world, but only 7 per cent of the arable land, under 5 per cent of the forest and pastures, and a mere 1–2 per cent of proved oil and natural gas reserves. To be sure, coal reserves should last many decades, even if the planned large increase in output is achieved, but the price is continuing high levels of atmospheric pollution. China is hard pressed to grow enough food for the population, is short of many raw materials, and has to import equipment for industrial development. It squeezes as much as possible out of the resources it has, to add value to limited materials, and to export various consumer goods which are luxuries in China.

The distribution of population and resources in China presents a serious problem for planners and has constantly threatened the implementation of socialism. In order to develop sophisticated industries, capable of exporting quality goods already widely produced in various smaller countries of East Asia, China would have to concentrate much of its investment in the modernisation and further expansion of the industries in coastal provinces, already much more highly industrialised than many interior ones and (relatively) much more affluent, thereby increasing disparities.

Trade between China and EC countries is still very small, considering the size of the two regions. In 1988 Chinese exports to the EC were worth 4.7 billion US dollars while imports from the EC reached 8.1 billion. About 10 per cent of all Chinese exports went to EC countries, but almost 15 per cent of imports came from the Community. If Hong Kong and Singapore are for convenience regarded as developed areas, then almost all of China's foreign trade is with the developed world, very little with Africa and Latin America. China still trades with CMEA countries, but in contrast to the 1950s, when its trade was dominated by the

293

USSR and its East European partners, these only accounted for a few per cent in 1988, and in view of the new situation there, the share could drop further.

China's relationship with the EC was soured in 1989 by the suppression of Beijing's pro-democracy movement and violations of human rights, even though it was comparatively limited in extent compared with oppression on other occasions both before and since 1949. It could take a decade for China to regain respectability in Western eyes and the uncertainty over the future of Hong Kong after 1997 is continuing to affect relations. Nevertheless, in the next century it could be exporting large quantities of cheap but reasonably high-quality manufactured goods, gaining an increasing share of markets in the rest of the developing world as well as penetrating both the EC and Japanese markets.

THE EC IN THE 1990s AND BEYOND

Before the late 1980s the EC was concerned largely with the development of its internal markets and the organisation of trade relations with the rest of the world. Suddenly it has become an identifiable global entity, with diplomatic representation in various quarters and a new role in international affairs (e.g. peace-keeping in Yugoslavia). The USSR refused to recognise the existence of the EC until the late 1980s. Now 145 countries have diplomatic missions to the EC with addresses in Brussels (see Landmarks 1991). Since Member States of the EC do not have diplomatic missions to the EC, whereas they do all have embassies, almost 20 countries have a diplomatic mission to the EC without having an embassy there, there being 138 embassies. Some of the diplomatic missions share premises with their embassies.

Further evidence of the growing importance of having a presence in Brussels is the fact that there are 64 subnational public missions with offices in Brussels, mostly representing regional or local government interests (see Table 12.10). The regions of origin of these missions are shown in Figure 12.3. Since these missions are 'on the spot' in Brussels to represent the interests of the regions that invested in establishing them there, it is of interest to speculate *why* some of them are

Table 12.10 Subnational public missions in Brussels, 1990

EC		Non-EC	
France	13	USA	12
Germany	12	Canada	1
UK	9	Sweden	1
Spain	8		
Belgium	4		
Denmark	3		
Netherlands	1		

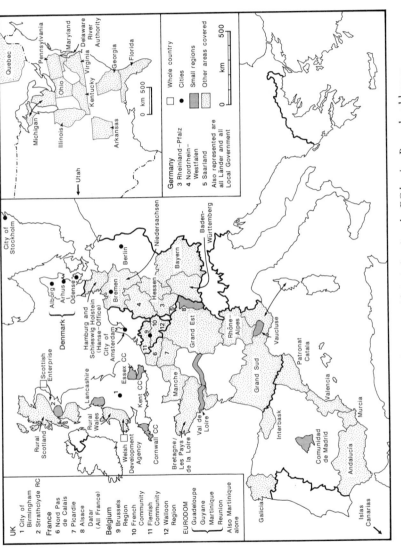

Figure 12.3 Subnational regions with 'missions' to the EC having Brussels addresses

Source: Landmarks 1991: 57–9

there, especially the ones from the USA such as the Commonwealth of Kentucky and the Delaware River Authority (actually in Antwerp). Brussels is at last showing that it is becoming a place of influence in the supranational superstate of the EC.

To conclude this chapter and the book, a number of themes are brought together and some possible future trends proposed. While the EC may carry less weight in world affairs than the combined power of individual Member States did in the nineteenth century, the culmination of Mackinder's Columbian epoch, its influence could be considerable.

In contrast to most of the rest of the world, the EC does not have any major demographic problems. All additional economic growth benefits the existing population, whereas in the developing countries, much of that achieved is immediately absorbed by increasing population. As a result, the EC is likely to face increasing pressures from outside from hopeful immigrants, while its high standard of living can be used as a claim for increased amounts of assistance for poorer countries. Its ability to produce surpluses of some types of agricultural products may oblige it, out of both self-interest and philanthropic motives, to provide food aid to less fortunate parts of the world. The alternative is to reform the Common Agricultural Policy and radically alter the livelihood of many of its farmers.

With regard to energy supplies, the EC is particularly vulnerable because it is unlikely that nuclear power and new types of energy produced in the Community will become the main source for some decades. The pressures from environmentalists to reduce the consumption of energy may indeed prove a useful incentive to the achievement of greater self-sufficiency. More serious in the next century may be the competition faced by traditional EC industries from the developing countries. The services sector, on the other hand, is more local in its operations and does not enter prominently in trade with the rest of the world, notwithstanding some important, 'invisible' exports.

Great uncertainty faces the defence activities and industries of the EC. It seems unlikely that the Member States of the EC will need to spend as much on defence as they have done since the Second World War, although regional if not global conflicts seem likely to proliferate. The decline in the manpower in the armed forces and in the associated civilian industries and services gives the Commission new problems of job losses acutely affecting a number of local areas in the EC.

After the accession of Spain and Portugal to the EC in 1986 and the signing of the Single European Act in the same year, it seemed that in a matter of a decade or so the Community would have become much more integrated than it had hitherto been. Attempts were made in 1991 to consolidate moves towards greater unity, but in a climate of great confusion in Central and Eastern Europe. As the 1990s unfold, however, it is becoming increasingly likely that the EC will accept new members, with a variety of cultural backgrounds and levels of development, thereby putting back the process of future integration for years if

Plate 21 Crossroads of Europe: an internationally
labelled waste bin in an Autobahn parking area,
southern Germany. Eight of the nine main EC languages
are represented, together with six others

not decades. While the achievements of the first 35 years of the Community will
continue to stand, it will become increasingly difficult to arrive at consensus over
an extension of Community power with a greater number of Member States.

In conclusion, the authors consider it appropriate to refer again to *Europe
2000*. Whatever path is followed by the countries of Europe, the need is recognised for a Committee on Spatial Development:

The establishment of procedures of consultation between Member States and the Commission would give the competent authorities opportunities to discuss ... information and provide a forum where possible conflicts might be resolved and complementarities promoted. ... Discussion would not be restricted to matters internal to particular sectors such as transport, environment, telecommunication, energy, etc., but would extend to consider their inter-relationships, and their impact on territorial development in the future.

(Commission of the EC 1991a: 198–9)

The need for a geographical approach to at least some of the problems of the EC is explicitly acknowledged in *Europe 2000*. It is hoped that the authors of the present book have made a contribution to this important subject, both by looking critically at some of the geographical problems and policies of the EC itself, and by pointing to new problems likely to arise from enlarged membership, whenever that comes.

FURTHER READING

HMSO (1991) *Japan and the European Community*, London.
World Bank (1990) *World Development Report 1990*, Oxford: Oxford University Press.

REFERENCES

Barney, G. O. (ed.) (1982) *The Global 2000 Report to the President*, Harmondsworth: Penguin Books.

Bassett, P. (1991) 'British Coal makes £78m and cuts jobs', *The Times*, 25 July, p. 21.

Belton, E. (1990) 'The banker who must mould Europe's money', *The European*, May 25–7, p. 19.

Bennett, N. (1991) 'City outstrips the Continentals', *The Times*, 5 Aug.

Birrell, I. and Skipworth, M. (1991) 'Airlines warned their fares are far too high', *The Sunday Times*, 24 Nov., p. 15.

Blake, D. (1991) 'Time to abolish Luxembourg?', *The European*, July 26–8, p. 10.

British Petroleum (BP) (1991) *Statistical Review of World Energy*, June, Corporate Communications Services (various years).

Buchan, D. and Wyles, J. (1990) 'The intolerance threshold nears', *Financial Times*, 12 March, p. 14.

Bureau of Mines (1985) *Mineral Facts and Problems*, Bulletin 675, Department of the Interior, Washington DC.

Calendario Atlante De Agostini 1990 (1989), Istituto Geografico De Agostini, Novara.

Carazzi, M. and Segre, A. (1989) 'Città e industria: alcune linee interpretative a proposito di Torino e Milano', *Bollettino della Società Geografica Italiana*, ser. XI, vol. VI, p. 197.

Casassus, B. (1991) 'Gulf war could fuel drive for the electric car', *The European*, 8–10 Feb., p. 25.

Cecchini, P. (1988) *The European Challenge 1992*, Aldershot: Wildwood House.

Charles, R. (1989) 'Canada – United States Free Trade Agreement: a Canadian's personal perspective', *National Westminster Bank Quarterly Review*, May, pp. 17–26.

Clark, J. P., and Flemings, M. C. (1986) 'Advanced materials and the economy', *Scientific American* 255(4): 42–9.

Clough, P. (1983) 'EEC: facing reality', *The Times*, 2 Dec., p. 14.

Cole, J. P. (1990) 'Europe: looking towards the 21st century', in M. J. Cipolato (ed.), *The Community and Europe*, Brussels: AD Consult S.P.R.L., pp. 23–30.

Cole, J. P. and Cole, F. J. (1990) 'German reunification, the EC and the USSR: an Autobahn too far?' Working Paper 8, Department of Geography, University of Nottingham.

COM 87-230 (1987) *Third Periodic Report from the Commission on the Social and Economic Situation and Development of the Regions of the Community*, Brussels, 21 May.

COM 89-564 (1990) *Communication on a Community Railway Policy*, Brussels, 25 Jan.

COM 90-609 (1991a) *The Regions of the 1990s*, Commission of the European Communities, Fourth Periodic Report . . ., Brussels, 9 Jan.

COM 91-100 (1991b) *The Development and Future of the CAP*, policy paper from Commission to Council, Brussels, 1 Feb.

COM 92-2000 (1992a) *From the Single Act to Maastricht and Beyond. The Means to Match Our Ambitions*, Brussels, 11 Feb.

COM 92-84 (1992b) *Community Structural Policies, Assessment and Outlook*, Brussels, 18 March.

Commission of the EC (1984) *The Regions of Europe* (Second Periodic Report ...), Luxembourg: Office for Official Publications of the European Communities.

—— (1985) *White Paper on Completing the Internal Market*, Brussels.

—— (1987) *The European Community Forests*, Luxembourg: Office for the Official Publications of the European Communities.

—— (1989) *European Regional Development Report*, Luxembourg: Office for Official Publications of the European Communities.

—— (1990), *Panorama of EC Industry 1990*, Luxembourg: Office for Official Publications of the European Communities.

—— (1991a) *Europe 2000 – Outlook for the Development of the Community's Territory*, Directorate-General for Regional Policy, Brussels/Luxembourg.

—— (1991b) *A Strategy for Enlargement*, Preliminary Report of the SG Study Group on Enlargement, Brussels, 14 Nov.

—— (1991c) *Employment in Europe 1991*, COM (91) 248 final, Directorate-General Employment, Industrial Relations and Social Affairs, Luxembourg.

—— (1992) *The Agricultural Situation in the Community*, 1991 Report, Brussels/Luxembourg.

CSO – Central Statistical Office (1990) *Regional Trends 25*, London: HMSO.

Davies-Gleizes (1991) 'US cleans up Europe's act', *The European*, 17–19 May, p. 24.

De Gucht, K. (1992) *Interim Motion for a Resolution on a Permanent Scheme for Allocating the Seats of Members of the European Parliament*, Committee on Institutional Affairs, 6 Feb., DOC EN/RE/202153.

Dynes, M. (1991) 'BR to pick final freight terminal for tunnel link', *The Times*, 11 Nov., p. 3.

—— (1992) 'Super-fast train shunted into sidings', *The Times*, 3 Jan., p. 5.

Economic Commission for Europe (1991) *Transport Information 1991*, Geneva. Published New York: United Nations.

ECSC, see Treaties (1987).

EEC, see Treaties (1987).

EPU (1991) *Treaty on European Union*, Maastricht 10 Dec., CONF-UP 1850/91 and SN 252/1/91 REV.1.

Euratom (also EAEC), see Treaties 1987.

European Communities (1988) *Disadvantaged Island Regions*, Economic and Social Consultative Assembly, Brussels, July.

European Parliament (1989, 1991) *Fact Sheets on the European Parliament and the Activities of the European Community*, Directorate-General for Research, Luxembourg.

—— (1990a) *List of Members*, Luxembourg: Office for Official Publications of the European Communities.

—— (1990b) *The Impact of German Unification on the European Community*, Directorate-General for Research, Working Document no. 1, 6-1990.

—— (1991) *On the State of the Environment in the Czech and Slovak Federative Republic* (CSFR), Delegation for Relations with Czechoslovakia. Committee on the Environment, Public Health and Consumer Protection, 26 March, SDI/CH/bs DOC-EN/RESRCH/106892.

Eurostat (1989a) *Basic Statistics of the Community*, 26th edition, Luxembourg: Office for Official Publications of the European Community.

—— (1989b) *Europe in Figures, Deadline 1992*, Brussels/Luxembourg: Office for Official Publications of the European Communities.

—— (1990) *Regions Statistical Yearbook 1989*, Brussels/Luxembourg.

—— (1991a) *Eurostatistics*, various numbers, Luxembourg: Office des publications officielles des Communautés européennes.

—— (1991b) *A Social Portrait of Europe*, Brussels/Luxembourg: Statistical Office of the EC.

—— (1991c) *Le Tourisme en Europe, tendances 1989*, Brussels/Luxembourg.

FAOTY – Food and Agriculture Organisation, *Trade Yearbook* (annual publication), United Nations Organisation.

FAOTY – Food and Agriculture Organisation *Trade Yearbook* (annual publication), United Nations Organisation.

Froment, R. and Lerat, S. (1989) *La France à l'aube des années 90* (3 vols), Paris: Bréal.

Gardner, D. (1991) 'Southern discomfort', *Financial Times*, 18 June, p. 16.

—— (1992) 'Row looms over EC budget', *Financial Times*, 12 Feb., p. 1.

Gilbert, S. and Horner, R. (1984) *The Thames Barrier*, London: Thomas Telford Ltd.

Gill, K. (1991) 'Conservation experts want 150,000 red deer culled', *The Times*, 17 Aug., p. 1.

Gunnemark, E. and Kenrick, D. (1985) *A Geolinguistic Handbook*, Gothenburg: Goterna.

Heilig, G., Büttner, T. and Lutz, W. (1990) 'Germany's population: turbulent past, uncertain future', Population Reference Bureau, *Population Bulletin* 45(4): 33.

Hornsby, M. (1991) 'Farmers urge nitrogen cut', *The Times*, 14 May, p. 5.

JETRO (1990) *Handy facts on EC–Japan Economic Relations*, Tokyo: Japanese External Trade Organisation.

Jones, P. D. and Wigley, T. M. L. (1990) 'Global warming trends', *Scientific American*, August, 263(2): 66–73.

Kadlec, J. (1991) *Nuclear Power in Czechoslovakia*, European Parliament, Delegation for Relations with Czechoslovakia, PE 150.206, 22 March.

Kuczynski, R. R. (1939) Living-Space and Population Problems, Oxford Pamphlets on World Affairs, no. 8, Oxford: Clarendon Press.

Landmarks (1991) *The European Public Affairs Directory*, Brussels: Landmarks sa/nv.

Langer, W. L. (1972) 'Checks on population growth: 1750–1850', *Scientific American* 226(2): 92–9.

Larson, E. D., Ross, M. H. and Williams, R. H. (1986) 'Beyond the era of materials', *Scientific American* 254(6): 24–31.

Le Bras, H. and Todd, E. (1981) *L'Invention de la France*, Paris: Collection Pluriel.

LUFPIG (1990) *A Future for Europe's Farmers and the Countryside*, Brussels: European Parliament.

Mackinder, H. J. (1904) 'The geographical pivot of history', *Geographical Journal* XXIII(4): 421–2.

McMillan-Scott, E. (1990) 'Greater Europe: 12 plus 6 plus 6', *Target Europe Papers* no. 4, Conservatives in the European Parliament.

—— (1991) *Draft Report of the Committee on Transport and Tourism on a Community Tourism Policy*, 21 Feb., DOC EN/PR/104766, European Parliament.

McVeigh, C. (1991) 'What the Japanese think of the EC', *The European*, 29 Nov.–1 Dec., p. 25.

Marchetti, R. (1985) *Quadro analitico complessivo dei risultati delle indagini condotte negli anni 1977–1980 sul problema dell' eutrofizzazione nelle acque costiere dell'Emilia-Romagna*, Regione Emilia-Romagna, Assessorato ambiente e difesa del suolo.

Marsh, J. S. (1991) *Hearing on the Reform of the Common Agricultural Policy*, European Parliament, Committee on Budgets, 26 June.

Mitchell, B. R. (1981) *European Historical Statistics 1750–1975*, London: Macmillan.

Murray, I. (1991) 'Rise in jobless widens German economic gap', *The Times*, 7 March, p. 12.

—— (1992) 'Rising flood of refugees pours into Germany', *The Times*, 5 Feb., p. 8.

National Audit Office (NAO) (1990) *Maternity Services*, London: HMSO, 16 March.

Nef, J. U. (1977) 'An early energy crisis and its consequences', *Scientific American* 237(5): 140–51.

OECD (1991) *The State of the Environment*, Paris: OECD.

Olins, R. and Lorenz, A. (1992) 'BR destination unknown', *The Sunday Times*, 12 Jan., p. 3–3.

Painton, F. (1990) 'Darkness at noon', *Time*, 9 April, pp. 24–32.

Palmer, R. and Rowland, J. (1990) 'North Sea chokes to death in its own filth', *The Sunday Times*, 4 March, p. A5.

Parry, M. (1990) *Climate Change and World Agriculture*, London: Earthscan Publications Ltd.

Paterson, T. (1991a) 'Death lurks in nuclear waste mountains', *The European*, 15–17 Feb. p. 6.

—— (1991b) 'Miners haul industry minister over the coals', *The European*, 2–4 Aug., p. 12.

PRB (Population Reference Bureau) (1991) *World Population Data Sheet (WPDS)*, Washington (various years).

Rand McNally (1987) *Goode's World Atlas*, Chicago: Rand McNally.

Romera, I. Alcazar (1991) *Draft Report on Community Policy on Transport Infrastructure*, European Parliament, Committee on Transport and Tourism, 22 Feb., DOC EN/PR/103678, PE 148.168.

SEA, see Treaties (1987).

Shloma, V. (1992) 'Ukraina: tyazholyye vremena' (The Ukraine: hard times), *Ekonomika i zhizn'*, May, no. 18, p. 11.

Soltau, R. H. (1935) *An Outline of European Economic Development*, London: Longmans, Green.

Thomas Cook (1991) *European Timetable*, July, Peterborough: Thomas Cook Publishing.

Treaties (1987) *Treaties Establishing the European Communities, Treaties Amending these Treaties, Single European Act*, Luxembourg: Office of Official Publications of the European Communities.

UNDP – United Nations Development Programme (1990) *Human Development Report 1990*, Oxford University Press.

UNSYB (1987) *Statistical Yearbook of the United Nations*, New York (various years).

United Nations (1991) *Transport Information 1991*, Economic Commission for Europe, Geneva, publisher UN, New York.

Walker, L. and Comfort, N. (1991) 'Europe braced for migrant invasion', *The European*, 10–12 May, p. 1.

White, C. (1991) 'Wanted: jobs in the West for 6 m. Soviets', *The European*, 20–2 Sept., p. 1.

Wijsenbeek, F. (1991) *Draft Report on Congestion and Urban Transport*, European Parliament, Committee on Transport and Tourism (PE 151.493 Or. NL/EN).

Ziegler, C. E. (1987) *Environmental Policy in the USSR*, London: Frances Pinter.

INDEX